# About This Book

## Why this topic is important

Although financial ROI has been measured for more than one hundred years to quantify the value of plants, equipment, and companies, the concept has only recently been applied to evaluate the impact of learning and development, human resources, technology, quality, marketing, and other support functions. In the learning and development field alone, the use of ROI has become routine in many organizations. In the past decade, hundreds of organizations have embraced the ROI process to show the impact of many different projects and programs.

Along the way, professionals and practitioners need help. They need tools, templates, and tips, along with explanations, examples, and details, to make this process work. Without this help, using the ROI Methodology to show the value of projects and programs is difficult. In short, practitioners need shortcuts and proven techniques to minimize the resources required to use this process. Practitioners' needs have created the need for this series, and this accompanying collection of case studies. This series will provide the detail necessary to make the ROI Methodology successful within an organization.

## Why this book is important

*ROI in Action Casebook* is a companion to the Measurement and Evaluation Series Six Pack, which describes the ROI Methodology, a methodical approach to evaluation that can be replicated throughout an organization, enabling comparisons of results between one program and another. The ROI Methodology is the most documented evaluation method in the world, and its implementation has been phenomenal, with more than 5,000 individuals participating in five-day certification programs designed for implementing it.

With this approach, every program is evaluated at some level. With executives asking for more accountability from program leaders and teams, the information in this book—and series—is critical. *ROI in Action*

*Casebook* shows fourteen real-world examples of how companies have used the ROI Methodology to prove the value of their programs, projects, and initiatives.

# How this book is organized

*ROI in Action Casebook* contains fourteen case studies which follow the ROI Process from beginning to end. Each case study provides an abstract describing the program being evaluated, a detailed background of the company, and the reasons for the evaluation. Each study then reveals in great detail how the ROI Methodology was used to collect data, isolate the effects of the program, calculate the monetary benefits, convert the data to money, and report the results to stakeholders. The authors then analyze the lessons learned throughout the process and present questions the reader can use to stimulate discussion about how the methodology was used.

Chapter 1 explores how a telecommunications equipment manufacturer measured the ROI in effective meeting skills. Chapter 2 shows how the ROI Methodology helped a global hotel chain measure the return on investment in its business coaching program.

Chapters 3, 5, and 9 show examples of how sales training programs were evaluated for a pharmaceutical company, an international hotel chain, and a nonprofit information technology company. An operational and quality training program is evaluated for a plastics manufacturing company in the prepared foods industry in Chapter 7.

The ROI is measured for a career development initiative for a global computer company in Chapter 4, while Chapter 6 shows the methodology at work in measuring the ROI in coaching for new-hire employee retention for a global media company.

The program diversity continues in Chapter 8 as a professional development day is evaluated for a technical college. Chapter 10 shows how the ROI of an electronic documentation tool was evaluated for a pharmacy benefit management company.

Chapter 11 is an ROI forecast of a performance improvement training program for a healthcare organization. Chapter 12 measures the return on investment in negotiations skills training for a mortgage company.

An automotive wheels manufacturing company measures the ROI for a manage by fact program in Chapter 13, while a global copper mining and manufacturing company uses the ROI Methodology to prove the value of its employee retraining program in Chapter 14.

The cases in this book present a variety of approaches to evaluating human resources, learning and development, and performance improvement programs. The cases focus on evaluation at the ultimate level—return on investment (ROI). Collectively, the cases offer a wide range of settings, methods, techniques, strategies, and approaches and represent manufacturing, service, and governmental organizations. Target groups for the programs vary from all employees to managers to technical specialists. As a group, these cases represent a rich source of information about the strategies of some of the best practitioners, consultants, and researchers in the field.

Each case does not necessarily represent the ideal approach for the specific situation. In every case it is possible to identify areas that might benefit from refinement or improvement. That is part of the learning process—to build on the work of others. Although the implementation processes are contextual, the methods and techniques can be used in other organizations.

Table I.1 presents basic descriptions of the cases in the order in which they appear in the book. This table can serve as a quick reference for readers who want to examine the implementation approach for a particular type of program, audience, or industry.

## How to use the cases

There are several ways to use this book. It will be helpful to anyone who wants to see real-life examples of the return on investment of specific programs. The editors recommend the following four uses:

1. This book will be useful to professionals as a basic reference of practical applications of measurement and evaluation. A reader can analyze and dissect each of the cases to develop an understanding of the issues, approaches, and, most of all, possible refinements or improvements.

**Table I.1. Overview of case studies**

| Case | Industry | Program | Target Audience |
|------|----------|---------|-----------------|
| Techno-Tel | Telecommunications | Effective Meeting Skills | Managers, Project Leaders |
| Nations Hotel Corporation | Hospitality | Business Coaching | Executives |
| Biosearch Pharmaceutical, Inc. | Pharmaceutical | Impact of Sales Training | Sales Staff |
| Innovative Computer, Inc. | Computer | Career Development Initiative | Managers |
| LeMeridien Hotels and Resorts | Hospitality | Sales Training Programme | Sales Directors, Meetings Champions, Regional Sales Staff |
| Ruche Media Company | Media | Coaching for New-Employee Retention | New Employees |
| Plastics Manufacturing Company | Prepared Foods | Operational and Quality Training | Managers |
| United Tribes Technical College | Education | Professional Development Day | Faculty and Staff Members |
| CompTIA | Information Technology | Sales Training in a Nonprofit Business | Sales Staff |
| Caremark/CVS Pharmacy Operations | Pharmaceutical | Electronic Documentation Tool | All Employees |
| The Hospital District | Healthcare | Performance Improvement Training Program | Employees at All Levels |
| ACC Capital Holdings | Mortgage | Negotiations Skills Training | Sales Staff |
| Quality Wheels International | Automobile Wheel Manufacturing | Manage by Fact Training | First- and Second-Level Managers |
| Codelco | Copper Mining and Manufacturing | Employee Retraining | Mining Equipment Operators, Extraction Truck Operators |

2. This book will be useful in group discussions in which interested individuals can react to the material, offer different perspectives, and draw conclusions about approaches and techniques. The questions at the end of each case can serve as a beginning point for lively and entertaining discussion.

3. This book will serve as a supplement to other textbooks. It provides the extra dimensions of real-life cases that show the outcomes of human resources, learning and development, and performance improvement programs.

4. Finally, this book will be extremely valuable for managers who do not have primary human resources, learning and development, or performance improvement responsibility. Because the managers provide support for these processes, it is helpful for them to understand the results that their programs can yield.

It is important to remember that each organization and its program implementation are unique. What works well for one may not work well for another, even if they are in similar settings. This book offers a variety of approaches and provides an arsenal of tools from which to choose when evaluating programs.

## Follow-up

Space limitations necessitated that some cases be shorter than the authors would have liked. Some information concerning background, assumptions, strategies, and results had to be omitted. If additional information on a case is needed, we are pleased for you to contact us directly at jack@roiinstitute.net or patti@roiinstitute.net.

The Measurement and Evaluation Series Editors
Patricia Pulliam Phillips, Ph.D., and Jack J. Phillips, Ph.D.

# About Pfeiffer

Pfeiffer serves the professional development and hands-on resource needs of training and human resource practitioners and gives them products to do their jobs better. We deliver proven ideas and solutions from experts in HR development and HR management, and we offer effective and customizable tools to improve workplace performance. From novice to seasoned professional, Pfeiffer is the source you can trust to make yourself and your organization more successful.

**Essential Knowledge** Pfeiffer produces insightful, practical, and comprehensive materials on topics that matter the most to training and HR professionals. Our Essential Knowledge resources translate the expertise of seasoned professionals into practical, how-to guidance on critical workplace issues and problems. These resources are supported by case studies, worksheets, and job aids and are frequently supplemented with CD-ROMs, websites, and other means of making the content easier to read, understand, and use.

**Essential Tools** Pfeiffer's Essential Tools resources save time and expense by offering proven, ready-to-use materials—including exercises, activities, games, instruments, and assessments—for use during a training or team-learning event. These resources are frequently offered in looseleaf or CD-ROM format to facilitate copying and customization of the material.

Pfeiffer also recognizes the remarkable power of new technologies in expanding the reach and effectiveness of training. While e-hype has often created whizbang solutions in search of a problem, we are dedicated to bringing convenience and enhancements to proven training solutions. All our e-tools comply with rigorous functionality standards. The most appropriate technology wrapped around essential content yields the perfect solution for today's on-the-go trainers and human resource professionals.

*Essential resources for training and HR professionals*

www.pfeiffer.com

# ROI in Action Casebook

## Measurement and Evaluation Series

Edited by
Patricia Pulliam Phillips, Ph.D.,
and Jack J. Phillips, Ph.D.

A Wiley Imprint
www.pfeiffer.com

Published by Pfeiffer
An Imprint of Wiley
989 Market Street, San Francisco, CA 94103-1741
www.pfeiffer.com

Readers should be aware that Internet websites offered as citations and/or sources for further information may have changed or disappeared between the time this was written and when it is read.

For additional copies/bulk purchases of this book in the U.S. please contact 800-274-4434.

Pfeiffer books and products are available through most bookstores. To contact Pfeiffer directly call our Customer Care Department within the U.S. at 800-274-4434, outside the U.S. at 317-572-3985, fax 317-572-4002, or visit www.pfeiffer.com.

Pfeiffer also publishes its books in a variety of electronic formats. Some content that appears in print may not be available in electronic books.

Library of Congress Cataloging-in-Publication Data

ROI in action casebook / edited by Patricia Pulliam Phillips, and Jack J. Phillips.
     p. cm.— (Measurement and evaluation series)
    Includes index.
    ISBN 978-0-7879-8717-6 (cloth)
1.   Employees—Training of—Cost effectiveness—Case studies. 2.
Employees—Training of—Evaluation—Case studies. 3.   Rate
of return—Evaluation. 4.   Personnel management—Evaluation. I. Phillips,
Patricia Pulliam. II. Phillips, Jack J.
    HF5549.5.T7.R5654 2008
    658.3'124—dc22
                                                        2007041052

Acquiring Editor: Matthew Davis
Marketing Manager: Brian Grimm
Director of Development: Kathleen Dolan Davies

Production Editor: Michael Kay
Editorial Assistant: Marisa Kelley
Editor: Rebecca Taff
Manufacturing Supervisor: Becky Morgan

Printed in the United States of America
Printing   10 9 8 7 6 5 4 3 2 1

# Contents

# List of Figures and Exhibits

# Preface

This is a collection of ROI case studies that represents the classic use of the ROI Methodology. Described in the book series known as "The ROI Six Pack," a series of books in the *Measurement in Action* series published by Pfeiffer, these six books illustrate the ROI Methodology. These case studies represent a variety of applications in human resources, learning and development, and performance improvement. Each case follows the methodology and describes in detail how it was used to show the value of a particular project, program, or initiative.

## Need for the Book

These case studies have been selected for use in ROI workshops, briefings, and in certification processes. They are designed to be teaching tools. In addition, these case studies are designed to be a self-learning experience. From the early beginnings of our introduction to this methodology we had requests for case studies. All audiences want to see real examples, ideally in their particular setting. The quest for case studies has led to a proliferation of published case studies. Yet the need continues. There are so many projects and programs and different types of situations and settings that practitioners want to see a variety of examples. They need to see how it works in a real setting with all the issues, concerns, and opportunities fully described.

## Target Audience

This book should interest anyone involved in human resources, learning and development, and performance improvement. The primary audience is practitioners who are struggling to determine the value of programs and to show how programs contribute to the strategic goals of the organization. These practitioners are the ones who request more real-world examples. This same group also expresses concern that there are too many models, methods, strategies, and theories, and too few examples to show if any of them have really made a difference. This publication should satisfy practitioners' needs by providing examples of the implementation of comprehensive evaluation processes.

Readers should find this casebook entertaining and engaging. Questions are placed at the end of each case to stimulate additional thought and discussion. The potential weaknesses of case studies are explored in the questions at the end of each case. One of the most effective ways to maximize the usefulness of this book is through group discussions, using the questions to develop and dissect the issues, techniques, methodologies, and results.

## The Cases

The case studies we selected met specific guidelines. Each case study includes data that can be converted to monetary values so that ROI can be calculated. The selected case studies provide a method of isolating the effects of the program. The isolation step is imperative in showing the true value of a program. The isolation methodologies included in the case studies presented in this book are control groups, trend line analysis, forecasting, and participant and manager estimates.

Although there was some attempt to structure cases similarly, they are not identical in style and content. It is important for the reader to experience the programs as they were developed and identify the issues pertinent to each particular setting and situation. The result is a variety of presentations with a variety of styles. Some cases are brief and to the point, outlining precisely what happened and what was achieved. Others provide more detailed background information, including how the need for the program was determined, the personalities involved, and how their backgrounds and biases created a unique situation.

## Acknowledgments

We would like to acknowledge the clients who allow us to publish these case studies. We greatly appreciate the help we have received from these clients as we have worked together in applying this methodology.

For a variety of reasons, some of the clients have elected not to include their names or the names of their organizations. In today's competitive world and in situations in which there is an attempt to explore new territory, it is understandable why an organization would choose not to be identified. Identification should not be a critical issue, however. They are based on real-world situations faced by real people.

## Suggestions

We welcome your input. We are involved in publishing many casebooks. If you have ideas or recommendations regarding presentation, case selection, or case quality, please send them to us. Contact us with your comments and suggestions at the ROI Resource Center, P.O. Box 380637, Birmingham, AL 35238–0637, www.roiinstitute.net.

Jack and Patti Phillips
ROI Institute, Inc.
2008

# Measuring ROI in Effective Meeting Skills

## A Telecommunications Equipment Manufacturer

Patricia Pulliam Phillips

## Abstract

Long, meaningless meetings can seriously impair workplace productivity. This case study presents the benefits that can be achieved by reducing the length of meetings, the number of meetings, and the number of meeting participants. The program evaluated is a two-day workshop intended to teach managers, supervisors, and project leaders skills in planning, managing, and facilitating the meeting process. A needs assessment, which included dialogue between the Chief Learning Officer and the President of Manufacturing, led to the identification of application and business impact measures. Pre-program data were collected using a meeting profile worksheet, and post-program data were collected using a comprehensive questionnaire. Participant estimates were used to isolate the effects of the workshop on the time savings resulting from less time in meetings, fewer meetings, and fewer people attending meetings. Standard values of time (salary and benefits) were used

Note: This case was prepared to serve as a basis for discussion rather than to illustrate either effective or ineffective administrative and management practices. All names, dates, places, and organizations have been disguised at the request of the authors or organization. A modified version of this case study previously was published *In ROI at Work: Effective Meeting Skills* (J.J. Phillips & P.P. Phillips. Alexandria, VA: ASTD, 2005, pp. 103–123).

to convert data to monetary values. Fully loaded program costs were developed.

## Program Need

TechnoTel Corporation is a maker of telecommunications equipment. Although the firm has twenty-two locations, this case study takes place in Frankfurt, Germany. A needs assessment targeting managerial and supervisory competencies revealed a lack of effective meeting skills, including the ability to prepare, conduct, facilitate, and follow up on meetings. This needs assessment was initiated by a conversation between the Chief Learning Officer (CLO) and the President of Manufacturing in Frankfurt.

The President of manufacturing explained to the CLO his concerns that the learning function placed too much emphasis on activity. An example of his observation was presented in a meeting with the CEO during which the CLO reminded executives how many programs the learning function was developing. He explained to her that in manufacturing the focus is on efficiencies—building more with less while improving quality.

PRESIDENT: In the manufacturing division we focus on efficiencies—building more with less, as well as ensuring quality. We recognize that, while the organization is doing well economically, there has to be some way to manage our resources. We want to make sure that we are getting the most for the investments we make, even when we make them in our people.

But, I look around and I see waste—time being one of the biggest waste factors. Meetings and training appear to be unproductive.

For example, my managers and supervisors, as good as they are technically, cannot run an effective meeting. They invite everyone they can think of, with half of the participants sitting around looking at their watches, checking BlackBerries, or con-figuring process design models. Once the meeting is underway, there is no structure and no agenda. The meetings invariably run over the time allotted. On top of this, there is a meeting on everything. My team spends more time meeting than any other group only to leave the meetings and do nothing as a result of them.

His concern was the time wasted in meetings. According to the president, there were:

- Too many meetings.
- Too many people attending the meetings.
- Meetings were too long.

He explained his concern that time in meetings meant money wasted and productivity lacking. While no definitive dollar amount was known, it was estimated that the cost of lost productivity due to time wasted was in the hundreds of thousands in U.S. dollars per year.

The conversation set the stage for further investigation as to why so many meetings were being held, why too many people were attending the meetings, and why the meetings were too long. With clear instructions not to disrupt productivity any more than necessary, the president agreed to allow the CLO to delve deeper into the cause of the meeting problem by asking some of his staff. Three focus groups, each including eight managers, supervisors, project leaders, and/or employees who participate in meetings on a routine basis, would be conducted to find the cause of the business problems identified by the president.

### Focus Groups

Prior to the focus group selection, the president initiated a commu-niqué explaining that the learning function was in the process of helping him identify the cause of so many meetings in the division. It was also communicated that if a cause was identified, consideration would be given to a variety of solutions. The decision as to which solution would be made was based on cost and convenience, as well as potential effectiveness.

Each focus group was scheduled at the plant for a maximum of two hours. Participants were randomly selected from 150 managers, supervisors, and project leaders, along with the employees at large, to participate in the focus group, then randomly assigned to the focus group in which they would participate. In some cases a person identified to participate in the focus group process would have a conflict and could not participate at the designated time. When this occurred, they would swap their time with someone scheduled for a more convenient time slot. In those few cases when a selected participant was unwilling, a new participant was selected.

The focus group was very structured, focusing specifically on the cause of each of the business problems identified by the president. Each business problem was written on separate pages on a flip chart. Each focus group participant was given a stack of large Post-it® Notes.

The facilitator explained the purpose of the focus groups, then flipped the page on the flip chart to the first business problem:

- There are too many meetings.

Each participant was given approximately two minutes to comment on this issue. Then the facilitator wrote a question on a second flip chart:

- What is happening or not happening on the job that is causing there to be too many meetings?

Focus group participants were asked to write their observations on the Post-it Notes, one per note. Then the facilitator would ask them to post their observations on the flip chart. The facilitator, along with participants, organized the responses into meaningful categories and discussed them to ensure clarity in the meaning of the observations.

The facilitator then wrote another question on the flip chart:

- What knowledge, skills, or information are needed in order to change what is happening or not happening on the job that is causing there to be too many meetings?

Again, the focus group participants wrote their answers on the Post-it Notes and the facilitator placed them on the flip chart. The responses were again categorized.

A final question was written on the flip chart:

- How best can the knowledge, skills, and information identified be presented so that they will change what is happening or not happening on the job that is causing there to be too many meetings?

Once again, participants provided their responses, and the responses were grouped into meaningful categories. This process of identifying job performance needs, learning needs, and preferences for acquiring knowledge was repeated for each of the other two business needs.

The facilitator, with the help of the CLO, reviewed the findings and developed a summary table that was presented to the president along with the proposed solution. Table 1.1 presents the summary of the focus group results.

**Table 1.1. Summary of Needs Assessment**

| Level of Need | Needs |
|---|---|
| Economic Need | What is the economic opportunity or problem? |
| | Specific dollar amount unknown. Estimate hundreds of thousands in U.S. dollars due to time wasted in meetings. |
| Business Need | What are the specific business needs? |
| | Too many meetings |
| | Too many people attending meetings |
| | Meeting are too long |
| Job Performance Need | What is happening or not happening on the job that is causing the business need? |
| | Meetings are not planned |
| | Agendas for meetings are not developed prior to the meeting |
| | Agendas for meetings are not being followed |
| | Consideration of time and cost of unnecessary meetings is lacking |
| | Poor facilitation of meetings |
| | Follow-up on actions resulting from the meeting is not taking place |
| | Conflict that occurs during meetings is not being appropriately managed |
| | Proper selection of meeting participants is not occurring |
| | Good meeting management practices are not implemented |
| | Consideration of cost of meetings is not taking place |
| Learning Need | What knowledge, skill, or information is needed in order to change what is happening or not happening on the job? |
| | Ability to identify the extent and cost of meetings |
| | Ability to identify positives, negatives, and implications of basic meeting issues and dynamics |
| | Effective meeting behaviors |
| Preferences | How best can this knowledge, skill, or information be communicated so that change on the job occurs? |
| | Facilitator-led workshop |
| | Job aids and tools provided |
| | Relevant and useful information a requirement |

### Solution

The summary of needs and a proposed two-day workshop were presented to the president. Program objectives suggest that upon completion of the workshop, participants would have:

- The tools and techniques to prepare, conduct, and follow up on meetings

- An understanding of the human dynamics of meetings

- Strategies for participating in or leading meetings more effectively

In addition to these program outputs, participation in the program was expected to lead to shorter meetings, fewer meetings, and fewer participants attending meetings.

## Program Design

To meet the identified objectives, the two-day Effective Meeting Skills workshop included a variety of knowledge-based exercises as well as skill-based practices and tasks. Figure 1.1 presents the complete outline for the program.

To assist the transfer of skills to the job, a brief action plan was required so that participants could identify specific new and enhanced behaviors and track their progress as they conduct future meetings. Although an important part of the program, the action plan was used primarily to assist participants in their tracking actual use of knowledge and skills.

Along with the action plan, a meeting profile was designed into the program to capture the current level and cost of meetings. It also provided baseline data for comparing improvements resulting from the program. Figure 1.2 presents the meeting profile.

1. Meeting activity profile completed by participants
2. Definition for an effective meeting
3. Criteria for effective meetings
4. Causes behind ineffective meetings
5. Tips for conducting effective meetings
   a. Determine purpose
   b. Recognize the type of meeting
   c. Arrange seating appropriately
   d. Set the agenda
   e. Assemble a set of all appropriate attendees
   f. Establish ground rules
   g. Bring closure and plan follow-up
6. Skill practices
7. Key roles in meetings
8. Meeting tasks
9. The human function in meetings
10. Debriefing model
11. Brainstorming
12. Decision making
13. Encouraging participation
14. Handling group dynamics
15. Dealing with difficult participants
16. Providing feedback
17. Handling conflict
18. Meeting simulations/exercises
19. Action plan requirements

**Figure 1.1. Outline for the Effective Meetings Program**

| Current Meeting Activity (Month Before Program) | | |
|---|---|---|
| • Number of meetings chaired each month | _____ | A |
| • Average number of individuals attending each meeting each month | _____ | B |
| • Average length of time for each meeting (in hours) | _____ | C |
| **Total Time Consumed in Meetings (A x B x C)** | _____ | D |
| • Average hourly compensation of attendees (salary plus benefits) | _____ | E |
| **Total Meeting Costs (D x E)** | _____ | F |

**Figure 1.2. Meeting Profile**

## Target Audience

While the target audience would include all managers, supervisors, and project leaders throughout TechnoTel, the more immediate need was in the Manufacturing Division. The president was interested in conducting the program for 150 of his managers. However, due to the concern about productivity interruption and the president's skepticism toward another training program, he wanted to ensure that the investment was achieving some return. He committed to allow three groups of twenty-four participants to be targeted for a comprehensive evaluation. Understanding that the benefits of the program would be reported for only the seventy-two participants and that the program costs would reflect only the costs of the seventy-two participants, the president saw value in the process and wanted confidence that training was more than an activity. He also made it clear that the value returned should exceed the investment being made in the program.

## Evaluation Need

The nature of the business and the president's interest in accountability led the president to request a comprehensive evaluation of the program. Not only was he interested in whether the program resulted in reduced meetings and fewer participants, but he expressed interest in whether the benefits of his putting his people through the program exceeded the costs.

The president's desire to ensure a positive return on his investment, as well as the corporate learning department's desire to gather data to improve the program overall, led the learning staff's plan of a comprehensive evaluation. Therefore the learning staff implemented the ROI Methodology in its entirety.

## Evaluation Methodology

The ROI Methodology (Phillips, 2003) had been integrated into TechnoTel's corporate learning function two years prior to the launch of the Effective Meeting Skills program. TechnoTel has successfully sustained the use of this process because it:

- Reports a balanced set of measures

- Follows a methodical step-by-step process

- Adheres to standards and philosophy of maintaining a conservative approach and credible outcomes

The ROI Methodology categorizes evaluation data into five levels as shown in Table 1.2. These five levels tell the complete story of program success. The five levels balance economic impact with measures that address individuals' perspectives of the program and success with the transfer of learning.

### Level 1: Reaction, Satisfaction, and Planned Action

This initial level of evaluation is the most commonly used within the TechnoTel learning environment. Reaction and satisfaction

Table 1.2.    The Evaluation Framework

| Level | Measurement Focus |
| --- | --- |
| Reaction, Satisfaction, and Planned Action | Measures participant satisfaction with the program and captures planned action |
| Learning | Measures changes in knowledge, skills, and attitudes |
| Application and Implementation | Measures changes in on-the-job behavior |
| Impact | Measures changes in critical business measures |
| Return-on-Investment (ROI) | Compares the monetary benefits to the costs |

data are collected using a standard end-of-course questionnaire. Planned actions are often collected using action plans, however, a question asking the participants' intent to use what they learned is included on the end-of-course questionnaire and suffices for the planned action measure when action plans are not used.

The TechnoTel learning environment is interested in a variety of measures at Level 1, some of which are relevant only to the learning staff and their efforts to improve the learning process. These measures address course design and delivery as well as participant perception of the learning environment. Because management is interested in potential use of all programs, TechnoTel's Level 1 evaluation also answers five important questions:

1. Is the program relevant to participants' jobs?

2. Is the program important to participants' jobs?

3. Do participants intend to use what they learned in the program?

4. Did the program provide participants with new information?

5. Would participants recommend the programs to others?

An acceptable rating, using a 1 to 5 rating scale (1 = Worst Case; 5 = Best Case), for all TechnoTel courses is 4.0 or above. Any measures that fall below this rating are flagged and actions are taken to improve them in future courses.

## Level 2: Learning

Participant understanding of the knowledge and skills taught in a program is imperative to their ability to change behavior. Learning measurement at TechnoTel takes place during the program through a variety of techniques such as tests, facilitator assessment, peer assessment, self-assessment, observation, and reflective thinking with documentation. The questions that TechnoTel strives to answer when measuring learning are:

1. Do participants understand what they are supposed to do and how to do it?
2. Are participants confident to apply their newly acquired knowledge and skills when they leave the classroom?

## Level 3: Application and Implementation

For many programs, TechnoTel's supervisors and managers are interested in what participants do with what they learn. When this is the case, programs are evaluated at Level 3 using a variety of techniques including self-administered questionnaires, 360-degree feedback, observations, focus groups, and interviews. Because there is more to learning transfer than just attending the program or course, it is important to TechnoTel to gather data related to how the organizational system (management, technology, and so forth) supports the transfer of training. With these considerations, three basic questions are answered at Level 3 for some TechnoTel learning initiatives:

1. How much have participants changed their approach, behavior, or performance?
2. If they are applying their knowledge and skills, what is supporting their effort?
3. If they are not applying their knowledge and skills, why not?

## Level 4: Impact

For many programs TechnoTel is interested in impact on output, quality, cost, and time-measures. For these programs, the organization may also want to know how programs influence customer satisfaction and employee satisfaction—measures that are critical to organizational success but not monetized and only tracked using corporate metrics. The ultimate question answered at Level 4 is, "So what?" By answering this basic question, stakeholders gain an understanding of the consequences of participant application of newly acquired knowledge and/or still.

## Level 5: ROI

This final measure of success answers the question: "Do the monetary benefits of the program exceed the costs?"

For some programs, the organization is not interested in calculating ROI. But for programs that are costly or high profile, that drive business impact, or that are of particular interest to management, ROI is important. A standard ROI target of 25 percent is set for programs being evaluated to this level. This represents a slightly higher ROI than the ROI being achieved by other investments made by TechnoTel.

The balanced set of measures that is yielded by answering the key questions posed at each level of evaluation provides TechnoTel's corporate learning department a complete story of program success. Through this story, the department not only improves the immediate learning process, but also enhances how the system as a whole works to ensure successful transfer of learning and the achievement of desired outcomes. TechnoTel uses all of this information in combination with the ROI metric to determine if a program is a wise investment—either alone or in comparison to alternative programs that may yield similar outcomes.

## Step-by-Step Process

The ten steps in the ROI Methodology constitute a methodical process to evaluation. As shown in Figure 1.3, the evaluation process begins with identifying program objectives and evaluation planning. From there, execution requires that data be collected and analyzed before developing a final report.

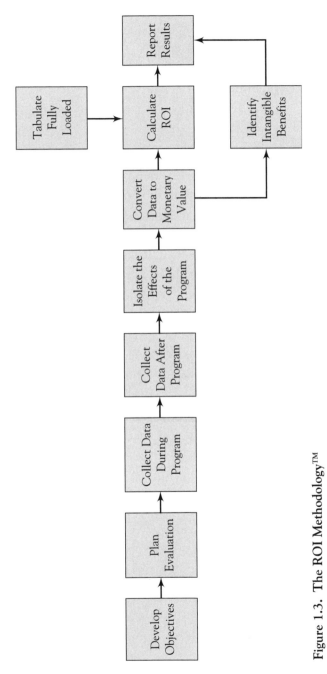

**Figure 1.3. The ROI Methodology™**
Copyright © ROI Institute, Inc.

## Data-Collection Procedures

A pragmatic approach to data collection was taken for the evaluation of the Effective Meeting Skills program. Because the cost of the program (as will be described in a later section) was not excessive, the corporate learning department staff determined that the prudent approach for this particular evaluation would be to keep the cost low while ensuring credible results. The data collection process began with a review of the objectives and measures of success, identification of the appropriate data collection methods and the most credible sources of data, and a determination of the timing of data collection.

### Program Objectives and Measures

The needs assessment identified the knowledge and skill deficiencies that kept managers from conducting effective meetings. Through the needs assessment process and the design of the Effective Meeting Skills program, specific outputs were defined, as well as specific impact measures that would result if participants applied their newly acquired knowledge and skills. Measures of success at Level 1 are standard (4.0 out of 5.0), as is the measure of success at Level 5 (25 percent); measures of success for the other levels of evaluation were dependent on the program or the client expectations. In this case, the president of the division implementing the workshop was interested in improvement in the impact measures; even though he did not specify what improvement he was looking for, he did indicate by his request that the benefits should exceed the cost of the program. Therefore, the improvement must be such that when converted to monetary value a positive ROI was achieved. Table 1.3 summarizes the program's objectives and the measures used to determine success.

### Data Collection Methods

Data were collected for this evaluation using multiple methods: end-of-course questionnaire, action plans, meeting profile, written

**Table 1.3.  Objectives and Measures of Success for the Effective Meeting Skills Program**

|  | Broad Objectives | Measures |
|---|---|---|
| Satisfaction Objectives | Positive reaction and planned action with the knowledge and skills presented in the course | Ranking of 4 out of 5 on:<br>• Relevance<br>• Importance<br>• Intent to use<br>• New information<br>• Recommendation to others |
|  | Planned action | Three different actions to be taken when returning to the job from each participant |
| Learning Objectives | Ability to identify the extent and cost of meetings | Given cost guidelines, determine the cost of last three meetings |
|  | Ability to identify positives, negatives, and implications of basic meeting issues and dynamics | From a list of 30 positive and negative meeting behaviors, correctly identify the implications of each behavior |
|  | Acquisition of effective meeting behaviors | Demonstrate appropriate responses to eight of ten active role play scenarios |
| Application Objectives | Use of effective meeting behaviors | Reported changes in behavior toward planning and conducting meetings |
|  | Barriers to application | Number and variety of barriers identified |
|  | Enablers to application | Number and variety of enablers identified |
| Impact Objectives | Shorter meetings | Reported time savings |
|  | Fewer meetings | Reported time savings |
|  | Fewer meeting participants | Reported time savings |
|  | Other benefits related to improvement in productivity | Reported times savings, cost savings, output improvement, quality improvement project turnaround, etc. |
| ROI | 25% |  |

test, skills practice observation, and a follow-up questionnaire. The successful meeting profile was designed into the program (see Figure 1.2). It was used at the beginning of the program to capture the current level and costs of meetings. When completed, this exercise showed participants how much time they spent in meetings and the overall cost of meetings. These data served as baseline for comparing improvements identified in the follow-up questionnaire. The written test measured the improvements in knowledge of basic issues and meeting dynamics, and skill practices measured success in using effective meeting skills.

The action plan was an important part of understanding how participants applied what they learned when they returned to the job; however, the follow-up questionnaire was the primary data collection method for Level 3 and Level 4 follow-up data. Figure 1.4 presents the follow-up questionnaire.

Because of their desire to limit the cost of the evaluation, the corporate learning department staff decided on the most feasible methods for data collection. Cost data were developed using company records. Table 1.4 summarizes the other data collection methods.

**Data Sources**

Data source selection is a critical step in data collection in that the source drives the credibility and validity of the study. Who knows best about the measures being taken? The primary source of data for the effective meeting skills evaluation was the participants. The managers and project leaders participating in the workshop know the extent to which they apply their knowledge and skills; they are the people who plan and lead the meetings; they are the people who recognize the cost of too many unproductive meetings (they are the ones calling the meetings). Although it may have been valuable to administer surveys to the professional staff participating in the meetings, this step would have added additional cost to the data collection process. The information

Are you currently in a people management role/capacity?    Yes ☐    No ☐

1. Listed below are the objectives of the Effective Meetings program. After reflecting on this program, please indicate the degree of success in meeting the objectives:

| As a result of this program, participants will have: | Failed | Limited Success | Generally Successful | Completely Successful |
|---|---|---|---|---|
| a. the tools and techniques to prepare for, conduct, and follow up on meetings. | ☐ | ☐ | ☐ | ☐ |
| b. an understanding of the human dynamics of meetings | ☐ | ☐ | ☐ | ☐ |
| c. strategies to participate in and lead meetings more effectively | ☐ | ☐ | ☐ | ☐ |

2. Did you develop and implement an on-the-job action plan for Effective Meetings? Yes ☐    No ☐
   If yes, please describe the nature and outcome of the plan. If not, explain why.

   _____

   _____

   _____

3. Please rate, on a scale of 1 to 5, the relevance of each of the program elements to your job, with (1) indicating no relevance and (5) indicating very relevant.

| | 1 | 2 | 3 | 4 | 5 |
|---|---|---|---|---|---|
| a. Interactive Activities | ☐ | ☐ | ☐ | ☐ | ☐ |
| b. Groups Discussions | ☐ | ☐ | ☐ | ☐ | ☐ |
| c. Networking Opportunities | ☐ | ☐ | ☐ | ☐ | ☐ |
| d. Reading Materials/Video | ☐ | ☐ | ☐ | ☐ | ☐ |
| e. Program Content | ☐ | ☐ | ☐ | ☐ | ☐ |

4. Have you used the written materials since you participated in the program? Yes ☐    No ☐
   Please explain.    _____

5. Please indicate the degree to which you have changed the use of the following items/actions/behaviors enhanced as a result of your participation in *Effective Meetings*:

| | No Change | Little Change | Some Change | Significant Change | Very Much Change | No Opportunity to Use Skill |
|---|---|---|---|---|---|---|
| a. Participating Effectively in Meetings | ☐ | ☐ | ☐ | ☐ | ☐ | ☐ |
| b. Avoiding Meetings Unless They Are Necessary | ☐ | ☐ | ☐ | ☐ | ☐ | ☐ |

**Figure 1.4. Effective Meeting Skills Follow-Up Impact Questionnaire**

| | | | | | | |
|---|---|---|---|---|---|---|
| c. Minimizing the Number of Participants Attending Meetings | ☐ | ☐ | ☐ | ☐ | ☐ | ☐ |
| d. Setting Objectives for Meetings | ☐ | ☐ | ☐ | ☐ | ☐ | ☐ |
| e. Developing an Agenda for Each Meeting | ☐ | ☐ | ☐ | ☐ | ☐ | ☐ |
| f. Controlling Time of Meetings | ☐ | ☐ | ☐ | ☐ | ☐ | ☐ |
| g. Enhancing Participant Satisfaction in Meetings | ☐ | ☐ | ☐ | ☐ | ☐ | ☐ |
| h. Arranging the Meeting Site for Maximum Effectiveness | ☐ | ☐ | ☐ | ☐ | ☐ | ☐ |
| i. Scheduling the Optimum Time for Meetings | ☐ | ☐ | ☐ | ☐ | ☐ | ☐ |
| j. Communicating the Ground Rules for Meetings | ☐ | ☐ | ☐ | ☐ | ☐ | ☐ |
| k. Assigning Appropriate Roles for Meeting Participants | ☐ | ☐ | ☐ | ☐ | ☐ | ☐ |
| l. Reaching Consensus in Meetings When Appropriate | ☐ | ☐ | ☐ | ☐ | ☐ | ☐ |
| m. Listening Actively to Meeting Participants | ☐ | ☐ | ☐ | ☐ | ☐ | ☐ |
| n. Encouraging Participation in Meetings | ☐ | ☐ | ☐ | ☐ | ☐ | ☐ |
| o. Using Brainstorming in Meetings When Appropriate | ☐ | ☐ | ☐ | ☐ | ☐ | ☐ |
| p. Dealing with Difficult Meeting Participants | ☐ | ☐ | ☐ | ☐ | ☐ | ☐ |
| q. Providing Feedback to Meeting Participants | ☐ | ☐ | ☐ | ☐ | ☐ | ☐ |
| r. Handling Conflict in Meeting | ☐ | ☐ | ☐ | ☐ | ☐ | ☐ |
| s. Keeping the Meeting on Focus | ☐ | ☐ | ☐ | ☐ | ☐ | ☐ |
| t. Accomplishing Meeting Objectives | ☐ | ☐ | ☐ | ☐ | ☐ | ☐ |
| u. Evaluating the Meeting Process | ☐ | ☐ | ☐ | ☐ | ☐ | ☐ |
| v. Implementing Action Plans | ☐ | ☐ | ☐ | ☐ | ☐ | ☐ |
| w. Planning a Follow-Up Activity | ☐ | ☐ | ☐ | ☐ | ☐ | ☐ |

6. List the five *Effective Meeting* behaviors or skills you have used most frequently as a result of the program.

_____

_____

_____

**Figure 1.4.  (Continued)**

7. What has changed about your meeting activity profile as a result of this program? (Fewer meetings, fewer participants, shorter meetings, etc.)

_____

_____

_____

8. Please estimate the following monthly time-saving measures. Use the most recent month compared to the month before attending this program. Provide only improvements directly related to this program and only when the time saved is used productively.

☐    Number of meetings avoided each month with improved
     planning and analysis                                        _____

☐    Average time saved per meeting per month (in hours)          _____

☐    Average number of participants reduced per meeting
     per month                                                    _____

9. What level of confidence do you place on the above estimations? (0 percent = No Confidence, 100 percent = Certainty)

_____ percent

10. Please identify any specific accomplishments/improvements that you can link to this program (on-time schedules, project completion, response times, better decisions, more ideas from group, etc.)

_____

_____

_____

11. What specific value in U.S. dollars can be attributed to the above accomplishments/improvements? Use first-year values only. While this is a difficult question, try to think of specific ways in which the above improvements can be converted to monetary units. Along with the monetary value, please indicate the basis of your calculation.

$_____

Basis _____

_____

12. What level of confidence do you place on the above estimations?

(0 percent = No Confidence, 100 percent = Certainty)

_____ percent

13. Other factors often influence improvements in performance. Please indicate the percent of the above improvement that is related directly to this program.

_____ percent

Please explain. _____

_____

**Figure 1.4.  (Continued)**

14. Do you think the **Effective Meetings** program represented a good investment for TechnoTel?

    Yes ☐   No ☐

    Please explain. _____

    _____

    Was it a good investment of your time?

    Yes ☐   No ☐

    Please explain. _____

    _____

15. Indicate the extent to which you think the **Effective Meetings** program has influenced each of these measures in your work unit, department, or business unit:

| | No Influence | Some Influence | Moderate Influence | Significant Influence | Very Much Influence |
|---|---|---|---|---|---|
| a. Productivity | ☐ | ☐ | ☐ | ☐ | ☐ |
| b. Customer Response Time | ☐ | ☐ | ☐ | ☐ | ☐ |
| c. Cost Control | ☐ | ☐ | ☐ | ☐ | ☐ |
| d. Employee Satisfaction | ☐ | ☐ | ☐ | ☐ | ☐ |
| e. Customer Satisfaction | ☐ | ☐ | ☐ | ☐ | ☐ |
| f. Quality | ☐ | ☐ | ☐ | ☐ | ☐ |
| g. Other _____ | ☐ | ☐ | ☐ | ☐ | ☐ |

16. What barriers, if any, have you encountered that have prevented you from using skills or knowledge gained in this program. Please explain, if possible.

    _____

    _____

17. What enablers, if any, are present to help you use the skills or knowledge gained from this program? Please explain.

    _____

    _____

18. What additional benefits have been derived from this program?

    _____

    _____

19. What specific suggestions do you have for improving this program?

    _____

    _____

20. Other comments:

    _____

    _____

**Figure 1.4.  (Continued)**

Table 1.4.  Data Collection Methods

| | Level 1 | Level 2 | Level 3 | Barriers/ Enablers | Level 4 | Costs |
|---|---|---|---|---|---|---|
| End-of-Course Questionnaire | X | | | | | |
| Meeting Profile | | X | | | | |
| Written Test | | X | | | | |
| Skill Practice Observation | | X | | | | |
| Action Plan | X | | X | | | |
| Questionnaire | | | X | X | X | |
| Company Records | | | | | | X |

they would have provided would have been valuable, but the perceived value of their input did not appear to outweigh the time and cost involved in collecting and analyzing the additional data. It was decided that the participants would serve as the source of data for this evaluation.

While the program was intended to be implemented to all 150 managers and supervisors, the president agreed to allow seventy-two people (three groups) to participate initially in the evaluation. This limitation would save cost and time of evaluation and would provide the president the data he needed to make a fair assessment of the success of the program. The evaluation results would be based on benefits dervied from the seventy-two and the costs of training those seventy-two.

## Data Collection Timing

When conducting a comprehensive evaluation such as that completed for the Effective Meeting Skills workshop, data is collected at two different timeframes: Levels 1 and 2 data are collected during the program, and Levels 3 and 4 data are collected after participants have had time to apply knowledge and skills on a routine basis. It was determined that, given the type of skills being developed in the

Effective Meeting Skills program and the numerous opportunities managers have to apply the skills, three months would be ample time for the acquired skills to be internalized and produce results. Therefore, three months after completing the program, participants would receive the follow-up questionnaire.

Figure 1.5 presents the complete data collection plan. The corporate learning staff presented the data collection plan and the ROI analysis plan (described in the next section) to the division president for concurrence prior to execution.

## Success with Data Collection

A data collection administration strategy is important for ensuring that the appropriate amount of data is provided. In the case of the Effective Meeting Skills workshop, the administrative strategy consisted of four primary actions:

1. The evaluation strategy was presented at the beginning of the program.

2. The facilitators reinforced the need for participants to respond to the follow-up questionnaire at the end of the program.

3. The division president signed a letter that was distributed three days prior to the questionnaires being mailed.

4. The questionnaire did not require that participants include their names or other demographic information; therefore, respondents remained anonymous.

All participants responded to the Level 1 and 2 evaluations; the follow-up for Levels 3 and 4 proved to be challenging, however. The overall response rate was 67 percent (forty-eight respondents), which was satisfactory to the evaluation team and the division president. Unfortunately, only 43 percent (thirty-one respondents) of the participants provided useable data on Questions 8, and 9 (see Figure 1.4). These two questions were directly related to follow-up

Evaluation Purpose: _____  Responsibility: _____  Date: _____
Program: Effective Meetings

| Level | Broad Program Objective(s) | Measures | Data Collection Method/Instruments | Data Sources | Timing | Responsibilities |
|---|---|---|---|---|---|---|
| 1 | REACTION/SATISFACTION & PLANNED ACTIONS<br>• Positive Reaction<br>• Planned Actions | • Average rating of at least 4.0 on 5.0 scale on quality, usefulness and achievement of program objectives.<br>• 100% submit planned actions | • End of Course Questionnaire<br>• Completed Action Plans | Participants | • End of Course | Facilitator |
| 2 | LEARNING<br>• Identify the extent and cost of meetings<br>• Identify positives, negatives, and implications of basic meeting issues and dynamics<br>• Acquisition of Effective Meeting behaviors | • Given cost guidelines, identify the cost of last three meetings<br>• From a list of 30 positive and negative meeting behaviors, correctly identify the implications of each behavior<br>• Demonstrate appropriate response to 8 of 10 active role play scenarios | • Meeting Profile<br>• Written Test<br>• Skill Practice Observation | Participants | • At the Beginning of Program<br>• At the Beginning of the Program (Pre)<br>• At the End of the Program (Post)<br>• During Program | Facilitator |
| 3 | APPLICATION/ IMPLEMENTATION<br>• Use of Effective Meeting behaviors<br>• Examine the need for a meeting and scrutinize the list of participants invited | • Reported actions to influence more effective meetings<br>• Reported use of effective meeting planning and meeting conduct behaviors | • Action Plan<br>• Questionnaire (for three groups) | Participants | 3 Months | Program Owner |
| 4 | BUSINESS IMPACT<br>• Time Savings from fewer meetings, shorter meetings, and fewer participants (Hours Saved Per Month)<br>• Variety of Business Impact Measures from more successful meetings | • Time savings<br>• Time savings, cost savings, output improvement, quality improvement, project turnaround, etc. as reported | • Questionnaire (for three groups) | Participants | 3 Months | Program Owner |
| 5 | ROI<br>Target ROI at least 25 percent | Comments: | | | | |

Figure 1.5. Data Collection Plan

on the impact measures. With the understanding that the results would reflect only that which occurred for those responding, the division president was satisfied with the response rate.

## Data Analysis Procedures

Data analysis comprises five key steps, each of which was carefully considered during the evaluation of this workshop:

1. Isolating the effects of the program
2. Converting data to monetary value
3. Tabulating fully loaded costs
4. Identifying intangible benefits
5. Comparing the monetary benefits to the costs

### Isolating the Effects of the Program

This step of the ROI Methodology answers the question, "How do you know it was your program that influenced the measures?" Isolating the effects of the program considers all other variables that may have influenced improvement in specific measures of success for a program. Four of the ten potential techniques were considered for the Effective Meeting Skills workshop: control group, trend line analysis, forecasting, and participant estimations.

Because only seventy-two of the 150 were being evaluated, it was first suggested that a control group arrangement could be used to isolate the effects of the program. The thought was that those managers and supervisors not participating in the evaluation process could serve as the control group. After much deliberation, however, it was agreed that it would be difficult to maintain the integrity of the experiment and it would be disruptive.

Participants completed a meeting profile during the program to determine the time, frequency, and participation of meetings, along with the costs. To collect similar data from the control group, its members would have to complete meeting profiles as well. This would not only contribute to the contamination of the experiment, but would require additional work for the control group members. It was important to the division president to keep the evaluation low key by not requiring too much additional work and by not disrupting the organization. For these reasons, the control group arrangement was eliminated as an option.

Historical data were not available for the primary measure (time savings), so trend line analysis and forecasting were inappropriate as well. The only remaining option was the use of participant estimations for isolating the effects of the workshop on the three impact measures: shorter meetings, reduced number of meetings, and fewer participants attending meetings.

### Converting Data to Monetary Value

When moving from Level 4 to Level 5 evaluation, this step is the most critical because it determines the numerator (top number) in the ROI equation. Ten techniques to convert data to monetary value are possible. For this evaluation, however, the technique was apparent. As the outcome measures were all time related, the standard value of hourly compensation (salary plus benefits) for the participant chairing the meeting, as well as those attending the meeting, was used. If other business measures improved due to the programs, they would be converted to money using participant estimates unless standard values were available.

### Tabulating Fully Loaded Costs

To calculate ROI, it is imperative to use the fully loaded costs of the program. Costs categories for the Effective Meeting Skills workshop were:

- Needs assessment (facilitator time, participant time, materials, refreshments)

- Program fee (facilitator costs, materials, program design and development)

- Travel, lodging, meals

- Facilities

- Participants' salaries and benefits for their time in the classroom

- Evaluation costs

### Identifying Intangible Benefits

Intangible benefits are any unplanned benefits derived from the program or any benefits not converted to monetary value. There were many intangible benefits of the Effective Meeting Skills workshop, which will be listed in the Evaluation Results section that follows.

## Calculating ROI

The ROI equation compares net benefits (earnings) to the program costs (investment). It can be reported as a BCR by comparing the benefits to the program costs. ROI is well-used within the TechnoTel organization. Managers and professionals recognize the acronym for what it is; therefore, to ensure that the corporate learning department speaks the same language as the business, the following equation is used to report ROI:

$$BCR = \frac{Benefits}{Costs}$$

$$ROI = \frac{Net\ Program\ Benefits}{Costs} \times 100$$

A 25 percent ROI target is standard for most programs being evaluated at this level. Because of the nature of the program, the evaluation team and the division president believed this to be a conservative target.

Figure 1.6 presents the completed ROI analysis plan. As in the case of the data collection plan, the ROI analysis plan was presented to the division president prior to implementing the evaluation. The division president concurred with the plan.

The ROI Methodology used for evaluating the Effective Meeting Skills program adhered to a set of operating standards or guiding principles, as presented in Table 1.5. These Twelve Guiding Principles keep the process consistent and conservative.

## Evaluation Results

The results of the study indicated that the program was successful. Participants enjoyed the workshop, but, even more important, they saw it as relevant and useful. Participants quickly grasped the ability to define meeting costs and began implementing the new knowledge and skills. Although there were some barriers to application, they were minimal. From the perspective of the division president, however, the impact on time spent in meetings was significant; the investment returned positive results.

### Level 1: Reaction, Satisfaction, and Planned Action

Level 1 objectives included reaction and satisfaction measures important to improving facilitation, content, and materials. The key measures of interest, however, addressed issues indicating intent to use, including three defined actions to be taken upon return to the job. The measure of success was a minimum score of 4.0 out of 5.0. Results were successful in regard to relevance, importance, intent to use, and willingness to recommend the workshop to others. Only one measure (new information) fell below the 4.0 target. This was anticipated, in that most of the concepts were familiar, but the packaging and tools provided a new perspective on the familiar topics.

| Data Items (Usually Level 4) | Methods for Isolating the Effects of the Program/Process | Methods of Converting Data to Monetary Values | Cost Categories | Intangible Benefits | Communication Targets for Final Report | Other Influences/Issues During Application | Comments |
|---|---|---|---|---|---|---|---|
| • Time Savings | • Participant's Estimate | • Hourly Wage and Benefits | • Needs Assessment<br>• Program Fee Per Participant<br>• Travel/Lodging Meals<br>• Facilities<br>• Participant Salaries Plus Benefits<br>• Evaluation Costs | • Improvement in Individual Productivity Not Captured Elsewhere<br>• Stress Reduction<br>• Improved Planning and Scheduling<br>• Greater Participation in Meetings | • Business Unit President<br>• Senior Managers<br>• Managers of Participants<br>• Participants<br>• Training and Development Staff | • Participants must see need for providing measurement<br>• Follow-up process will be explained to participants during program<br>• Three groups will be measured | • Participants will identify specific improvements as a result of meetings being conducted more effectively |
| • Miscellaneous Business Measures | • Participant's Estimate | • Participant's Estimate (Using Standard Values when available) | | | | | |
| | | | | | | | |
| | | | | | | | |

Figure 1.6. ROI Analysis Plan

29

**Table 1.5.    Twelve Guiding Principles of ROI**

1. When conducting a higher-level evaluation, collect data at lower. levels.
2. When planning a higher-level evaluation, the previous level of evaluation is not required to be comprehensive.
3. When collecting and analyzing data, use only the most credible sources.
4. When analyzing data, select the most conservative alternative for calculations.
5. Use at least one method to isolate the effects of a project.
6. If no improvement data are available for a population or from a specific source, assume that little or no improvement has occurred.
7. Adjust estimates of improvement for potential errors of estimation.
8. Avoid use of extreme data items and unsupported claims when calculating ROI.
9. Use only the first year of annual benefits in ROI analysis of short-term solutions.
10. Fully load all costs of a solution, project, or program when analyzing ROI.
11. Intangible measures are defined as measures that are purposely not converted to monetary values.
12. Communicate the results of ROI Methodology to all key stakeholders.

The participants listed three defined actions they planned to take when returning to the job. The most noted action was implementing the meeting activity profile as a routine tool when reflecting on meetings each month. Also, participants indicated they would follow the seven steps to conducting an effective meeting as listed in the program outline (see Figure 1.1).

**Level 2: Learning**

Level 2 objectives suggested that participants should be able to:

- Identify the extent and cost of meetings

- Identify positives, negatives, and implications of basic meeting issues and dynamics

- Acquire effective meeting behaviors

The meeting profile identifying costs of meetings was successfully completed by participants. They felt comfortable with the tool and indicated the ability to complete similar items during the follow-up. A simple multiple-choice test was administered to ensure that participants understood the basic issue of meetings. The average score the test was a 92 out of a possible 100.

Exercises and skill practice indicated that participants were equipped with the knowledge and skills to successfully conduct meetings while reducing the cost of meetings by conducting shorter meetings, fewer meetings, and including fewer meeting participants.

**Level 3: Application and Implementation**

The follow-up evaluation (see Figure 1.4) took place three months after the workshop. Questions 4, 5, 6, 16, and 17 related to application of knowledge and skills. The fundamental question with regard to application was Question 5, which assessed how much participants had changed their approach to planning and conducting meetings using the knowledge and skills they learned from the workshop. Table 1.6 summarizes the degree of change in behavior that occurred. For the most part, participants did change their meeting practices; some measures, however, indicated that little change occurred in some areas. Providing feedback to meeting participants (item Q), evaluating the meeting process (item U), and planning follow-up activity (item W) appeared to be the least used skills.

Examining the barriers (Question 16) to the use of the knowledge and skills learned in the workshop shed some light on the reasons why there was less change in some areas than in others.

**Table 1.6. Level 3 Evaluation Responses**

| | No Change | Little Change | Some Change | Significant Change | Very Much Change | No Opportunity to Use Skill |
|---|---|---|---|---|---|---|
| a. Participating Effectively in Meetings | 0 | 0 | 25% | 44% | 31% | 0 |
| b. Avoiding Meetings Unless They Are Necessary | 0 | 0 | 19% | 46% | 35% | 0 |
| c. Minimizing the Number of Participants Attending Meetings | 0 | 0 | 19% | 50% | 31% | 0 |
| d. Setting Objectives for Meetings | 0 | 0 | 25% | 42% | 33% | 0 |
| e. Developing an Agenda for Each Meeting | 0 | 4% | 27% | 44% | 25% | 0 |
| f. Controlling Time of Meetings | 0 | 0 | 6% | 44% | 50% | 0 |
| g. Enhancing Participant Satisfaction in Meetings | 0 | 10% | 31% | 44% | 15% | 0 |
| h. Arranging the Meeting Site for Maximum Effectiveness | 0 | 0 | 4% | 65% | 31% | 0 |
| i. Scheduling the Optimum Time for Meetings | 0 | 0 | 25% | 42% | 33% | 0 |
| j. Communicating the Ground Rules for Meetings | 0 | 4% | 27% | 44% | 25% | 0 |
| k. Assigning Appropriate Roles for Meeting Participants | 0 | 0 | 6% | 44% | 50% | 0 |
| l. Reaching Consensus in Meetings When Appropriate | 0 | 0 | 13% | 52% | 35% | 0 |
| m. Listening Actively to Meeting Participants | 0 | 0 | 4% | 65% | 31% | 0 |
| n. Encouraging Participation in Meetings | 0 | 0 | 25% | 42% | 33% | 0 |
| o. Using Brainstorming in Meetings When Appropriate | 0 | 4% | 27% | 44% | 25% | 0 |
| p. Dealing with Difficult Meeting Participants | 0 | 0 | 6% | 44% | 50% | 0 |
| q. Providing Feedback to Meeting Participants | 0 | 19% | 56% | 25% | 0 | 0 |
| r. Handling Conflict in Meeting | 0 | 4% | 31% | 50% | 15% | 0 |
| s. Keeping the Meeting on Focus | 0 | 0 | 25% | 42% | 33% | 0 |
| t. Accomplishing Meeting Objectives | 0 | 4% | 27% | 44% | 25% | 0 |
| u. Evaluating the Meeting Process | 0 | 10% | 38% | 38% | 15% | 0 |
| v. Implementing Action Plans | 0 | 2% | 33% | 46% | 19% | 0 |
| w. Planning a Follow-Up Activity | 0 | 6% | 42% | 35% | 17% | 0 |

The most often cited barrier was time. Some participants indicated they did not have the time to evaluate the success of the meeting or follow up with meeting participants; however, others indicated that both of these actions were a valuable part of the meeting process.

Enabling factors (Question 17) supported the use of meeting skills learned in the workshop. The most often cited enabling factors were the job aids and materials participants took with them from the course. The workbook was cited as being the most valuable tool. Some participants indicated that senior management's interest in the tools and the workshop encouraged them to take the application of what they learned seriously.

### Level 4: Impact

The intended outcomes of the Effective Meeting Skills workshop were shorter meetings, fewer meetings, and fewer meeting participants. Other measures of improvement were of interest, but the president was specifically interested in the payoff of the program with respect to these measures. By applying the knowledge and skills learned in the workshop, improvement in these three time-related measures did occur. Figure 1.7 presents a comparison of the original meeting profile data obtained from participants during the program to the average post-program data. The average amounts taken from Question 8 are subtracted from the average pre-program data to get the average post-program data. Only thirty-one participants (43 percent) responded to Questions 8 and 9; the average confidence in the estimates for the group responding was 81 percent. The figure shows that the intended outcomes (reduction in the number of meetings, less time spent in meetings, and fewer participants attending meetings) were achieved as a result of the program.

Other measures improved as a result of the program as well. Respondents indicated improvement in overall productivity and quality of the meetings, and six managers placed monetary values on these measures. However, the monetary payoff of the program is based on the time savings from the above measures. The other

| Current Meeting Activity (Month Before Program) | | Average Pre-Program Data | Average Post-Program Data |
|---|---|---|---|
| Number of meetings chaired each month | A | 6.5 | 5.2 |
| Average number of individuals attending each meeting each month | B | 7.2 | 5.1 |
| Average length of time for each meeting (in hours) | C | 2.6 | 1.7 |
| **Total Time Consumed in Meetings (A × B × C)** | D | 121.68 | 45.1 |

| Averaged Responses to Question 8 (Follow-Up Questionnaire) | |
|---|---|
| **Meetings Avoided** | |
| Estimate of number of meetings avoided each month | 1.3 |
| **Shorter Meetings** | |
| Estimate of average time saved per meeting (in hours) | 0.9 |
| **Reduced Number of Participants in Meetings** | |
| Estimate of number of participants reduced for each meeting | 2.1 |
| Number completing programs | 72 (three groups) |
| Number of questionnaires Returned | 48 (67 percent) |
| Number of questionnaires with usable data for Questions 8 and 9 | 31 (43 percent) |
| Average value of confidence level from Question 9 | 81 percent |

**Figure 1.7. Improvement in Time Spent on Meetings**

measures were reported as "other benefits" because they were not as credible as the time savings.

## Level 5: ROI

The ROI for the Effective Meeting Skills workshop was calculated based on time savings. To calculate the ROI, improvement in time savings due to shorter meetings, fewer meetings, and fewer meeting participants were converted to monetary value and then compared to the costs of the program.

## Monetary Benefits

The data conversion technique used was a standard value of time, which equates to average hourly compensation of attendees plus the benefits factor of 32 percent. The average hourly cost of an attendee was calculated to be $31. As shown in Figure 1.8, an average monthly savings in meeting costs based on the three measures was $2,373.98. This amount represents the difference in pre-program costs ($3,772.08) and post-program costs ($1,398.10).

| Current Meeting Activity (Month Before Program) | | Average Pre-Program Data | Average Post-Program Data | |
|---|---|---|---|---|
| Number of meetings chaired each month | A | 6.5 | 5.2 | |
| Average number of individuals attending each meeting each month | B | 7.2 | 5.1 | |
| Average length of time for each meeting (in hours) | C | 2.6 | 1.7 | |
| **Total Time Consumed in Meetings (A × B × C)** | D | 121.68 | 45.1 | |
| Average hourly compensation of attendees (salary plus benefits) | E | $31.00 | $31.00 | |
| **Total Meeting Costs (D × E)** | F | $3,772.08 | $1,398.10 | |
| **Meetings Avoided** | | | | |
| Estimate of number of mettings avoided each month | | | 1.3 | G |
| **Shorter Meetings** | | | | |
| Estimate of average time saved per meeting (in hours) | | | 0.9 | H |
| **Reduced Participants in Meetings** | | | | |
| Estimate of number of participants reduced for each meeting | | | 2.1 | I |
| **Total Savings** | | | | |
| **Monthly Meeting Savings (Pre–Post Costs)** | | | $2,373.98 | J |
| **Annual Savings (J × 12)** | | | $28,487.76 | K |

**Figure 1.8. Monetary Benefits of Time Savings**

The ROI is an annual value, and the division president wanted to see a payoff within the first year. The savings were annualized using this monthly average, yielding a monetary benefit of $28,487.76 for one participant.

To calculate the full benefits of the program, the monthly value was multiplied by the number of participants who provided useable data (thirty-one); the confidence adjustment was also considered (81 percent). The full value of the Effective Meeting Skills workshop was: ($28,487.76 × 31) × 0.81 = $715,327.65

### Fully Loaded Costs

Program costs included the program fee, which incorporated materials and facilitator costs; travel, lodging, and meals for participants; facilities; participants' time in the workshop (salaries and benefits); and evaluation costs. The needs assessment of $5,000 was also included. However, since the program was intended to go out to the entire 150 managers and supervisors, these costs were prorated over the number of people attending the program, and calculated only for the seventy-two in the evaluation. Even though the benefits were calculated only for those responding, program costs accounted for all participant costs. The fully loaded costs of the Effective Meeting Skills workshop are shown in Table 1.7.

The return on investing in the Effective Meeting Skills workshop was 470 percent, as shown by the calculation below.

$$\text{BCR} = \frac{\$715,327.65}{\$125,408} = 5.7{:}1$$

$$\text{ROI} = \frac{\$715,327.65 - \$125,408}{\$125,408} \times 100 = 470\%$$

The ROI told the division president that for every dollar spent on the workshop, TechnoTel received $4.70 after costs. On the surface, the ROI seemed high in comparison to other investments. But because the division president knew the value of time and knew how much time had been wasted in meetings in the past,

**Table 1.7.  Costs Used in the ROI Calculation for the Effective Meeting Skills Workshop**

| Item | Calculation | Cost |
|---|---|---|
| Needs Assessment | $5,000 prorated over 150 participants | $2,400 |
| Program Fee | $800 per participant × 72 | $57,600 |
| Travel, Lodging, Meals | $245 × 72 | $17,640 |
| Facilities | $190 × 6* | $1,140 |
| Participant Time | $219 per day × 1.32 × 2 × 72)** | $41,628 |
| Evaluation Costs |  | $5,000 |
| | **Total Costs** | **$125,408** |

*Facilities cost $190 per day; the workshop required two days and was offered to three groups.

**Participant time includes average salaries of $219 per day multiplied by the benefits factor of 32 percent. Each participant was in the workshop for two days; the cost accounts for all seventy-two participants.

the ROI calculation was believable. The evaluation team had been diligent in advising the division president of the evaluation process and keeping him abreast of the findings, thereby enhancing the credibility of the ROI process.

## Intangible Benefits

The financial impact to TechnoTel was an important outcome of the evaluation. However, other important outcomes occurred as well. Along with improvement in overall productivity and quality of meetings, employees and their supervisors in TechnoTel were becoming happier in the work setting due to the reduction in wasteful meetings. The groups who had attended the Effective Meeting Skills workshop took the process seriously and had a keen desire to improve their meeting process; therefore, tools were being implemented. This also helped improve customer satisfaction—both external and internal customers. Respondents to the evaluation reported being more accessible and more focused on customer concerns.

An interesting unexpected benefit of the program was that the division president began using the meeting profile worksheet as a tool to manage the cost of his own meetings. He asked that his senior leaders do the same. The tool has become a time management tool throughout this division of TechnoTel.

## Communication Strategy

The success of the ROI study at TechnoTel can be attributed to the continuous communication throughout the process. From the outset, the division president was kept informed of the progress with the study. He was involved in the planning stage and data collection. As results at Levels 3 and 4 began rolling in, the evaluation team kept him informed. Once the study was completed and the division president was aware of the results, the senior management team participated in a one-hour briefing. Because there were several new senior managers who were unfamiliar with the evaluation practice at TechnoTel, a full presentation was conducted. The presentation topics included:

- Need for effective meetings
- Program design
- Need for evaluation
- Evaluation methodology
- Evaluation results

At the end of the presentation, each person received a copy of the complete report, as well as a summary copy.

Based on the questions and the response to the presentation, the senior management saw the evaluation process as credible. Even more important, they saw the value of the Effective Meeting Skills workshop and asked that the program be implemented in other areas of TechnoTel.

## Lessons Learned

Regardless of the number of evaluation studies conducted, there are always lessons to learn. Because the evaluation team thought there was an understanding of the evaluation process, they did not spend enough time explaining Questions 8 and 9. Had they done a better job covering those questions on the questionnaire, they might have achieved a greater response rate.

Because evaluation is routine at TechnoTel, the questionnaire administration strategy seemed appropriate. However, with only a 67 percent response rate, there was room for improvement.

*Questions for Discussion*

1. Was the president justified in asking for a comprehensive evaluation of an effective meetings skills workshop?
2. How could the needs assessment have been improved?
3. What steps could have been taken to ensure a higher response rate, especially for Questions 7, 8, and 9 on the questionnaire?
4. How credible are the time savings data?
5. How would you have approached the evaluation strategy for the Effective Meeting Skills workshop?

## About the Author

**Patricia Pulliam Phillips, Ph.D.,** President and CEO of the ROI Institute, Inc., Patti earned her doctoral degree in international development and her master's degree in public and private management. Early in her professional career, Patti was a corporate manager who observed performance improvement initiatives from the client perspective and knew that results were imperative. Since 1997 Patti has embraced the ROI Methodology as a tool to show value for and improve program and policy implementation.

She has contributed to the development of the ROI Methodology through research and application. Internationally known as an accountability, measurement, and evaluation expert, Patti facilitates workshops all over the world and consults with U.S. and international organizations—public, private, nonprofit, and educational—on implementing the ROI Methodology™. Patti is co-author of *Show Me the Money* (Berrett-Koehler, 2007), *The Value of Learning* (Pfeiffer, 2007), and the author of *The Bottomline on ROI* (CEP Press, 2002), which won the 2003 ISPI Award of Excellence. She is editor or co-author of *ROI Basics* (ASTD, 2006), *ROI at Work: Best-Practice Case Studies from the Real World* (ASTD, 2005), *Proving the Value of HR: How and Why to Measure ROI* (SHRM, 2005), *The Human Resources Scorecard: Measuring the Return on Investment* (Butterworth-Heinemann, 2001), and *Measuring ROI in the Public Sector* (ASTD, 2002).

# 2

# Measuring ROI in Business Coaching
## A Global Hotel Chain

Jack J. Phillips

## Abstract

The leadership and development team at the Nations Hotel Corporation was challenged to identify learning needs to help executives find ways to improve efficiency, customer satisfaction, and revenue growth in the company. A key component of the program was the development of a formal, structured coaching program, Coaching for Business Impact. The corporate executives were interested in seeing the actual ROI for the coaching project. This case study provides critical insights into how coaching creates value in an organization including ROI.

## Background

Nations Hotel Corporation (NHC) is a large U.S.-based hotel firm with operations in fifteen countries. The firm has maintained

Note: This case was prepared as a basis for discussion, rather than to illustrate either effective or ineffective administrative and management practices. All names, dates, places, and organizations have been disguised at the request of the authors or organizations. This is an update of a case study originally published in *ROI at Work: Best Practice Case Studies from the Real World*, (Phillips, J.J., & Phillips, P.P., American Society for Training and Development, Alexandria, VA, 2005).

steady growth to include more than three hundred hotels in cities all over the world. NHC enjoys one of the most recognized names in the global lodging industry, with 98 percent brand awareness worldwide and 72 percent overall guest satisfaction.

The hospitality industry is very competitive, cyclical, and subject to swings with the economy. Room rentals are price sensitive, and customer satisfaction is extremely important for NHC. Profits are squeezed if operating costs get out of hand. NHC top executives constantly seek ways to improve operational efficiency, customer satisfaction, revenue growth, and retention of high-performing employees. Executives—particularly those in charge of individual properties—are under constant pressure to show improvement in these key measures.

The learning and development function, the Nations Hotel Learning Organization (NHLO), conducted a brief survey of executives to identify learning needs to help them meet some of their particular goals. NHLO was interested in developing customized learning processes, including the possibility of individual coaching sessions. Most of the executives surveyed indicated that they would like to work with a qualified coach to assist them through a variety of challenges and issues. The executives believed that this would be an efficient way to learn, apply, and achieve results. Consequently, NHLO developed a formal, structured coaching program—Coaching for Business Impact (CBI)—and offered it to the executives at the vice president level and above.

As the project was conceived, the senior executive team became interested in showing the value of the coaching project. Although they supported coaching as a method to improve executive performance, they wanted to see the actual ROI. The goal was to evaluate twenty-five executives, randomly selected (if possible) from the participants in CBI.

## The Program

Figure 2.1 shows the steps in the new coaching program from the beginning to the ultimate outcomes. This program involves fourteen discrete elements and processes.

1. *Voluntary participation:* Executives had to volunteer to be part of this project. Voluntary commitment translates into a willing participant who is not only open to changing, improving, and applying what is being learned, but who is also willing to provide the necessary data for evaluating the coaching process. The voluntary nature of the coaching program, however, meant that not all executives who needed coaching would be involved. When compared to mandatory involvement, however, the volunteer effort appeared to be an important ingredient for success. It was envisioned that, as improvements were realized and executives reflected on the positive perceptions of coaching, other executives would follow suit.

2. *The need for coaching:* An important part of the process was a dialog with the executive to determine whether coaching was actually needed. In this step, NHLO staff used a checklist to review the issues, needs, and concerns about the coaching agreement. Along with establishing a need, the checklist revealed key areas where coaching could help. This step ensured that the assistance desired by the executive could actually be provided by the coach.

3. *Self-assessment:* As part of the process, a self-assessment was taken from the individual being coached, his or her immediate manager, and direct reports. This was a typical 360-degree assessment instrument that focused on areas of feedback, communication, openness, trust, and other competencies necessary for success in the competitive hospitality environment.

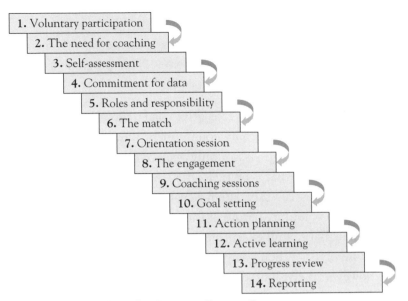

**Figure 2.1. Coaching for Business Impact Steps**

4. *Commitment for data:* As a precondition, executives had to agree to provide data during coaching and at appropriate times following the engagement. This up-front commitment ensured that data of sufficient quality and quantity could be obtained. The data made evaluation easier and helped executives see their progress and realize the value of coaching.

5. *Roles and responsibility:* For both the coach and the executive, roles and responsibilities were clearly defined. It was important for the executive to understand that the coach was there to listen, provide feedback, and evaluate. The coach was not there to make decisions for the executive. This clear distinction was important for productive coaching sessions.

6. *The match:* Coaches were provided from a reputable business coaching firm where NHLO had developed a productive relationship. Coach profiles were presented to executives and a tentative selection was made on a priority listing. The respective coach was provided background information on

the executive and a match was made. After this match, the coaching process began.

7. *Orientation session:*  The executive and coach formally met during an orientation session. Here, the NHLO staff explained the process, requirements, timetable, and other administrative issues. This was a very brief session, typically conducted in a group; however, it could also be conducted individually.

8. *The engagement:*  One of the most important aspects of the process involved making sure that the engagement was con-nected to a business need. Typical coaching engagements focused on behavioral issues (e.g., an executive's inability to listen to employees). To connect to the business impact, the behavior change must link to a business consequence. In the initial engagement, the coach uncovered the business need by asking a series of questions to examine the conse-quences of behavior change. This process involved asking "so what?" and "what if?" as the desired behavior changes were described. As the business needs were identified, the measures must be in the categories of productivity, sales, effi-ciency, direct cost savings, employee retention, and customer satisfaction. The engagement should be connected to corre-sponding changes in at least three of those measures. With-out elevating the engagement to a business need, it would have been difficult to evaluate coaching with this level of analysis.

9. *Coaching sessions:*  Individual sessions were conducted at least once a month (usually more often) lasting a minimum of 1 hour (sometimes more), depending on the need and issues at hand. The coach and executive met face to face, if possible. If not, coaching was conducted in a telephone conversa-tion. Routine meetings were necessary to keep the process on track.

10. *Goal setting:* Although individuals could set goals in any area needing improvements, the senior executives chose five priority areas for targeting: sales growth, productivity/operational efficiency, direct cost reduction, retention of key staff members, and customer satisfaction. The executives selected one measure in at least three of these areas. Essentially, they would have three specific goals that would require three action plans, described next.

11. *Action planning:* To drive the desired improvement, the action planning process was utilized. Common in coaching engagements, this process provided an opportunity for the executive to detail specific action steps planned with the team. These steps were designed to drive a particular consequence that was a business impact measure. Figure 2.2 shows a typical action planning document used in this process. The executive was to complete the action plan during the first two to three coaching sessions, detailing step-by-step what he or she would accomplish to drive a particular improvement. Under the analysis section, Parts A, B, and C are completed in the initial development of the plan. The coaches distributed action plan packages that included instructions, blank forms, and completed examples. The coach explained the process in the second coaching session. The action plans could be revised as needed. At least three improvement measures were required out of the five areas targeted with the program. Consequently, at least three action plans had to be developed and implemented.

12. *Active learning:* After the executive developed the specific measures in question and the action plans, several development strategies were discussed and implemented with the help of the coach. The coach actually facilitated the efforts, utilizing any number of typical learning processes, such as reading assignments, self-assessment tools, skill practices,

Name: _____ Coach: _____ Date _____

Impact
Objective: _____

Evaluation
Period: _____ to _____

Improvement
Measure: _____

Current
Performance: _____

Target
Performance: _____

| Action Steps | Analysis |
|---|---|
| 1. _____ | A. What is the unit of measure? _____ |
| 2. _____ | B. What is the value (cost) of one unit? $ _____ |
| 3. _____ | C. How did you arrive at this value? |
| 4. _____ | _____ |
| 5. _____ | _____ |
| 6. _____ | D. How much did the measure change during the evaluation period? (monthly value) _____ |
| 7. _____ | E. What other factors could have contributed to this improvement? value) _____ |
| 8. _____ | F. What percent of this change was actually caused by this program? _____ percent |
| Intangible Benefits: _____ | G. What level of confidence do you place on the above information? (100 percent = Certainty and 0 percent = No Confidence) _____ Percent |
| Comments: _____ | |

Figure 2.2. Action Plan Form

47

video feedback, journaling, and other techniques. Coaching is considered to be an active learning process where the executive experiments, applies, and reflects on the experience. The coach provides input, reaction, assessment, and evaluation.

13. *Progress review:*  At monthly sessions, the coach and executive reviewed progress and revised the action plan, if necessary. The important issue was to continue to make adjustments to sustain the process.

14. *Reporting:*  After six months in the coaching engagement, the executive reported improvement by completing other parts of the action plan. This includes Parts D, E, F, and G and intangible benefits and comments. If the development efforts were quite involved and the measures driven were unlikely to change in the interim, a longer period of time was utilized. For most executives, six months was appropriate.

These elements reflected a results-based project appropriately called "Coaching for Business Impact."

**Objectives**

An effective ROI study flows from the objectives of the particular project being evaluated. For coaching, it is important to clearly indicate the objectives at different levels. Figure 2.3 shows the detailed objectives associated with this project. The objectives reflect the four classic levels of evaluation plus a fifth level for ROI. Some of the levels, however, have been adjusted for the coaching environment. With these objectives in mind, it becomes a relatively easy task to measure progress on these objectives.

**Planning for Evaluation**

Figure 2.4 shows the completed data collection plan for this project. The plan captures the following techniques and strategies used to collect data for this project:

**Level 1. Reaction Objectives**
After participating in this coaching program, the executive will:

1. Perceive coaching to be relevant to the job

2. Perceive coaching to be important to job performance at the present time

3. Perceive coaching to be value added in terms of time and funds invested

4. Rate the coach as effective

5. Recommend this program to other executives.

**Level 2. Learning Objectives**
After completing this coaching program, the executives should improve their understanding of or skills for each of the following:

1. Uncovering individual strengths and weaknesses

2. Translating feedback into action plans

3. Involving team members in projects and goals

4. Communicating effectively

5. Collaborating with colleagues

6. Improving personal effectiveness

7. Enhancing leadership skills.

**Level 3. Application Objectives**
Six months after completing this coaching program, executives should

1. Complete the action plan

2. Adjust the plan accordingly as needed for changes in the environment

**Level 3. Application Objectives (continued)**

3. Show improvements on the following items:

   a. uncovering individual strengths and weaknesses

   b. translating feedback into action plans

   c. involving team members in projects and goals

   d. communicating effectively

   e. collaborating with colleagues

   f. improving personal effectiveness

   g. enhancing leadership skills.

4. Identify barriers and enablers

**Level 4. Impact Objectives**
After completing this coaching program, executives should improve at least three specific measures in the following areas:

1. Sales growth

2. Productivity/operational efficiency

3. Direct cost reduction

4. Retention of key staff members

5. Customer satisfaction.

**Level 5. ROI Objective**
The ROI value should be 25 percent.

**Figure 2.3. Objectives of Business Impact Coaching**

Program: Coaching for Business Impact   Responsibility: Jack Phillips   Date: _____

| Level | Objective(s) | Measures/Data | Data Collection Method | Data Sources | Timing | Responsibilities |
|---|---|---|---|---|---|---|
| 1 | **Reaction/Satisfaction**<br>• Relevance to job<br>• Importance to job success<br>• Value add<br>• Coach's effectiveness<br>• Recommendation to others | • 4 out of 5 on a 1 to 5 rating scale | • Questionnaire | • Executives | • Six months after engagement | • NHLO Staff |
| 2 | **Learning**<br>• Uncovering strengths/weaknesses<br>• Translating feedback into action<br>• Involving team members<br>• Communicating effectively<br>• Collaborating with colleagues<br>• Improving personal effectiveness<br>• Enhancing leadership skills | • 4 out of 5 on a 1 to 5 rating scale | • Questionnaire | • Executives<br>• Coach | • Six months after engagement | • NHLO Staff |
| 3 | **Application/Implementation**<br>• Complete and adjust action plan<br>• Identify barriers and enablers<br>• Show improvements in skills | • Checklist for action plan<br>• 4 out of 5 on a 1 to 5 rating scale | • Action Plan<br>• Questionnaire | • Executive<br>• Coach | • Six months after engagement | • NHLO Staff |
| 4 | **Business Impact (3 of 5)**<br>1. Sales growth<br>2. Productivity/efficiency<br>3. Direct cost reduction<br>4. Retention of key staff members<br>5. Customer satisfaction | 1. Monthly revenue<br>2. Varies with location<br>3. Direct monetary savings<br>4. Voluntary turnover<br>5. Customer satisfaction index | • Action Plan | • Executive | • Six months after engagement | • NHLO Staff |
| 5 | ROI<br>• 25 percent | | | | | |

**Comments:** *Executives are committed to providing data. They fully understand all the data collection issues prior to engaging into the coaching assignment.*

Figure 2.4. Completed Data Collection Plan

1. *Objectives:* The objectives are listed as defined in Figure 2.3 and are repeated only in general terms.

2. *Measures:* Additional definition is sometimes needed beyond the specific objectives. The measures used to gauge progress on the objective are defined.

3. *Methods:* This column indicates the specific method used for collecting data at different levels. In this case, action plans and questionnaires are the primary methods.

4. *Sources:* For each data group, sources are identified. For coaches, sources are usually limited to the executive, coach, manager of the executive, and the individual/team reporting to the executive. Although the actual data provided by executives will usually come from the records of the organization, the executive will include the data in the action plan document. Thus, the executive becomes a source of the data to NHLO.

5. *Timing:* The timing refers to the time for collecting specific data items from the beginning of the coaching engagement.

6. *Responsibility:* The responsibility refers to the individual(s) who will actually collect the data.

The data integration plan (Figure 2.5) shows how the various types of data are collected and integrated to provide an overall evaluation of the program.

| Data Category | Executive Questionnaire | Senior Executive Questionnaire | Action Plan | Company Records |
|---|---|---|---|---|
| Reaction | X | | | |
| Learning | X | X | | |
| Application | X | X | X | |
| Impact | | | X | X |
| Costs | | | | X |

**Figure 2.5. Data Integration Plan for Evaluating the Program**

Figure 2.6 shows the completed plan for data analysis. This document addresses the key issues needed for a credible analysis of the data and includes the following:

1. *Data items:* The plan shows when business measures will be collected from one of the five priority areas.

2. *Isolating the effects of coaching:* The method of isolating the effects of coaching on the data is estimation, where the executives actually allocate the proportion of the improvement to the coaching process (more on the consequences of this later). Although there are more credible methods, such as control groups and trend line analysis, they are not appropriate for this situation. Although the estimates are subjective, they are developed by those individuals who should know them best (the executives), and the results are adjusted for the error of the estimate.

3. *Converting data to monetary values:* Data is converted using a variety of methods. For most data items, standard values are available. When standard values are not available, the input of an in-house expert is pursued. This expert is typically an individual who collects, assimilates, and reports the data. If neither of these approaches is feasible, the executive estimates the value.

4. *Cost categories:* The standard cost categories included are the typical costs for a coaching assignment.

5. *Communication targets:* Several audiences are included for coaching results, representing the key stakeholder groups: the executive, the executive's immediate manager, the sponsor of the program, and the NHLO staff. Other influences and issues are also detailed in this plan.

## Evaluation Results

The careful data collection planning allowed the coaching program to be evaluated at all five levels.

ROI Analysis Plan

Program: Coaching for Business Success    Responsibility: Jack Phillips    Date: _____

| Data Items (Usually Level 4) | Method for Isolating the Effects of the Program | Methods of Converting Data to Monetary Values | Cost Categories | Intangible Benefits | Communication Targets for Final Report | Other Influences/ Issues During Application | Comments |
|---|---|---|---|---|---|---|---|
| • Sales growth | Estimates from executive | • Standard value<br>• Expert input<br>• Executive estimate | • Needs assessment<br>• Coaching fees<br>• Travel costs | • Increased commitment<br>• Reduced stress | • Executives<br>• Senior executives | A variety of other initiatives will influence the | It is extremely important to secure |
| • Productivity/ operational efficiency | (Method is the same for all data items) | (Method is the same for all data items) | • Executive time<br>• Administrative support | • Increased job satisfaction<br>• Improved customer service | • Sponsors<br>• NHLO staff<br>• Learning & Development Council | impact measure including our Six Sigma process, service excellence | commitment from executives to provide accurate data in a timely manner. |
| • Direct cost reduction | | | • Administrative overhead<br>• Communication expenses | • Enhanced recruiting image | • Prospective participants for CBI | program, and our efforts to become a great place to work. | |
| • Retention of key staff members | | | • Facilities<br>• Evaluation | • Improved teamwork<br>• Improved communication | | | |
| • Customer satisfaction | | | | | | | |

Figure 2.6. The ROI Analysis Plan for Coaching for Business Impact

53

## Reaction

Reaction to the coaching program exceeded expectations of the NHLO staff. Comments received for Level 1 evaluation included these:

- "This program was very timely and practical."

- "My coach was very professional."

On a scale of 1 to 5 (1 = unacceptable and 5 = exceptional), the average rating of five items was 4.1, exceeding the objective of 4.0. Table 2.1 shows the items listed.

## Learning

As with any process, the executives indicated enhancement of skills and knowledge in certain areas:

- "I gained much insight into my problems with my team."

- "This is exactly what I needed to get on track. My coach pointed out things I hadn't thought of and we came up with some terrific actions."

Table 2.2 shows seven items with inputs from both the executives and their coaches. For this level, it was considered appropriate

Table 2.1.  Executive Reaction to Coaching

| Level 1 Evaluation | Rating* |
| --- | --- |
| Relevance of Coaching | 4.6 |
| Importance of Coaching | 4.1 |
| Value of Coaching | 3.9 |
| Effectiveness of Coach | 3.9 |
| Recommendation to Others | 4.2 |

*Scale 1 to 5, where 1 = Unacceptable, 5 = Exceptional

Table 2.2.  Learning from Coaching

| Measures | Executive Rating * | Coach Rating * |
|---|---|---|
| Understanding strengths and weaknesses | 3.9 | 4.2 |
| Translating feedback into action plans | 3.7 | 3.9 |
| Involving team members in projects and goals | 4.2 | 3.7 |
| Communicating effectively | 4.1 | 4.2 |
| Collaborating with colleagues | 4.0 | 4.1 |
| Improving personal effectiveness | 4.1 | 4.4 |
| Enhancing leadership skills | 4.2 | 4.3 |

*Program value scale 1 to 5.

to collect the data from both groups, indicating the degree of improvement. The most accurate, and probably most credible, is the input directly from the executive. The coach may not be fully aware of the extent of learning.

## Application

For coaching to be successful, the executive had to implement the items on the action plans. The most important measure of application was the completion of the action plan steps. Eighty-three percent of the executives reported completion of all three plans. Another 11 percent completed one or two action plans.

Also, executives and the coach provided input on questions about changes in behavior from the use of skills. Here are some comments they offered on the questionnaires:

- "It was so helpful to get a fresh, unique point of view of my action plan. The coaching experience opened my eyes to significant things I was missing."

- "After spending a great deal of time trying to get my coach to understand my dilemma, I felt that more effort went into this than I expected."

- "We got stuck in a rut on one issue and I couldn't get out. My coach was somewhat distracted and I never felt we were on the same page."

The response rates for questionnaires were 92 percent and 80 percent for executives and coaches, respectively. Table 2.3 shows a listing of the skills and the rating, using a scale of 1 to 5, where 1 was "no change in the skill" and 5 was "exceptional increase."

### Barriers and Enablers

With any process, there are barriers and enablers to success. The executives were asked to indicate the specific barriers (obstacles) to the use of what was learned in the coaching sessions. Overall the barriers were weak, almost nonexistent. Also, they were asked to indicate what supported (enablers) the process. The enablers were very strong. Table 2.4 shows a list of the barriers and enablers.

### Impact

Specific business impact measures varied with the individual but, for the most part, were in the categories representing the five priority areas. Table 2.5 shows the listing of the actual data reported in the action plans for the first measure only. The table identifies the executive and the area of improvement, the monetary value, the

### Table 2.3.  Application of Coaching

| Measures | Executive Rating * | Coach Rating * |
|---|---|---|
| Translating feedback into action plans | 4.2 | 3.9 |
| Involving team members in projects and goals | 4.1 | 4.2 |
| Communicating more effectively with the team | 4.3 | 4.1 |
| Collaborating more with the group and others | 4.2 | 4.2 |
| Applying effective leadership skills | 4.1 | 3.9 |

*Program value scale 1 to 5, where: 1 = No change in skills, 5 = Exceptional increase

**Table 2.4.  Barriers and Enablers of the Coaching Process**

| Barriers | Enablers |
|---|---|
| Not enough time | Coach |
| Not relevant | Action plan |
| Not effective when using the skill | Structure of CBI |
| Manager didn't support it | Support of management |

basis of the improvement, the method of converting the monetary value, the contribution from coaching, the confidence estimate of the contribution, and the adjusted value. Since there are three measures, a total of all three tables are developed. The total for the three is $1,861,158.

Figure 2.7 shows a completed action plan from one participant, Caroline Dobson (executive number 11). In this example, Caroline reduced annual turnover to 17 percent from 28 percent—an improvement of 11 percent. This represented four turnovers on an annual basis. Using a standard value of 1.3 times base salaries for the cost of one turnover and adding the total base salaries yields a total cost savings of $215,000.

As mentioned earlier, the estimates were used to isolate the benefits of coaching. After the estimates were obtained, the value was adjusted for the confidence of the estimate. Essentially, the executives were asked to list other factors that could have contributed to the improvement and allocate the amount (on a percentage basis) that was directly attributable to coaching. Then, using a scale of 0 percent (no confidence) to 100 percent (total certainty), executives provided the confidence levels for their estimates.

## ROI

The costs were fully loaded and included both the direct and indirect costs of coaching. Estimates were used in some cases. Table 2.6 shows the costs of coaching for all twenty-five executives in the study.

**Table 2.5. Business Impact from Coaching**

| Exec Number | Measurement Area | Total Annual Value | Basis | Method for Converting Data | Contribution Factor | Confidence Estimate | Adjusted Value |
|---|---|---|---|---|---|---|---|
| 1 | Revenue growth | $ 11,500 | Profit margin | Standard value | 33% | 70% | $ 2,656 |
| 2 | Retention | 175,000 | 3 turnovers | Standard value | 40% | 70% | 49,000 |
| 3 | Retention | 190,000 | 2 turnovers | Standard value | 60% | 80% | 91,200 |
| 4 | Direct cost savings | 75,000 | From cost statements | Participant estimate | 100% | 100% | 75,000 |
| 5 | Direct cost savings | 21,000 | Contract services | Standard value | 75% | 70% | 11,025 |
| 6 | Direct cost savings | 65,000 | Staffing costs | Standard value | 70% | 60% | 27,300 |
| 7 | Retention | 150,000 | 2 turnovers | Standard value | 50% | 50% | 37,500 |
| 8 | Cost savings | 70,000 | Security | Standard value | 60% | 90% | 37,800 |
| 9 | Direct cost savings | 9,443 | Supply costs | N/A | 70% | 90% | 5,949 |
| 10 | Efficiency | 39,000 | Information technology costs | Participant estimate | 70% | 80% | 21,840 |
| 11 | Retention | 215,000 | 4 turnovers | Standard value | 75% | 90% | 145,125 |

| # | Category | Value | Description | Source | % | % | Amount |
|---|---|---|---|---|---|---|---|
| 12 | Productivity | 13,590 | Overtime | Standard value | 75% | 80% | 8,154 |
| 13 | Retention | 73,000 | 1 turnover | Standard value | 50% | 80% | 29,200 |
| 14 | Retention | 120,000 | 2 annual turnovers | Standard value | 60% | 75% | 54,000 |
| 15 | Retention | 182,000 | 4 turnovers | Standard value | 40% | 85% | 61,880 |
| 16 | Cost savings | 25,900 | Travel | Standard value | 30% | 90% | 6,993 |
| 17 | Cost savings | 12,320 | Administrative support | Standard value | 75% | 90% | 8,316 |
| 18 | Direct cost savings | 18,950 | Labor savings | Participant estimate | 55% | 60% | 6,253 |
| 19 | Revenue growth | 103,100 | Profit margin | Participant estimate | 75% | 90% | 69,592 |
| 20 | Revenue | 19,500 | Profit | Standard value | 85% | 75% | 12,431 |
| 21 | Revenue | 21,230 | Profit % | Standard value | 80% | 70% | 18,889 |
| 22 | Revenue growth | 105,780 | Profit margin | Standard value | 70% | 50% | 37,023 |
| | TOTAL $ 1,716,313 | | | | | | TOTAL $ 817,126 |

2nd Measure Total $649,320

3rd Measure Total $394,712

TOTAL Benefits $1,861,158

## ACTION PLAN

Name: _Caroline Dobson_   Coach: _Pamela Mills_

Objective: _Improve retention for staff_

Improvement Measure: _Voluntary turnover_

|  | Current Performance | Evaluation Period: _January_ | Target Performance | Follow-Up Date | _1 September_ |
|---|---|---|---|---|---|
|  | | _28% Annual_ | _15% Annual_ | to _July_ | |

| Action Steps | | Analysis |
|---|---|---|
| 1. _Meet with team to discuss reasons for turnover – using problem-solving skills._ | _31 Jan_ | A. What is the unit of measure? _One voluntary turnover_ |
| 2. _Review exit interview data with HR– look for trends and patterns._ | _15 Feb_ | B. What is the value (cost) of one unit? _Salary × 1.3_ |
| 3. _Counsel with "at-risk" employees to correct problems and explore opportunities for improvement._ | _1 Mar_ | C. How did you arrive at this value? _Standard Value_ |
| 4. _Develop individual development plan for high-potential employees._ | _5 Mar_ | D. How much did the measure change during the evaluation period? _11%_ (annual %) _(four turnovers annually)_ |
| 5. _Provide recognition to employees with long tenure._ | _Routinely_ | E. What other factors could have contributed to this improvement? _Growth opportunities, changes in job market_ |
| 6. _Schedule appreciation dinner for entire team._ | _31 May_ | F. What percent of this change was actually caused by this program? _75%_ |
| 7. _Encourage team leaders to delegate more responsibilities._ | _31 May_ | G. What level of confidence do you place on the above information? (100% = Certainty and 0% = No Confidence) _90%_ |
| 8. _Follow-up with each discussion and discuss improvement or lack of improvement and plan other action._ | _Routinely_ | |
| 9. _Monitor improvement and provide recognition when appropriate._ | _11 May_ | |

Intangible Benefits: _Less stress on team, greater job satisfaction_

Comments: _Great Coach – He kept me on track with this issue._

**Figure 2.7. An Example of an Executive's Completed Action Plan**

Table 2.6.    Costs of Coaching Twenty-Five Executives

| Item | Cost |
|---|---|
| Needs Assessment/Development | $   10,000 |
| Coaching Fees | 480,000 |
| Travel Costs | 53,000 |
| Executive Time | 9,200 |
| Administrative Support | 14,000 |
| Administrative Overhead | 2,000 |
| Telecommunication Expenses | 1,500 |
| Facilities (Conference Room) | 2,100 |
| Evaluation | 8,000 |
| **Total** | **$ 579,800** |

Only a small amount of initial assessment cost was involved, and the development cost was minor, as well, because the coaching firm had developed a similar coaching arrangement previously. The costs for sessions conducted on the phone were estimated, and sometimes a conference room was used instead of the executive offices.

Using the total monetary benefits and total cost of the program, two ROI calculations can be developed. The first is the benefit-cost ratio (BCR), which is the ratio of the monetary benefits divided by the costs:

$$BCR = \frac{\$1,861,158}{\$579,800} = 3.21 : 1$$

This value suggests that for every dollar invested, $3.21 was generated in benefits. The ROI formula for investments in training, coaching, or any human performance intervention is calculated in the same way as for other types of investments: earnings divided by investment. For this coaching solution, the ROI was calculated thus:

$$ROI(\%) = \frac{\$1,861 - \$579,000}{\%579,800} \times 100 = 221\%$$

In other words, for every dollar invested in the coaching program, the invested dollar was returned and another $1.21 was generated. In this case, the ROI exceeded the 25 percent target.

### Intangibles

As with any project, there were many intangibles revealed by this analysis. Intangibles were collected on both the follow-up questionnaire and the action plan. Two questions were included on the questionnaire; one involved other benefits from this process and the other asked for comments about the program. Some individuals indicated intangibles when they listed the comments. Also, the action plan contained a place for comments and intangibles. The intangible benefits identified through these data sources included:

- Increased commitment

- Improved teamwork

- Increased job satisfaction

- Improved customer service

- Improved communication

Note that this list includes only measures that were identified as being an intangible benefit by at least four of the twenty-five executives. In keeping with the conservative nature of the ROI Methodology, it was decided that intangibles identified by only a couple of executives would be considered extreme data items and not credible enough to list as an actual benefit of the program.

### Credibility of the ROI Analysis

The critical issue in this study is the credibility of the data. The data were perceived to be very credible by the executives, their immediate managers, and the coaches. Credibility rests on eight major issues:

1. The information for the analysis was provided directly by the executives. They had no reason to be biased in their input.

2. The data was taken directly from the records and could be audited.

3. The data collection process was conservative, with the assumption that an unresponsive individual had realized no improvement. This concept—no data, no improvement—is ultraconservative with regard to data collection. Three executives did not return the completed action plans.

4. The executives did not assign complete credit to this program. Executives isolated only a portion of the data that should be credited directly to this program.

5. The data was adjusted for the potential error of the above estimate.

6. Only the first year's benefits were used in the analysis. Most of the improvements should result in second- and third-year benefits.

7. The costs of the program were fully loaded. All direct and indirect costs were included, including the time away from work for the executives.

8. The data revealed a balanced profile of success. Very favorable reaction, learning, and application data were presented along with business impact, ROI, and intangibles.

Collectively, these issues made a convincing case for the CBI program.

## Communication Strategy

To communicate appropriately with the target audiences outlined in the ROI analysis plan, three specific documents were produced. The first report was a detailed impact study showing the approach, assumptions, methodology, and results using all the data categories. In addition, barriers and enablers were included, along with conclusions and recommendations. The second report was an eight-page executive summary of the key points, including a one-page overview of the methodology. The third report was a brief, five-page summary of the process and results. These documents were presented to the different groups according to the plan in Figure 2.8.

Because this was the first ROI study conducted in this organization, face-to-face meetings were conducted with the sponsor and other interested senior executives. The purpose was to ensure that executive sponsors had a clear understanding of the methodology, the conservative assumptions, and each level of data. The barriers, enablers, conclusions, and recommendations were an important part of the meeting. In the future, after two or three studies have been conducted, this group will receive only a one-page summary of key data items.

A similar meeting was conducted with the learning and development council. The council consisted of advisors to NHLO—usually middle-level executives and managers. Finally, a face-to-face meeting was held with the NHLO staff at which the complete impact study was described and used as a learning tool.

As a result of this communication, the senior executive decided to make only a few minor adjustments in the program and continued to offer CBI to others on a volunteer basis. They were very pleased with the progress and were delighted to have data connecting coaching to the business impact.

| Audience | Document |
|---|---|
| Executives | Brief summary |
| Managers of executive (senior executives) | Brief summary |
| Sponsor | Complete study, executive summary |
| NHLO staff | Complete study |
| Learning and development council | Complete study, executive summary |
| Prospective participants | Brief summary |

**Figure 2.8. NHLO's Plan for Communicating Evaluation Results**

## Questions for Discussion

1. How did the decision to conduct an ROI study influence the design of the coaching program?

2. Critique the evaluation design and method of data collection.

3. Discuss the importance of getting participants committed to provide quality data.

4. What other strategies for isolating the impact of the coaching program could have been employed here?

5. Discuss the importance of credibility of data in an ROI study.

6. How can the outcomes of coaching be linked to your organization's business objectives?

## About the Author

As a world-renowned expert on measurement and evaluation, **Jack J. Phillips** is chairman of ROI Institute. Through the Institute, Phillips provides consulting services for *Fortune* 500 companies and workshops for major conference providers throughout the world.

Phillips is also the author, co-author, or editor of more than sixty books—at least twenty about measurement and evaluation—and more than one hundred articles. Books most recently authored by Jack Phillips include *The Value of Learning* (Pfeiffer, 2007); *Show Me the Money: How to Determine ROI in People, Projects, and Programs* (Berrett-Koehler, 2007); *Proving the Value of Meetings & Events: How and Why to Measure ROI* (ROI Institute, MPI, 2007); *Building a Successful Consulting Practice* (McGraw-Hill, 2006); *Investing in Your Company's Human Capital: Strategies to Avoid Spending Too Much or Too Little* (AMACOM, 2005); *Proving the Value of HR: How and Why to Measure ROI* (SHRM, 2005); *The Leadership Scorecard* (Elsevier Butterworth-Heinemann, 2004); *Managing Employee Retention* (Elsevier Butterworth-Heinemann, 2003); *Return on Investment in Training and Performance Improvement Programs* (2nd ed.) (Elsevier

Butterworth-Heinemann, 2003); *The Project Management Scorecard*, (Elsevier Butterworth-Heinemann, 2002); and *How to Measure Training Results* (McGraw-Hill, 2002). Dr. Phillips served as series editor for ASTD's *In Action* casebook series, an ambitious publishing project featuring thirty titles. He currently serves as series editor for Elsevier Butterworth-Heinemann's Improving Human Performance series and for Pfeiffer's new series on Measurement and Evaluation. He can be reached at jack@roiinstitute.net.

# 3

# Measuring ROI in Sales Training
## *A Pharmaceutical Company*

### Ron Drew Stone

## Abstract

In the highly competitive marketplace of pharmaceutical prescription drugs, success in selling a new product is dependent
upon the reputation of the product from clinical trials and the
skill of the sales person in convincing customers that their
product is superior in meeting patient needs. When physicians
are the targeted customer population, the sales representative
often has only a fifteen-to-twenty-minute window to make a
convincing case for the product. This case study demonstrates
how a focused training effort and the proper supporting environment can result in a successful initiative to influence physician
choices. It also demonstrates how the return on investment can be
calculated.

Note: This case was prepared to serve as a basis for discussion rather than
an illustration of either effective or ineffective administrative and management
practices. All names, dates, places, and data may have been disguised at the
request of the author or organization.

## Background

### Need for the Program

Biosearch Pharmaceutical Incorporated (BPI) is a worldwide company headquartered in the U.S. with autonomous sales offices in many countries. BPI is involved in the research and marketing of both prescription and over-the-counter consumer medication. Almost 40 percent of sales originate from outside the U.S. More than 60,000 employees in fifty countries are involved in research, development, and sales. Salustatin is BPI's statin product, which has been on the market for two years. Prescription medications in the "statin drug family" are prescribed by physicians when patients have certain indications of heart disease. BPI has experienced substantial competition in the statin market that prevented the organization from achieving market share and reaching sales potential with Salustatin. Initial marketing research activities were directed to determine why the goals are not being met and to identify the problem areas.

The following conclusions came from the marketing research report:

- Physicians are not well educated about Salustatin, do not understand the benefits of Salustatin, and do not believe it to be superior in performance.

- There is no consistent message being delivered to physicians regarding the benefits of Salustatin.

- Sales representatives are not proficient in handling physicians' questions and objections about the product.

- It is widely believed that physicians do not view the sales representative as a credible resource regarding Salustatin.

- Since the physicians' current attitude regarding Salustatin may not be favorable, researchers believe that an extension of effective meeting time with physicians may be necessary to tell the Salustatin story.

- Since there are competing statin products in the market, the prescribing physicians are the key to achieving market share. Physicians determine which product to prescribe based on their belief in the effectiveness of the product.

## Overview of the Performance Solution

The deficiencies noted in the marketing research report led to the formation of the USA Field Force Effectiveness team, charged with the responsibility of verifying the findings and recommending a solution. The manager of sales force effectiveness training was a member of this group. Following a more detailed needs assessment, the group soon reached the conclusion that a focused training effort was needed for sales representatives and open educational seminars would be recommended for physicians. Management at BPI had high expectations for this initiative. The Field Force Effectiveness team expressed significant concern regarding how to ensure that sales representatives would transfer skills to the work setting. Their research indicated that the district sales managers should be involved to enhance the possibility of transfer.

*Training Design for Sales Representatives*    The Field Force Effectiveness team made three demands for the training design.

- *First,* the training would be facilitator-led, and there must be some transfer component designed into the training to influence execution in the work setting. Action planning was determined to be the method of choice, with the format and approach left to the judgment of the training design team.

- *Second*, post-training involvement of the first-line managers (usually a district sales manager) is a necessity.

- *Third*, first-line managers should also be trained to assist them in performing their role as they interact with the sales representatives to improve sales.

The Field Force Effectiveness team determined that all attendees must be in a sales capacity when selected to participate and would attend the training sessions on company time. Product knowledge would be a prerequisite with Salustatin product training already being available online. Money was budgeted for a two-day training program for sales representatives and an additional two-day training program for first-line managers. First-line managers would also monitor the training of their sales representatives and act as supporters, assessors, and evaluators during the training.

The Field Force Effectiveness team's recommendations led to the implementation of the Salustatin Promotional Program (SPP). The SPP was comprised of three components:

1. A focused sales program provided to BPI sales representatives in the U.S. market. It was a two-day training program titled "Essential Selling Skills," conducted on back-to-back days.

2. First-line managers were provided training on performance observation and coaching, in addition to other related topics.

3. SPP also included physician seminars provided independently by regional marketing specialists throughout local markets. These local seminars were educational in nature and focused on the scientific research and medical successes of Salustatin during controlled studies.

*Training Program for First-Line Managers (FLM)*    First-line managers (FLMs) participated in the two-day training program prior
to the training for representatives. Prior to this program, all levels of sales management and marketing agreed upon standards
of performance for delivery of the core promotional message and
the handling of the most frequently heard physician objections to
Salustatin. During their training, FLMs were trained on:

- The standards of performance

- Delivery of the core promotional message

- Handling of the most frequently heard objections

- Observing performance, comparing performance to
  standards, and providing coaching

*Training Program for Sales Representatives*    During the two-day
Essential Selling Skills Training, sales representatives reconfirmed
standards of performance established by management and practiced
delivery of the promotional message and handling objections. The
FLM was involved in the sales training as they critiqued role-play
situations. The training was designed to improve the essential
selling skills of representatives as follows:

- Establishing specific call objectives

- Delivering a credible core promotional message to
  physician customers

- Handling objections properly to influence physician
  prescribing behavior

- Emphasis placed on skill development

Skill building was emphasized by using videotaped role-play situations to give feedback to the sales representative. The initial training included 220 sales representatives in the United States. All of the attendees were in a sales capacity when selected to participate in the training. Employees attended the training sessions on company time during the month of June.

## Need for Evaluation

The executive team expressed a strong desire to evaluate the post-intervention success of every aspect of the Salustatin Promotional Program, including feedback from physicians. However, the budget placed limitations on the scope of an evaluation study. The Field Force Effectiveness team recommended that the Essential Selling Skills Training for sales representatives be evaluated for three reasons:

1. It was considered the most crucial element to the success of the Salustatin Promotion Program (SPP).

2. Management needed to know whether the sales representatives were applying what they learned.

3. It was the most resource intensive component of the SPP.

The executive team agreed with the recommendation to evaluate only the Essential Selling Skills Training for sales representatives. Expressing concerns about objectivity, the Field Force Effectiveness team recommended that an independent study was needed to determine the impact of the program. An external measurement expert certified in the Phillips ROI Methodology was selected to determine the impact of the Essential Selling Skills program. The measurement consultant was tasked with designing the aforementioned Action Plan, recommending the strategy for follow-up evaluation, and designing and implementing the evaluation.

## Evaluation Methodology

The Phillips ROI Methodology was used to design the study, collect data, analyze data, and report the results. This systematic methodology is the most thorough and credible process in use today to evaluate training and performance improvement programs. It is used in more than forty countries. Thousands of studies have been completed by certified professionals using the methodology. Data is collected at five levels, as illustrated in Table 3.1.

The evaluation levels are an inherent framework for the ROI Methodology. The methodology includes techniques to isolate the effects of the training solution being studied. The ROI Model is illustrated in Figure 3.1.

The impact study was designed to evaluate the success of the Essential Selling Skills Training Program. The study had four specific objectives:

1. Determine the extent to which participants applied the skills they learned during the training to the sales detail job setting.

Table 3.1.   Evaluation Levels

| Level | Measurement Focus |
| --- | --- |
| 1. Reaction and Planned Action | Measures participant satisfaction with the program and captures planned actions, if appropriate. |
| 2. Learning | Measures changes in knowledge, skills, and attitudes related to the project. |
| 3. Application | Measures changes in on-the-job behavior or actions as the project is applied, implemented, or utilized. |
| 4. Business Impact | Measures changes in business impact variables. |
| 5. Return on Investment | Compare project benefits to the costs. |

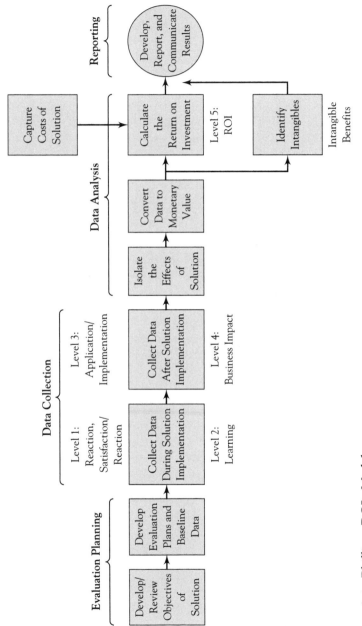

**Figure 3.1. Phillips ROI Model**

2. Verify that representatives received coaching from managers on the targeted skills.

3. Identify specific barriers that hindered successful application of the skills.

4. Identify the business impact on specific sales measures and calculate the ROI of the training.

These objectives were met through the implementation of a comprehensive data collection and analysis strategy that was developed after the objectives were approved by the Field Force Effectiveness Team. The strategy is captured in the Data Collection Plan process tool, illustrated in Figure 3.2 and the ROI Analysis Plan in Figure 3.3.

*Level 1 and Level 2 Data Collection*

Level 1 data was collected in the typical fashion at the end of the training with the use of a questionnaire. The focus for Level 1 was program relevance and effectiveness of delivery. The Level 1 instrument is shown in Table 3.2.

Level 2 data were collected from facilitators and managers after observation of skill practice in the classroom. During their two days of training, managers learned to observe performance and compare performance to standards. During Essential Selling Skills training, the checklist in Table 3.3 was used to observe and record the performance of sales representatives as they applied varying scenarios. It included the six skills, which were the focus of the training with assessment standards of "satisfactory," "role model," and "unsatisfactory."

While subjective, this assessment was planned and carried out to provide evidence of learning progress and to evaluate skill practice performance. This evidence of learning satisfied evaluators that execution in the work setting was a reasonable expectation as a next step.

Project: Biosearch Essential Selling Skills Training - *Salustatin in USA*                    Date: June

| Level | Broad Program Objective(s) | Measures | Evaluation Methods /Instruments | Data Sources | Timing | Responsibilities |
|---|---|---|---|---|---|---|
| I Reaction, Satisfaction, and Planned Action | 1. Satisfaction with course content and instructor delivery<br>2. Satisfaction with the coaching and feedback<br>3. Plan to apply K&S | 1. and 2. Average at least 4.5 on a five-point scale<br>3. At least 80 percent of participants plan to apply K&S to their job | • Questionnaire instrument for manager and participants | • Participants | • Immediately at end of: two-day Core Sales Team training. | • Administration by session leader |
| II Learning | 1. Demonstrate the K&S identified by objectives of Salustatin training<br>2. Develop and document action plan for transferring learning to the work setting and communicate plan to manager as necessary | 1. During role play, acceptable delivery of core promotional message, uncover hidden objections, and demonstrate how to handle three of six most frequent objections<br>2. Action plan completed per criteria | 1. Observation of skills through role plays<br>2. Action plan.<br>Note: Product knowledge assessment administered prior to training | 1. Participants are observed by instructors and managers<br>2. Facilitator reviews action plan for clarity and completeness | • During learning sessions | • Learner, coach/manager, instructor |

76

| | | | | | |
|---|---|---|---|---|---|
| **III Job Application** | 1. Sales reps apply K&S appropriately and consistently in the field<br>2. Managers provide coaching<br>3. Sales reps provide input on barriers and enablers to job application transfer | 1. 80% of physicians score at least 7 of 9-point scale on: quality of interaction with rep; confidence in rep; responsiveness; etc<br>1 and 2. Use of skills reported by managers and reps.<br>3. 80% of participants and managers provide input on barriers and enablers to rep performance | 1. Physician focus groups before and after training at various sites<br>1 and 2. Action planning process<br>1 and 2. Managers observe sales reps in field<br>1, 2, and 3. Follow-up focus group and questionnaires | 1. Sampling of physicians<br>1, 2, and 3. Participant and sales manager | – Action plan results 90 days after training.<br>– Manager review and update plan every thirty days<br>– Focus groups and questionnaires 90 to 120 days after training | – Observation by sales manager<br>– Physician focus groups by FFE<br>– Questionnaires by evaluation specialist<br>– Action plan by manager and rep. |
| **IV Business Results** | 1. Increase revenue of product line<br>2. Increase in market share<br>3. Increase revenue per physician<br>4. Improve customer satisfaction | 1. Revenue increase of at least 20 percent<br>2. 10 percent increase in penetration by Oct 30<br>3. Revenue increase of at least 10 percent per physician<br>4. Physician satisfaction on six key questions at least 7 on 9-point scale | 1 and 2. BPI records<br>3. Pharmacy utilization<br>4. Physician focus groups | 1 and 2. BPI performance records<br>3. New script report (Pharma sales report)<br>3 and 4. (same two focus group sessions as in L-3) | 1 and 2. From 90 to 120 days after training<br>3. 120 days after training<br>4. Prior to training and from 90 to 120 days after | 1, 2, and 3. FFE gains access to data and provides to evaluation specialist<br>4. FFE administers focus groups |

Figure 3.2. Data Collection Plan

**Table 3.2. Level 1 Course Evaluation**

| Effectiveness | Strongly Disagree | Disagree | Somewhat Agree | Agree | Strongly Agree |
|---|---|---|---|---|---|
| The course objectives were met | 1 | 2 | 3 | 4 | 5 |
| The content was focused and targeted | 1 | 2 | 3 | 4 | 5 |
| The facilitator's presentation was effective | 1 | 2 | 3 | 4 | 5 |
| The course materials were useful and well organized | 1 | 2 | 3 | 4 | 5 |

| Relevance | Strongly Disagree | Disagree | Somewhat Agree | Agree | Strongly Agree |
|---|---|---|---|---|---|
| The content was relevant to my job | 1 | 2 | 3 | 4 | 5 |
| The activities and practice were relevant | 1 | 2 | 3 | 4 | 5 |
| This content presented is important to my job | 1 | 2 | 3 | 4 | 5 |

| Value | Strongly Disagree | Disagree | Somewhat Agree | Agree | Strongly Agree |
|---|---|---|---|---|---|
| The course delivered high value for my time invested | 1 | 2 | 3 | 4 | 5 |
| Attending this course will enhance my work performance when I apply what I learned | 1 | 2 | 3 | 4 | 5 |
| I would recommend this course to others | 1 | 2 | 3 | 4 | 5 |

**Planned Improvements:** Indicate what actions you will take in your job as a result of what you learned during this course (please be specific). _____

_____

_____

**Table 3.3.  Level 3 Assessment Guide**

| SKILL PRACTICE CHECKLIST | | | |
|---|---|---|---|
| Name: _____ | | Observer: _____ | |
| Skill to Be Demonstrated | Unsatisfactory | Satisfactory | Role Model |
| Use of Questioning Techniques | | | |
| Uncovering Hidden Objections | | | |
| Handling Objections | | | |
| Command of Product Knowledge | | | |
| Communicating the Core Promotional Message | | | |

## Level 3 and Level 4 Data Collection

As documented on the Data Collection Plan, the evaluation strategy included collecting data from several sources using several methods. In addition to the Action Plan (implemented by the sales representative and monitored by the manager), a follow-up questionnaire and focus groups were planned to determine the extent to which participants used the training and achieved on-the-job success. The questionnaire was also the principle source to determine the coaching effectiveness of the manager. To remain objective, action plan and follow-up questionnaire data were collected anonymously only from the people who experienced the training.

Although follow-up data (Level 3 and Level 4) from the instruction team may be available and may be objective and helpful, it is essential that input be free from any perceived bias. These steps helped to ensure that the process was unbiased, objective, and contained minimal errors. Finally, sales data (Level 4) were monitored from BPI sales records before and after the program to determine whether scripts were indeed being written showing how much the Salustatin sales had changed.

**Focus Group: Physicians**. While there was a plan and a desire to collect sales call performance data from physicians, management had a change of heart before this was administered. It was determined that additional contact with physicians was a sensitive issue, and it was not supported as the study progressed toward implementation. Management was of the opinion that sufficient data were being collected from internal sources, so the planned focus groups with physicians were cancelled.

**Focus Group: Sales Representatives**. The plan to conduct focus groups was set aside for three reasons:

1. Sales representatives were being observed on the job and coached by their managers, and managers would have input into the action planning process.

2. The action plan and a follow-up questionnaire would be two rich sources of data. The follow-up questionnaire to be used was comprehensive, and it was noted that management support should ensure a good completion and return rate.

3. The opportunity to observe actual sales on a monthly basis could be used as a trigger to determine the need for additional data. If sales were not trending upward, then a decision to administer the focus groups could be made and sales representatives could then provide meaningful insight regarding their use of the skills on sales details. Therefore, the expense of this additional data collection method (focus groups) was postponed and would be administered only if actual sales were not meeting expectations.

**Questionnaire: Managers**. While sales managers initially agreed to respond to a follow-up questionnaire, as the training was being rolled out they asked for this requirement to be cancelled. They felt that they had sufficient involvement and input with assessments during the training, the follow-up observation and coaching, and the follow-up action planning process.

**Questionnaire: Sales Representatives**. Overall, 220 individuals participated in the training and were identified to receive a questionnaire. To assure confidentiality, the questionnaire was mailed to the homes of participants and returned to a third party in an anonymous manner. Generally, by ensuring anonymous feedback, participants are more likely to provide valid data since they are under no pressure to exaggerate the data to impress the boss. The questionnaire was field tested and then reviewed with participants during the training so that items could be clarified. The questionnaire included numerous questions to determine on-the-job application and business impact. The questionnaires and action plans were returned to the measurement partner for analysis.

**Multiple Use Action Plan: Sales Representatives**. Participants were required to use the action planning process to track progress and collect actual performance data for a three-month period after the training session. Sales managers (FLMs) were involved in the application in the work setting through appropriate follow-up and coaching. In addition to the action plan (implemented by the rep and monitored by the manager), each FLM was asked to use the action plan with each of their representatives to establish three follow-up dates to discuss the application of five specific skills and behaviors that were intended to influence physicians' decisions. These five skills and behaviors were the focal point of the training program. In many instances, the manager observed sales calls, later debriefed the calls, and provided coaching with the sales representative as needed.

While this is not an exact measure, it includes the input from the representative and the manager and is their best judgment after close contact with the customer and assessment in the work setting. It provides another strong link to increased sales and is a positive statement on how the manager, sales representative, and the training program combined to achieve the intended results. The action plan is shown and explained in Figures 3.4, 3.5, 3.6, and 3.7.

*Data Analysis*

The key decisions in applying the ROI Methodology involve selecting specific methods to collect data, isolate the effects of training, determine the extent of application on the job, and compare the value of the specific post-program sales measures to the pre-program measures. To calculate ROI, at least one of the Level 4 business measures must be converted to a monetary value.

The fifth level of evaluation, return on investment, was requested for the project. At Level 5 (ROI), the monetary benefits of the program using Level 4 results data are compared to the cost of the program. Improvement in business variables (Level 4) are used to determine business impact. Adjustments are made to the sales data by calculating the sales gain and applying the isolation strategy to determine the extent of influence on the gain due to the training and other influencing factors.

The ROI Analysis Plan (Figure 3.3) is the planning instrument used to document methods to isolate the effects, convert data to a monetary value, capture cost categories and communication targets, and other important information. The first step in completing the ROI Analysis Plan was to transfer the Level 4 measures from the Data Collection Plan to the first column of the ROI Plan. Then a decision was made regarding how to isolate the effects and how to convert data to a monetary value for each Level 4 measure.

The methods used to isolate the effects and convert data are shown in Figure 3.3. Note that while all three Level 4 measures are to be reported, only the revenue increase (measure 1) is used to calculate ROI. Use of the other measures to calculate ROI would represent double counting since they are contributors to the revenue in metric 1.

Project: Biosearch Essential Selling Skills Training - *Salustatin in USA*                    Date: June

| Data Items | Methods to Isolate Training | Methods to Convert Data | Cost Categories | Intangible Benefits | Other Influences/Issues | Communication Targets |
|---|---|---|---|---|---|---|
| 1. Revenue increase of at least 20 percent in the product line | 1. Trend analysis, participant estimate, and manager estimate | 1. Monetary value of profit margin | • Needs assessment and development cost prorated<br>• Delivery costs<br> – Training materials<br> – Instructor's and participants' salaries and benefits<br> – Travel and other<br>• Opportunity cost of training participation<br>• Coordination<br>• Evaluation<br>• Overhead within training and development | • Sales rep relationship improvement with customer<br>• Each product rollout drives sales of other products<br>• Closer partnership between sales manager and sales rep | Issues:<br>• Trust<br>• Customer sales dependent on number and severity of patients<br>• Sales environment not completely replicated in training<br>• Potential for sales rep information overload | • Senior executives headquarters<br>• National sales managers, sales managers, and sales reps<br>• FFE staff |
| 2. 10 percent increase in market penetration by October 30 | 2. Industry trend analysis and manager estimate | 2. Data reported, but conversion not necessary since #1 above is the only measure used for ROI calculation | | | | |
| 3. Revenue increase of at least 10 percent per physician | 3. Trend analysis, participant estimate, and manager estimate | 3. Data reported, but conversion not necessary since #1 above is the only measure used for ROI calculation | | | | |

Figure 3.3. ROI Analysis Plan

A control group was considered to isolate the effects, but was quickly dismissed because it was not feasible. Management did not want to withhold the solution from any group of sales representatives, and a comparison group would be difficult to find. Trend line analysis was quickly dismissed as a possibility because it addresses only one influencing factor. There were a variety of internal and external factors influencing sales in the BPI environment.

*Design and Implementation of the Action Planning Process*

The customized action plan was used to accomplish two objectives. First, because of the concern for transfer to the work setting, the action plan was designed as a performance tool to encourage the sales representatives to focus attention on relevant skills and behaviors deemed important to a successful sales call. This process linked sales representative behavior to desirable physician responses. The process was also used to achieve immediate and continuing application of these relevant behaviors and skills so that the sales representative's sales detail habits would change soon and permanently. Sales managers (FLMs) were purposely linked into the process as they worked with sales reps to establish objectives, assess progress, and coach the appropriate application of behavior and skills. Assessment reviews and coaching were accomplished through observation and follow-up by the managers and were considered an extension of the training process.

Second, participants were required to use the action planning process to track progress and collect actual performance data for a specified period of time after the training session. This design also served as a data collection tool for the evaluation.

Figure 3.4 and Figure 3.5 include the complete action plan form. A cut-down version is shown in Figure 3.6 and Figure 3.7 for purposes of explaining how the sales representative and FLM used the performance tool. Explanations are included within each of the two figures.

Name _____ Instructor Signature _____ FLM Signature _____

**PLAN OF ACTION:** <u>Salustatin Essential Selling Skills</u>

Current Number of BPI prescriptions in the market _____

Number of BPI prescriptions necessary to achieve goals _____

| Section 1 - Sales Representative Key Behavior/Skill | Section 2 - Sales Representative action steps (from key behavior/skill) |
|---|---|

**Date of First Follow-Up _____**

1. Setting specific call objectives ..............
2. Communicating the core promotional message ..............
3. Use of support brochures/materials ..............
4. Handling objections ..............
5. Command of product knowledge ..............

<u>Keep Doing This</u>☜ | ☞<u>Reinforce or Improve</u>

| 1. _____ | 1. _____ |
| 2. _____ | 2. _____ |
| 3. _____ | 3. _____ |
| 4. _____ | 4. _____ |
| 5. _____ | 5. _____ |

**Date of Second Follow-Up _____**

1. Setting specific call objectives ..............
2. Communicating the core promotional message ..............
3. Use of support brochures/materials ..............
4. Handling objections ..............
5. Command of product knowledge ..............

<u>Keep Doing This</u>☜ | ☞<u>Reinforce or Improve</u>

| 1. _____ | 1. _____ |
| 2. _____ | 2. _____ |
| 3. _____ | 3. _____ |
| 4. _____ | 4. _____ |
| 5. _____ | 5. _____ |

**Date of Third Follow-Up _____**

1. Setting specific call objectives ..............
2. Communicating the core promotional message ..............
3. Use of support brochures/materials ..............
4. Handling objections ..............
5. Command of product knowledge ..............

<u>Keep Doing This</u>☜ | ☞<u>Reinforce or Improve</u>

| 1. _____ | 1. _____ |
| 2. _____ | 2. _____ |
| 3. _____ | 3. _____ |
| 4. _____ | 4. _____ |
| 5. _____ | 5. _____ |

**Figure 3.4. Action Plan Sections 1 and 2**

Your Signature _____     Manager's Signature _____     Page _____ of _____

Section 3 PLAN OF ACTION - Salustatin Promotional Program (SPP)

*Circle the appropriate answers under each key behavior/skill. Circle more than one if appropriate:*
*Legend: Y = Yes     N = No     NS = Not Sure/Do Not Know*

|  | Sales Representative Skill/Behavior | | | | | |
| --- | --- | --- | --- | --- | --- | --- |
| ☞ How did sales representatives behavior/skills influence physician's decisions? | 1. Call Objectives | 2. Core Message | 3. Promotional Support | 4. Handling Objections | 5. Product Knowledge | 6. Other |
| A. Physician is a better listener? | N Y NS | N Y NS | N Y NS | N Y NS | N Y NS | N Y NS |
| B. Physician is ready to extend effective meeting time? | N Y NS | N Y NS | N Y NS | N Y NS | N Y NS | N Y NS |
| C. Physician is using the representative as a resource? | N Y NS | N Y NS | N Y NS | N Y NS | N Y NS | N Y NS |
| D. Physician better understands the benefits of Salustatin? | N Y NS | N Y NS | N Y NS | N Y NS | N Y NS | N Y NS |
| E. Physician is more convinced that Salustatin is superior? | N Y NS | N Y NS | N Y NS | N Y NS | N Y NS | N Y NS |
| F. Physician is more convinced that representative understands the needs of his/her practice? | N Y NS | N Y NS | N Y NS | N Y NS | N Y NS | N Y NS |

☞ In my view, my contact with physicians during this reporting period will result in: *Check only one response below:*

☐ No change in physician prescribing behavior
☐ A modest improvement in physician prescribing behavior in favor of BPI
☐ A significant improvement in physician prescribing behavior in favor of BPI

The behavior/skill that has worked best for me: _____

Your Signature: _____

Manager's (FLM) Signature: _____

Comments: _____

Figure 3.5.  Action Plan Section 3

| PLAN OF ACTION: Essential Selling Skills | Current # of BPI prescriptions in the market _____ <br> # of BPI prescriptions necessary to achieve goals _____ |
|---|---|
| **Section 1-Sales Representative Key Behavior/Skill** | **Section 2-Sales Representative action steps From each key behavior/skill** |
| **Date of First Follow-Up** <br> 1. Setting specific call objectives ................. <br> 2. Communicating the core promotional message ...... <br> 3. Use of support brochures/materials ......... <br> 4. Handling objections ................. <br> 5. Command of product knowledge ............ | **Keep Doing This →** <br> 1. _____ <br> 2. _____ <br> 3. _____ <br> 4. _____ <br> 5. _____ <br><br> **Reinforce or Improve →** <br> 1. _____ <br> 2. _____ <br> 3. _____ <br> 4. _____ <br> 5. _____ |

(see **Figure 4: Action Plan Sections 1 and 2** for the complete document)

**Explanation of Sections 1 and 2.** The FLM reviews the Action Plan with reps prior to the training to establish expectations and goals. Following the training, the sales rep and FLM meet initially and then meet at least two additional times over a three-month period to discuss how the rep is applying the key behaviors/skills (1 through 5) from Section 1 of the plan. They agree on what the rep should "keep doing" and "reinforce or improve" and the rep makes simple notes for reference. These are not maintained, but are used for dialog between the rep and FLM. The rep then makes numerous sales calls with specific improvements in mind. Following a series of sales calls, the rep completes Section 3 by assessing customer response to the behaviors/skills.

Figure 3.6.  Action Plan (Sections 1 and 2) Utilization as a Performance Tool

SECTION 3 PLAN OF ACTION - Salustatin Essential Selling Skills

*Circle the appropriate answers under each key behavior/skill. Circle more than one if appropriate*

**Legend: Y = Yes   N = No   NS = Not Sure/Do Not Know**

| | Sales Representative Skill/Behavior | | |
| --- | --- | --- | --- |
| | 1. Call Objectives | 2. Core Message | 3. Promotional Support |
| ☞ How did sales representatives' behavior/skills influence physician's decisions? | | | |
| A. Physician is a better listener? | N  Y  NS | N  Y  NS | N  Y  NS |
| B. Physician is ready to extend effective meeting time? | N  Y  NS | N  Y  NS | N  Y  NS |

(see **Figure 5: Action Plan Section 3** for complete document and additional items C through F and 4 through 6)

☞ In my view, contact with physicians during this reporting period **will result in:** *Check only one response below:*

☐ No change in physician prescribing behavior
☐ A modest improvement in physician prescribing behavior in favor of BPI
☐ A significant improvement in physician prescribing behavior in favor of BPI

**The behavior/skill that has worked best for me:** _____

**Explanation of Section 3.** Following a series of physician sales calls, using the criteria in Section 3, the rep conducts a self-assessment to evaluate progress in each skill/behavior area (1 through 5) and its impact on physician behavior (A through F). For example, the rep would estimate how each applied skill/behavior such as "delivering the core message" influenced the physicians' response such as "being a better listener."

On at least one occasion, the FLM accompanies the rep on a series of sales calls so there can be better understanding of the sales relationship and a joint assessment and opportunity for coaching. Section 3 also requires the rep to forecast the improved prescribing behavior of physicians following sales calls and to indicate the behavior/skill that worked best. The Section 3 assessment is then discussed during the next rep meeting with the FLM.

Figure 3.7.  Action Plan (Section 3) Utilization as a Performance Tool

## Evaluation Results

The Phillips Methodology uses Twelve Guiding Principles as an inherent part of collecting, analyzing, and reporting data. These guiding principles were applied to help ensure a conservative approach to collecting and analyzing the data. In addition to ensuring that the reported results are not overstated, the principles (standards) also helped to ensure that the process was applied in a consistent way.

### Level 1 and Level 2 Results

The Level 1 data were collected and analyzed using mean scores. Items were also reviewed for extreme responses, and there were none. Mean scores were as follows: Effectiveness 4.87; Relevance 4.95; and Value 4.88. Eighty-seven percent of the participants reported actions they would take (planned improvements) as a result of the training.

The Level 2 data is a consolidation of responses from facilitators and FLMs reporting on the progress made by participants during the training engagement. Table 3.4 illustrates the checklist that was used to evaluate learning. The consolidated results are shown as a percentage of sales representatives who met the standard of "satisfactory" and "role model," and the percentage of "unsatisfactory" that failed to meet standards in each skill area.

These results were viewed as a success by the Field Force Effectiveness Team, the managers, and the client. Sales representatives who scored unsatisfactory on the skill practice met separately with their managers to create an action plan for improvement that typically involved additional coaching.

### Level 3 and Level 4 Results

Following the training, FLMs and participants completed sales call assessments and discussed the list of behaviors documented on the action plan. Participants discussed sales call assessments with their FLMs on three occasions at specified intervals during the

**Table 3.4.  Level 2 Evaluation Results**

| Level 2 SKILL PRACTICE CHECKLIST N = 220 | | | |
|---|---|---|---|
| Skill to Be Demonstrated | Unsatisfactory | Satisfactory | Role Model |
| Use of Questioning Techniques | 0% | 72.7% | 27.3% |
| Uncovering Hidden Objections | 2.3% | 79.5% | 18.2% |
| Handling Objections | 6.9% | 81.7% | 11.4% |
| Command of Product Knowledge | 4.5% | 91% | 4.5% |
| Communicating the Core Promotional Message | 2.3% | 86.4% | 11.3% |

ninety-day follow-up data collection period. The specific timing of these discussions was left to the discretion of the FLM and sales reps. In addition to the action plan, a follow-up questionnaire was used to determine the extent to which participants used the training and achieved on-the-job success. The questionnaire included numerous questions to determine on-the-job application and business impact.

The final action plan documentation was returned to the measurement partner for analysis, along with the completed questionnaire. Table 3.5 shows a breakdown of the participants that received and returned the questionnaire and action plans. The results of the training process are reflective of what this group of participants accomplished.

**Table 3.5.  Response Profile**

| Data Collection Document | Number Administered | Number Responding | Percent Returned |
|---|---|---|---|
| Action Plan Documents | 220 | 163 | 74% |
| Questionnaires | 220 | 187 | 85% |

Level 4 business impact data (sales) were monitored from BPI records before and after the program to determine how much the Salustatin sales had changed. Responses to the questionnaires provided a good source of data because of the extensive number of write-in comments and quality of data supplied. The 85 percent return rate of completed questionnaires and 74 percent return rate of action plans adds to the credibility of the data.

The data provided by the action plans was of good quality and provided substantial information to use in determining application and performance improvement in the job setting. Exhibit 3.1 shows the consolidated results of Section 3 of the action plans. The skills reported by sales representatives as most useful in influencing physician behavior were "Communicating the Core Message" and "Handling Objections."

Selected results of the sales representatives' application of the training as reported in the follow-up questionnaire are presented below in Table 3.6, Training's Influence on Performance Measures, and Table 3.7, Accomplishments and Business Impact Linked to the Training.

In Question 5 of the questionnaire, participants were given a list of performance measures and asked to indicate the extent (1 to 5 scale) to which this course had a positive influence on these measures. The results are shown in Table 3.6.

Participants were asked in Question 6 to provide written comments to identify specific accomplishments/improvements linked to the training and the resulting business impact. A representation of the comments is listed in Table 3.7.

The data in Tables 3.6 and 3.7 and other data from Exhibit 3.1 of the action plans confirmed the success of learning transfer. Handling objections and communicating the core promotional message were consistently reported as the most successful behavior/ skills.

| How the Sales Representatives' Skill/Behavior Influenced the Physician's Behavior ➜ | Setting Specific Call Objectives | | | Communicating the Core Message | | | Use of Support Brochures/Materials | | | Handling Objections | | | Command of Product Knowledge | | |
|---|---|---|---|---|---|---|---|---|---|---|---|---|---|---|---|
| | | | | | | | N = No; Y = Yes; NS = Not Sure | | | | | | | | |
| | N | Y | NS | N | Y | NS | N | Y | NS | N | Y | NS | N | Y | NS |
| A. Is a better listener | 2 | 115 | 46 | 1 | 149 | 13 | 9 | 98 | 56 | 3 | 129 | 31 | 2 | 101 | 60 |
| Percentage Responding | 1.23% | 70.55% | 28.22% | 0.61% | 91.41% | 7.98% | 5.52% | 60.12% | 34.36% | 1.84% | 79.14% | 19.02% | 1.23% | 61.96% | 36.81% |
| B. Is ready to extend effective meeting time? | 15 | 71 | 77 | 15 | 99 | 49 | 10 | 81 | 72 | 3 | 129 | 31 | 1 | 99 | 63 |
| Percentage Responding | 9.20% | 43.56% | 47.24% | 9.20% | 60.74% | 30.06% | 6.13% | 49.69% | 44.17% | 1.84% | 79.14% | 19.02% | 0.61% | 60.74% | 38.65% |
| C. Is using the sales rep as a resource? | 15 | 55 | 93 | 7 | 92 | 64 | 8 | 98 | 57 | 2 | 122 | 39 | 1 | 124 | 38 |
| Percentage Responding | 9.20% | 33.74% | 57.06% | 4.29% | 56.44% | 39.26% | 4.91% | 60.12% | 34.97% | 1.23% | 74.85% | 23.93% | 0.61% | 76.07% | 23.31% |
| D. Better understands benefits of Salustatin? | 2 | 121 | 40 | 0 | 153 | 10 | 3 | 110 | 50 | 0 | 129 | 34 | 2 | 99 | 62 |
| Percentage Responding | 1.23% | 74.23% | 24.54% | 0.00% | 93.87% | 6.13% | 1.84% | 67.48% | 30.67% | 0.00% | 79.14% | 20.86% | 1.23% | 60.74% | 38.04% |
| E. Is more convinced Salustatin is superior? | 5 | 90 | 68 | 1 | 127 | 35 | 13 | 74 | 76 | 2 | 123 | 38 | 3 | 81 | 79 |
| Percentage Responding | 3.07% | 55.21% | 41.72% | 0.61% | 77.91% | 21.47% | 7.98% | 45.40% | 46.63% | 1.23% | 75.46% | 23.31% | 1.84% | 49.69% | 48.47% |
| F. Is more convinced rep understands the needs of his/her practice? | 8 | 74 | 81 | 9 | 64 | 90 | 8 | 58 | 97 | 1 | 71 | 91 | 2 | 65 | 96 |
| Percentage Responding | 4.91% | 45.40% | 49.69% | 5.52% | 39.26% | 55.21% | 4.91% | 35.58% | 59.51% | 0.61% | 43.56% | 55.83% | 1.23% | 39.88% | 58.90% |
| Cumulative responses by Column | 47 | 526 | 405 | 33 | 684 | 261 | 51 | 519 | 408 | 11 | 703 | 264 | 11 | 569 | 398 |

Exhibit 3.1. Action Plan Section 3 Results—Sales Representative Behaviors

**Table 3.6. Training's Influence on Performance Measures**

| Measure | No Influence/ 1 | Little Influence/ 2 | Some Influence/ 3 | Moderate Influence/ 4 | Significant Influence/ 5 | N = 187/ Mean |
|---|---|---|---|---|---|---|
| a. Increased confidence level of sales representative | 1.7% | 10.7% | 22.0% | 28.2% | 37.3% | 3.89% |
| b. Improved my ability to influence physician prescribing behavior | 0.6% | 3.4% | 34.1% | 34.1% | 27.9% | 3.85% |
| c. Improved my ability to tailor sales situations and activities to individual physician needs | 2.3% | 10.5% | 28.1% | 32.2% | 26.9% | 3.71% |
| d. Improved job satisfaction | 2.8% | 11.9% | 29.4% | 22.6% | 33.3% | 3.72% |
| e. Improved my ability to adapt to changing needs and business issues of physicians | 2.8% | 11.4% | 32.4% | 24.4% | 29.0% | 3.65% |
| f. Increase in quality time with customer | 3.4% | 16.9% | 26.4% | 25.3% | 28.1% | 3.58% |
| t. Increased revenue from the sales of Salustatin | 0.6% | 8.7% | 49.7% | 19.7% | 21.4% | 3.53% |
| h. Improved customer satisfaction | 2.8% | 17.6% | 29.5% | 27.8% | 22.2% | 3.49% |
| i. Improved ability to sell as a team | 5.3% | 11.2% | 42.6% | 16.0% | 24.9% | 3.44% |
| j. Increase in market share | 1.1% | 16.1% | 39.7% | 27.6% | 15.5% | 3.40% |
| k. Improved relationship between representative and physician | 6.2% | 22.7% | 21.6% | 24.4% | 25.0% | 3.39% |
| l. Closer partnership between sales manager and sales representative | 9.1% | 21.7% | 25.7% | 20.6% | 22.9% | 3.26% |
| m. Increase in sales of other BPI prescription products | 4.8% | 25.9% | 38.0% | 20.5% | 10.8% | 3.07% |
| n. Reduction in sales rep voluntary turnover | 33.3% | 26.0% | 13.3% | 8.7% | 18.7% | 2.53% |

Table 3.7.  Accomplishments and Business Impact Linked to the Training

| Comments from Questionnaire Item 6 | N = 187 (multiple answers) Number of Responses |
|---|---|
| 1. More meaningful communication due to consistent and aggressive core promotional message | 82 responses |
| 2. Better handling of objections | 77 responses |
| 3. Better skills to influence physician prescribing behavior | 68 responses |
| 4. Increased sales (another twelve predicted sales would increase) | 68 responses |
| 5. Better able to evaluate physician needs | 56 responses |
| 6. Better quality of call time spent with physicians | 41 responses |
| 7. Improved listening | 29 responses |
| 8. More satisfied customers | 22 responses |
| 9. Better strategic call objectives | 19 responses |

*Barriers to Application*

When asked in Question 8 about barriers to the job application of skills learned, the participants responded that "time" was the most significant barrier. Write-in comments indicate that there is support from BPI for the application of the training in the work setting, but the customer often presents barriers. Thirty-seven comments described the biggest barrier as, "physicians are in a hurry" and therefore there is insufficient time for sales calls. Twelve comments indicated that "multi-group physicians and stand-up calls were also a barrier." Table 3.8 includes the complete results.

*Measurable Business Impact*

Each FLM was asked to use the action plan with each of their representatives to establish three follow-up dates to discuss the

Table 3.8.  Barriers to Application

| Item | Number of Participants Selecting |
|---|---|
| A. Not enough time | 86 |
| B. My work environment does not support these skills | 27 |
| C. I have no opportunity to use the skills | 16 |
| D. My manager does not support this type of course | 6 |
| E. This material does not apply to my job situation | 5 |
| F. Other (Please specify) | 5 |

application of five specific skills and behaviors that were intended to influence physicians' decisions. These five skills and behaviors were the focal point of the training program. In many instances, the manager observed sales calls, later debriefed the calls, and provided coaching with the sales representative as needed.

While this is not an exact measure, it includes the input of the representative and the manager and is their best judgment after close contact with the customer and assessment in the work setting. It provides another strong link to increased sales and is a positive statement that the manager, sales representative, and the training program combined to achieve the intended results.

*Isolating the Effects of Training*

Several strategies were considered to isolate the effects of training, but some of the methods were not appropriate in this situation. It was agreed that input directly from the participants (estimates) would be the most appropriate and credible way to isolate the effects. Although subjective, participant estimates of training impact are a reliable indicator when appropriate steps are taken to collect the data. The participants are the closest individuals to the performance improvement and are often aware of other influences that impact the performance measures. Therefore, for this study, participants were asked to indicate the degree to which a specific improvement was caused by the training program. Item 8 on the questionnaire was used to capture this data.

Sales reps were asked to review the potential influencing factors and indicate a percentage attributable to each as appropriate by spreading 100 percent across all applicable factors. Table 3.9 illustrates the consolidated responses and is used to isolate the effects of the training on the Level 4 business metrics.

Of all the factors that contributed to performance improvement, the Essential Selling Skills training was ranked number 1 and coaching by sales managers was ranked number 3. These two components were a direct result of the implementation of the Salustatin Promotional Program.

**Table 3.9.  Factors Contributing to Performance Improvement**

| Please select the items that you feel are appropriate by writing in your estimated percentages as they apply. | Percentage Improvement Attributed |
|---|---|
| A.  Physician seminars promoting Salustatin | 21.17% |
| B.  Other local promotions of Salustatin | 9.02% |
| C.  Essential Selling Skills training for sales representatives | 24.32% |
| D.  Coaching by my sales manager | 18.90% |
| E.  Salustatin physicians seeing more patients with associated indications | 6.18% |
| F.  Improved sales brochures supporting the core promotional message | 12.13% |
| G.  Lack of competing products from our competitors | 4.58% |
| H.  Other training initiatives: _____ *please specify* | 2.44% |
| I.  Other: _____ *please specify* | 1.26% |
| Total of all selected items must = 100 percent | Total 100% |

**Table 3.10.  Confidence Level**

| Q9. What level of confidence do you place on the above estimations? (0% = No Confidence, and 100% = Certainty) | Average Confidence Level 70% |
|---|---|

Question 9 on the questionnaire asked participants what level of confidence they placed on their estimates, with 0 percent = No Confidence, and 100 percent = Certainty. The question and the average response is shown in Table 3.10.

Since learning transfer has been achieved, pre- and post-sales data are available, the influence of the training has been isolated, and confidence level has been determined, the business impact at Level 4 can now be determined. Business performance data (sales) was collected during the twelve-month period before and after the training.

*Calculating the Revenue Gain*

Salustatin revenue from sales was examined for the twelve-month period before and after the training. This established the change in revenue during the post-training time period of July (Year 2) to June (Year 3). While the sales figures could have been used after three or four months following the training and then annualized, the Field Force Effectiveness team and BPI management elected to wait and report the ROI based on actual twelve-month sales figures. Table 3.11 shows the comparison.

*Data Conversion*

Since revenue data includes the "cost of goods sold" (research costs, administrative costs, production costs, distribution costs, overhead costs, etc.), an adjustment must be made to reduce it to the amount equal to its profit contribution. The contribution is usually based on a percentage of revenue and is often tied to product line and/or customer segment. Communication with the chief analyst in BPI's

Table 3.11.  Comparison of Revenue

| (Prior to Training) Salustatin Revenue July, Year 1 Through June, Year 2 | Salustatin Revenue July, Year 2 Through June, Year 3 (One Month After Training Through One Year After Training) | Post-Training Gain in Revenue from Sales of Salustatin After One Year |
|---|---|---|
| $79,432,678 | $97,401,702 | $17,969,024 |

finance department revealed that the margin factor for Salustatin in the first five years of its life cycle is 21.5 *percent* of total revenue.

After adjustments, total monetary benefits attributable to Essential Selling Skills training = **$657,695**. Using the post-training value of $17,969,024 from Table 3.11, the calculation is as follows:

*Step One:* $17,969,024 × .215 (margin factor) = $3,863,340 profit

*Step Two:* $3,863,340 × 0.2432 (isolation factor - Table 3.9) = $939,564

*Step Three:* $939,564 × 0.7 (confidence level - Table 3.10) = **$657,695**

*Calculating Program Costs*

The fully loaded cost of the Essential Selling Skills training was $326,000. Utilization of sales managers during delivery added to the cost significantly. The detailed cost breakdown is not presented here, but it included all front-end research, design, and development costs associated with the training, salaries and benefits of staff and 220 participants, as well as others assisting in delivery, administrative and coordination costs, materials costs, overhead costs (including training facility), meals and refreshments, travel expense, and evaluation costs.

## ROI Calculation

The return on investment for the Essential Selling Skills Training was calculated at 102 percent. Prior to the calculation, the profit contribution, the isolation factor, and confidence level were adjusted and applied to the revenue. Only the first year of benefits were used in calculating the ROI (net benefits compared to fully loaded costs). After the above adjustments, the results were reported to management.

$$\text{ROI} = \frac{\text{Net Benefits}}{\text{Costs}} = \frac{\$657,695 - \$326,000}{\$326,000} = \times 100 = 102\%$$

# Communication Strategy

The communication strategy was planned up-front with the USA Field Force Effectiveness Team (FFE) buying in to the approach. An executive overview report of about three pages was presented to senior executives by the FFE. Each of the five FFE members made a stand-up presentation to his or her respective senior executive. The FFE received the full report and a two-hour presentation on the results.

The full report was also provided to the training function. A modified version was provided to national sales managers, sales managers, and sales representatives. The modified report focused extensively on Level 3 data.

The ROI data was not available until the end of the first year and was ultimately reported through a conference call with senior executives and short briefings with other stakeholders. One senior executive wanted a follow-up explanation with more detail about the guiding principles. The training manager met with her independently and explained the principles in detail and how they were applied to the study. As a result, this executive adopted the principles for her group when conducting research activities.

## Lessons Learned

Impact studies are almost always a victim of circumstances and constraints. This one was no exception. First, there was agreement that six methods would be used to collect data from four different sources. After considering the disruption that physicians would experience when asked to provide data, senior management dictated that this effort be abandoned. This left the evaluation team with three sources, the sales records, data from the sales manager, and data from the sales representative.

Additionally, the sales managers opted out of the questionnaire, and the focus group for sales representatives was cancelled. In hindsight, our appetite was probably too big for data. As it turned out, we had plenty of data with the action plans, questionnaires, and the data from the sales record. It is a difficult balancing act to determine how much data is enough. The answer is usually not known until the data analysis phase actually begins.

The organization has a much larger appetite for Level 3 data than we initially thought. We were asked several times by different executives to drill deeper with the Level 3 results. Three executives indicated a desire to see the focus group data and expressed disappointment that we abandoned the effort. Perhaps we should have been more insistent on collecting this data. Our next data collection effort will include soliciting the needs of the executive group before making final decisions on data collection strategy and methods.

*Questions for Discussion*

1. What would be the additional benefit in evaluating the other two components of the Salustatin Promotional Program (physician seminars and training of first-line managers)?

2. Is the amount of organization support for data collection provided in this BPI case normal or rare? What is your position

on the cancellation of the two focus group initiatives (physicians and sales representatives) and the questionnaire for
managers?

3. What are your opinions and concerns about using the action
   planning process with training programs in your organization
   to collect data and influence transfer to the work setting?

4. Should the fully loaded training costs include the cost of
   managers' "coaching on the job"? Why or why not?

5. The isolation factor in Table 3.9 attributed 18.9 percent to
   coaching. Can this 18.9 percent be used to calculate an additional gain for the ROI? Why or why not?

## Resources

Phillips, P., Phillips, J., Stone, R., & Burkett, H. (2006). *The ROI fieldbook:
Strategies for implementing ROI in HR and training*. Burlington, MA:
Butterworth-Heinemann.

Phillips, J., & Stone, R. (2002). *How to measure training results: A practical guide
to tracking the six key indicators*. New York: McGraw-Hill.

## About The Author

**Ron Drew Stone** is an author, international consultant, and
presenter, and one of the world's most recognized and accomplished
authorities on improving and measuring performance improvement
initiatives. Mr. Stone is a senior vice president with ROI Institute,
where he engages in the international consulting practice. While
working with Jack and Patti Phillips as a partner since 1995,
Mr. Stone has made significant contributions to perfecting the
ROI Process. He has conducted more than one hundred return
on investment studies and directed hundreds more. He provides
consulting services in performance improvement, linking training
to organization business measures, designing training for results and
ROI, and developing measurement and evaluation strategies. He

also conducts ROI Certification workshops, certifies practitioners in the ROI Methodology, and conducts a full range of public and in-house performance improvement, measurement, and needs assessment workshops. He is a certified change consultant.

Mr. Stone has twenty-five years of experience in engineering and economic development and in human resource management and training in the aerospace and electric utility industries. He has considerable experience in employment processes, performance management, managing the training function, designing healthcare delivery systems, budgeting and account classification processes, training curriculum design, safety, organizational development, executive development, needs assessment, measurement, and evaluation.

He co-authored *The ROI Fieldbook: Strategies for Implementing ROI in HR and Training* (Butterworth-Heinemann, 2006); *How to Measure Training Results—A Practical Guide to Tracking the Six Key Indicators* (McGraw-Hill, 2002); and *The Human Resources Scorecard* (Butterworth-Heinemann, 2001). He has contributed several case studies to the ASTD *In-Action Casebook* Series, *Measuring Return on Investment* (2005 and 1997), *Measuring ROI in the Public Sector* (2002), and *Measuring Learning and Performance* (1999) and is a contributing author to other ASTD publications. Mr. Stone received his BBA from Georgia State University. He can be reached at 205.980.1642 or drewroi@aol.com

# 4

# Measuring ROI in a Career Development Initiative

## A Global Computer Company

Holly Burkett

## Abstract

This case study describes the evaluation effort for a career develop-ment initiative implemented as a pilot performance improvement strategy in a dynamic manufacturing environment for a global com-pany employing more than 9,600 employees worldwide. Strategic goals for implementation included enhanced operational capacity and bench strength; enhanced work climate for engaging employ-ees; and increased labor efficiency. Components of this initiative included an action learning workshop with performance objectives aligned to business needs; Self and Manager assessments of pilot par-ticipants' Critical Skills; and a Development Discussion action plan to assist participants in applying Critical Skills toward execution of operational performance priorities. Evaluation results showed a positive link between participants' applied knowledge/skills and desired business results.

Note: This case was prepared to serve as a basis for discussion rather than an illustration of either effective or ineffective administrative and management practices. All names, dates, and places have been disguised at the request of the author or organization.

## Organizational Profile

Since its inception as a two-person operation to a global company employing more than 9,600 employees worldwide, Innovative Computer, Inc. (actual name disguised upon request) has been a leader of technological innovation in the microcomputer industry. It was the first in color graphics, sound, mass production, expandability, disk data storage, Pascal, bitmapped graphics, and integrated software since its incorporation as a business in 1977. It has a vigorous, dedicated commitment to its mission of bringing the best personal computing products and support to students, educators, designers, scientists, engineers, business persons, and consumers in more than 140 countries around the world. At the time of this study, Innovative Computer, Inc., owned manufacturing facilities in the United States, Ireland, and Singapore and had distribution facilities located in the United States, Europe, Canada, Australia, Singapore, and Japan. This initiative was deployed at the Operations Center, which then served as the sole company-owned production facility for all desktop computers sold in North and South America.

## Background and Program Objectives

The Career Development initiative began as a strategy to build organizational capacity and bench strength due to the ongoing challenge of retaining top management and technical talent. Given a shrinking labor pool of experienced managers, rising costs of recruiting outside talent, and an alarming lack of organizational depth in developing leaders from within, this was deemed a business-critical issue. The intent of the initiative, then, was to use development planning as a means of partnering with employees to fill leadership gaps and create capacity-building solutions that would enhance the viability of the organization as both a world-class operation and as an employer of choice. In light of the business need and the operation director's interest in accountability, this initiative applied the Phillips's ROI Methodology to measure the business impact and cost/benefit of the solution. This particular initiative had components that fit the typical criteria for measuring programs at higher levels of evaluation, which included:

- Long-term viability
- Importance to overall strategic objectives
- High visibility
- Senior management interest

## ROI Planning: The Linking Process

With the ongoing competition for resources in a dynamic, resource-constrained environment, it was important to provide stakeholders with clear direction about the schedule, scope, and resource requirements of this results-based evaluation effort. In this case, preliminary planning included defining business needs and linking those to specific objectives and measures through a documented data collection plan.

As shown in Figure 4.1, this plan served to communicate the type of data to be collected, how it would be collected, when it would be collected, and who was responsible for collecting it. This approach helped ensure that the solution design had built-in evaluation components and that the pilot was developed with a systemic view of aligning performance requirements across organizational, job, and process levels (Figure 4.2).

### Solution Components

Based on needs assessment input derived from interviews and historical data (including exit interviews), a Career Development program was implemented as one component of a comprehensive talent management strategy meant to increase capacity,

| Evaluation Level | Objective(s) | Data Collection Method | Data Sources | Timing | Responsibilities |
|---|---|---|---|---|---|
| 1 | **Reaction/Satisfaction/Planned Action**<br>• Achieve 4.0 on Overall Satisfaction and Relevance rating(s)<br>• Achieve 4.0 on Relevance of program<br>• 80% identify planned actions | • Reaction Questionnaire<br>• Impact Questionnaire | Participants' Managers, Supervisors<br>Steering Committee | • After each session<br>• During session<br>• 30, 60 days | • HRD consultant<br>• Participants<br>• Managers<br>• Steering Committee |
| 2 | **Learning**<br>• Identify individual skills, talents, and development opportunities per Self & Manager assessment inventories<br>• Demonstrate proficiency with Development Discussion guidelines | • Skill Practice Exercises, Simulations<br>• Skill Assessment Pre-Work (Self, Manager) | Participants<br>Managers<br>HRD facilitator | • During session<br>• Before/during<br>• One week after | • Participants<br>• Managers<br>• HRD consultant |
| 3 | **Application/Implementation**<br>• Conduct Development Discussion with manager within 60 days of program completion<br>• Apply critical skills/knowledge to prioritized development projects within 60 days of program completion | • Individual Action and Development Plans<br>• Action Projects<br>• Follow-Up Session(s) | Participants<br>Steering Committee<br>Managers | • During action plan implementation<br>• 2 months after program | • HRD consultant<br>• Project Sponsor<br>• Steering Committee<br>• Participants<br>• Managers |
| 4 | **Impact**<br>• To measure extent to which applied critical skills/knowledge impacted strategic goal of increasing labor efficiency<br>• Increased operational capacity, increased labor efficiency | • Performance Monitoring<br>• Impact Questionnaire | Steering Committee<br>Department Recorder Data<br>Participants | • 2 months after action plan implementation | • HRD consultant<br>• Subject-matter experts<br>• Participants<br>• Managers |
| 5 | **ROI**<br>• To measure return on investment with performance improvement strategy<br>• Achieve 120% ROI or greater | | | | |

**Figure 4.1. Data Collection Plan**

Copyright © ROI Institute, Inc.

**Alignment at Three Levels**

| Organization | Process | Performer |
|---|---|---|
| ▪ Solution supports strategic business objectives<br>▪ Business and/or performance impact measures have been defined by stakeholders<br>▪ Gap between desired and current state supports performance improvement solution<br>▪ Solution supports causal linkage between stated performance objectives and desired operational results<br>▪ Solution design addresses environmental factors influencing performance<br>▪ Appropriate incentives established for achievement of performance objectives<br>▪ Solution defines methods for using results for continuous improvement purposes | ▪ Development process communicates to those who need to use it and/or support it<br>▪ Process provides environmental support for performance to occur<br>▪ Participant selection process ensures participants/managers are sufficiently capable to complete a Development Discussion plan<br>▪ Instructional design process allows sufficient time for development, review, and completion of plans<br>▪ Development Planning process fully integrated into supporting business processes (mid-term, annual performance reviews, bonus plans, Metrics Meetings, Business Plans, Job Rotations) | ▪ Process provides participants with adequate feedback, time, and resources to complete Development action plans<br>▪ Development Plan clearly defines performance specifications<br>▪ Consequences, incentives for Development plan completion defined<br>▪ Process defines how participants' performance improvement data will be used<br>▪ Process promotes skill development and transfer of learning to real-world, on-the-job projects, tasks<br>▪ Includes provisions for participants to identify environmental enablers/barriers to planned actions |

**Figure 4.2. Alignment of Performance Improvement Solution**

build employee engagement, and enhance reputational capital. Pre-work included self/manager assessments of participants' critical skills, skill gaps, job characteristics, and performance priorities. The primary output of the program was an employee-driven Development Discussion Plan focusing on the following categories:

- *Talents:* Manager and I agree about my strengths

- *Job Gaps:* Manager and I don't agree about skill's importance

- *Skill Gaps:* Manager and I don't agree about my skill level

- *Development Needs:* Manager and I agree that my skill level is lower than job requires

The target audience for the pilot was a select pool of fifty high-potential, high-performing professionals in business-critical, hard-to-fill positions. The Development Discussion planning process was meant to enhance employees' leadership skills and development options by providing clarity about:

- Organizational and job performance priorities

- Skill strengths

- Skill gaps

- Growth opportunities

The employee-initiated Development Plan also gave both employees and their managers a structured feedback tool and process which emphasized the following: (a) individual employees' have primary responsibility for their career development and job satisfaction; (b) the best opportunities for increased development and satisfaction are through action learning assignments or rotations within one's current position; (c) organizational and individual capacity is best attained by building on strengths; (d) structured reflection about individual talents and strengths provides clarity about personal motivators and is a value-added input to development discussion goal-setting; and (e) effective manager/employee feedback and communication is crucial to high performance, high morale, and attraction/retention of top talent.

The Development Discussion planning process was considered a "best-in-class" component of effective leadership development since it focused on (1) careful selection of candidates to assure a future pipeline of qualified leaders; (2) quality action learning and real-time assignments to support both individual development and the delivery of optimal business results; and (3) advance communication planning of a career development discussion with clearly defined, targeted outcomes.

**Implementation Strategy**

The following objectives were communicated to pilot participants in briefing sessions led by HRD and members of the senior executive steering committee. Specifically, the business purpose was conveyed as follows: "This . . . [effort] . . . ensures our viability and agility as a world-class factory. . . . The end result will be a supportive work environment, with a flexible workforce, capable of supporting our strategic vision, executing our mission, and building our reputational capital."

Given the important role of managers in reinforcing this initiative and providing constructive, timely feedback, a Transfer strategy was developed as part of the evaluation plan. Figure 4.3 shows the Transfer Strategy Matrix used in this effort. This *"Before, During, After"* implementation approach was rolled out in initial briefings about the project, had strong senior management support, and was instrumental in holding managers accountable for supporting employees' performance objectives throughout all phases

| Role | Planning<br>Before | Implementation<br>During | Evaluation<br>After |
|---|---|---|---|
| **Steering Committee** | • Help define performance, business objectives<br>• Participate in assessing skill gaps<br>• Determine pilot selection criteria<br>• Co-faciliate "kick-off" sessions or briefings<br>• Require attendance at scheduled briefings | • Attend, co-facilitate select implementation sessions<br>• Communicate importance of learning, performance, and business objectives<br>• Assist in collecting, analyzing, converting data<br>• Ensure managers fulfill coaching/advising roles | • Participate in reviewing evaluation plan<br>• Reinforce follow-up and application of Action Plan<br>• Recognize individuals for successful completions<br>• Assist in removing barriers to application<br>• Provide incentives<br>• Determine viability of enterprise-wide roll-out of program |
| **Managers, Supervisors** | • Support HRD in defining performance objectives<br>• Attend briefing sessions prior to implementation<br>• Reinforce trainee participation<br>• Complete pre-work assessments | • Remove barriers to employees' attendance<br>• Provide coverage for individuals in training<br>• Attend sessions as available<br>• Directly discuss Development Discussion action plan<br>• Ask employees about workshop progress | • Reinforce follow-up and application of Development Discussion action plans<br>• Assist in removing barriers to application<br>• Conduct Development Discussion meetings<br>• Serve as mentor, coach, resource<br>• Work with HRD around development options<br>• Monitor performance progress |
| **Human Resource Development** | • Align objectives with identified needs (organization, process, performer)<br>• Customize curriculum to meet desired objectives<br>• Incorporate benchmarked transfer strategies into course design<br>• Design data collection instruments, evaluation plan(s)<br>• Conduct briefings with pilot groups | • Communicate importance of learning, performance, and business objectives<br>• Assess trainees for reaction, learning, and skill/knowledge transfer<br>• Facilitate Pre-work<br>• Teach the Development Discussion and action planning process<br>• Implement evaluation plan/tools; collect, analyze, report results data | • Continue implementing evaluation plan<br>• Conduct action planning sessions<br>• Facilitate 60-day follow-up sessions<br>• Report results to key stakeholders<br>• Use results for continuous improvement<br>• Determine viability of enterprise-wide roll-out of program |
| **Participants** | • Assist HRD in job/task analysis<br>• Attend briefing sessions<br>• Complete pre-assessment survey and pre-work | • Attend full program<br>• Complete self-assessment inventories<br>• Demonstrate active participation in skill practices<br>• Complete Development Discussion action plan | • Apply critical skills on the job<br>• Seek support from supervisor in implementing Development Plan<br>• Initiate Development Discussion<br>• Identify barriers to application<br>• Complete 60-day Impact Questionnaire |

**Figure 4.3. Transfer Strategy Matrix for Career Development Initiative**
Adapted from Broad and Newstrom, 1992

of solution implementation. In communicating for the vision a results-based effort, the transfer strategy was instrumental in dispelling the notion of evaluation as an "add-on" activity occurring at the end of a training program. Defining specific responsibilities of stakeholders was a critical success factor. It also established a foundation of shared ownership for solution results.

## Evaluation Results

### Level 1: Reaction, Satisfaction, Planned Action

Level 1 results were collected at the end of the program and again during the Impact Questionnaire administered sixty days later. Participants, sponsors, and managers were asked to indicate their level of agreement or disagreement with statements based on the following 5-point scale: strongly agree (5), agree (4), partly agree/partly disagree (3), disagree (2), and strongly disagree (1). The measure of success was a minimum score of 4.0 out of 5.0 with key measures of interest addressing areas of relevance, intent to use, and willingness to recommend the program to others. The average score of all participant ratings received in these key areas are listed below:

- I was satisfied with this program (4.8)

- This program was relevant to my work (4.5)

- I would recommend this program to others (4.8)

- This program was a worthwhile investment of my time (4.5)

Results were successful with 92 percent of participants indicating a planned intent to conduct a Development Discussion with their manager within thirty to sixty days of workshop completion.

## Level 2: Learning

Level 2 objectives focused on participants' demonstrated ability to:

- Define critical skills required for job effectiveness

- Define skill gaps

- Identify talents

- Identify developmental needs

- Demonstrate proficiency with Development Discussion guidelines

Success with learning objectives was measured during the program through skill practices, role plays, and training simulations. Learning exercises focused on participants' demonstrated ability to identify the critical skills needed to execute around defined performance priorities, as well as participants' demonstrated ability to conduct a Development Discussion with their managers, in accordance with the Development Discussion guidelines provided. In addition, participants completed a structured self-assessment of skills, gaps, talents, and development needs. Exercises and observations indicated that participants were equipped with the necessary knowledge and skills to successfully initiate a Development Discussion plan. Significant learning outcomes included:

- I have a better understanding of my Performance Priorities for the next six to twelve months (4.4)

- I have a better awareness of my Development Needs as they relate to my current position (4.3)

- I am confident in my ability to apply knowledge/skills gained from this program (4.6)

## Level 3: Application and Implementation

Developmental Action Plans and follow-up Impact Questionnaires were used to capture application results. As shown in Figure 4.4, the Development Action Plan was initiated to address the following fundamental questions:

- What steps or action items will be taken as a result of learning?

- What on-the-job improvements or accomplishments will be realized with applied knowledge/skill?

The Impact Questionnaire, Figure 4.4, administered sixty days after program completion, was also used to capture application data. Specifically, participants were asked to identify: (1) the extent and frequency with which they applied the planned actions defined in their Development Action Plans; (2) the extent of effectiveness in applying learned knowledge/skill on a scale of 1 to 5, with 5 being "Completely" and 1 being "Not Effective"; (3) the criticality of applied knowledge/skill to job success on a scale of 1 to 5, with 5 being "Completely" and 1 being "Not Critical"; (4) the extent to which desired specific knowledge/skills were changed on a scale of 1 to 5, with 5 being "Very Significant" and 1 being "No Change"; (5) the result of their actions on specific work measures; (6) barriers/enablers to application; and (7) intangible benefits of applied knowledge/skills.

Table 4.1 shows application data captured in the Impact Questionnaire (Q – 3).

Table 4.2 summarizes the degree to which participants enhanced or changed their approach to discussions with their managers about performance priorities and career development needs.

The most commonly cited barriers to application of skills/ knowledge were time constraints, marginal support from some

**Impact Questionnaire**

1. After reflecting upon your experience with the Career Development Program, please indicate your degree of agreement with the following.

| | Strongly Disagree 1 | 2 | 3 | 4 | Strongly Agree 5 | N/A |
|---|---|---|---|---|---|---|
| a. I'd recomend this program to others | ☐ | ☐ | ☐ | ☐ | ☐ | ☐ |
| b. The program was a worthwhile investment of my time | ☐ | ☐ | ☐ | ☐ | ☐ | ☐ |
| c. I learned new knowledge/skills from participation in this program | ☐ | ☐ | ☐ | ☐ | ☐ | ☐ |
| d. As a result of this program, I have a better understanding of my Performance Priorities for the next 6–12 months | ☐ | ☐ | ☐ | ☐ | ☐ | ☐ |
| e. As a result of this program, I have a better understanding of my Development Needs as they relate to my current position | ☐ | ☐ | ☐ | ☐ | ☐ | ☐ |
| f. I am confident in my ability to apply the knowledge/skills gained from this program | ☐ | ☐ | ☐ | ☐ | ☐ | ☐ |

2. Please rate, on a scale of 1–5, with 1 being "Low" and 5 being "High", the relevance of the following program elements to your job.

| Self-Assessments | 1 | 2 | 3 | 4 | 5 |
|---|---|---|---|---|---|
| a. Critical Skills | ☐ | ☐ | ☐ | ☐ | ☐ |
| b. Job Gaps | ☐ | ☐ | ☐ | ☐ | ☐ |
| c. Skill Gaps | ☐ | ☐ | ☐ | ☐ | ☐ |
| d. Development Needs | ☐ | ☐ | ☐ | ☐ | ☐ |
| e. Career Values/Motivators | ☐ | ☐ | ☐ | ☐ | ☐ |

| Manager Assessments | 1 | 2 | 3 | 4 | 5 |
|---|---|---|---|---|---|
| a. Critical Skills | ☐ | ☐ | ☐ | ☐ | ☐ |
| b. Job Gaps | ☐ | ☐ | ☐ | ☐ | ☐ |
| c. Skill Gaps | ☐ | ☐ | ☐ | ☐ | ☐ |
| d. Development Needs | ☐ | ☐ | ☐ | ☐ | ☐ |

| Other | 1 | 2 | 3 | 4 | 5 |
|---|---|---|---|---|---|
| • Workshop Content | ☐ | ☐ | ☐ | ☐ | ☐ |
| • Development Discussion Plan | ☐ | ☐ | ☐ | ☐ | ☐ |
| • Resource Materials | ☐ | ☐ | ☐ | ☐ | ☐ |

3. Did you implement a Development Discussion action plan with your manager?
Yes ☐        No ☐
If not, why not: _____

Figure 4.4.  Impact Questionnaire

4. Please indicate the degree to which you've applied knowledge/skills from the program.

| | Infrequent | | | | Exceptional | No Opportunity to Apply |
|---|---|---|---|---|---|---|
| | 1 | 2 | 3 | 4 | 5 | |
| a. How frequently did you use the knowledge/skills from this program on your job? | ☐ | ☐ | ☐ | ☐ | ☐ | ☐ |

| | Not Effective | | | | Completely | No Opportunity to Apply |
|---|---|---|---|---|---|---|
| | 1 | 2 | 3 | 4 | 5 | |
| b. How effective are you in using the knowlegdge/skills gained from this program? | ☐ | ☐ | ☐ | ☐ | ☐ | ☐ |

| | Not Effective | | | | Completely | N/A |
|---|---|---|---|---|---|---|
| | 1 | 2 | 3 | 4 | 5 | |
| c. How effective is your manager in using the Development Discussion Planning process? | ☐ | ☐ | ☐ | ☐ | ☐ | ☐ |

| | Not Critical | | | | Completely | N/A |
|---|---|---|---|---|---|---|
| | 1 | 2 | 3 | 4 | 5 | |
| d. How critical is applying the knowledge/skills from this program to your job success? | ☐ | ☐ | ☐ | ☐ | ☐ | ☐ |

5. Please indicate the extent to which the following behaviors have been changed or enhanced as a result of your participation in the Career Development program.

| | No Change | | | | Very Significant | No Opportunity to Apply |
|---|---|---|---|---|---|---|
| | 1 | 2 | 3 | 4 | 5 | |
| a. Communicating with my manager about performance priorities | ☐ | ☐ | ☐ | ☐ | ☐ | ☐ |
| b. Maintaining focus on short-term performance priorities | ☐ | ☐ | ☐ | ☐ | ☐ | ☐ |
| c. Maintaining focus on long-term performance priorities | ☐ | ☐ | ☐ | ☐ | ☐ | ☐ |
| d. Communicating with my manager about barriers in achieving performance priorities | ☐ | ☐ | ☐ | ☐ | ☐ | ☐ |
| e. Implementing a Development Action plan to close Skill Gaps | ☐ | ☐ | ☐ | ☐ | ☐ | ☐ |
| f. Communicating with my manager about Job Gaps | ☐ | ☐ | ☐ | ☐ | ☐ | ☐ |

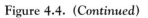

Figure 4.4.  (Continued)

| | No Change | | | | Very Significant | No Opportunity |
|---|---|---|---|---|---|---|
| | 1 | 2 | 3 | 4 | 5 | to Apply |
| g. Making good use of internal systems, groups, and/or resources for improved job effectiveness | ☐ | ☐ | ☐ | ☐ | ☐ | ☐ |
| h. Enlisting management support in identifying development options | ☐ | ☐ | ☐ | ☐ | ☐ | ☐ |

6. What has changed about your approach to career development at Innovative Computer as a result of this program?

_____

_____

7. What has changed about your perceptions of career development opportunities at Innovative Compter as a result of this program?

_____

_____

8. What, if anything, has changed about your perceptions regarding the company's interest in your career growth and development as a result of this program?

_____

_____

9. Indicate the extent to which your utilization of knowledge, skill, or resource support gained from participation in the Career Development Program has had a positive influence in the following areas of your own work unit or your department's work. *Please check the appropriate response beside each measure.*

| | No Influence | Low Influence | Some Influence | Significant Influence | Very Significant Influence |
|---|---|---|---|---|---|
| Increased capacity to support strategic operational goals | ☐ | ☐ | ☐ | ☐ | ☐ |
| Increased labor efficiencies in business processes and project management practices | ☐ | ☐ | ☐ | ☐ | ☐ |

10. What specific work improvements, if any, can be attributed to your participation in the Career Development Program?
    Examples:
    • Improved time savings
    • On-time schedules
    • Less rework or duplication of efforts
    • Improved cross-collaboration
    • Improved response times
    • Improved decision making due to better planning and analysis of prioritized tasks

_____

_____

**Figure 4.4.** (*Continued*)

11. As a result of the changes noted above, please **estimate** the monetary benefits to your department over a one-month period.  $_____

12. What is the basis of your estimate?
_____
_____

13. What level of confidence, expressed as a percentage, do you place on the above estimate? (**100% = Certainty** and **0% = No Confidence**)_____ %

14. What other factors, besides participation in the Career Development Program, may have contributed to the monetary benefits noted above?

| Influencing Factor | Percent of Influence |
| --- | --- |
| ☐ Career Development Program | _____% |
| ☐ Other (please specify) | _____% |
| Total Must Be 100% | _____100% |

15. Other factors influence improvement. Which of the following barriers deterred or prevented you from applying knowledge/skills, tools, or resource support gained from this program?
*Check all that apply.*
☐ My level of commitment was not high
☐ Work environment systems/processes did not support application of knowledge/skills
☐ I have not had enough time to apply the learning
☐ Lack of management support
☐ Lack of support from peers, team members
☐ The timing of this project was not right
☐ Other (please specify):

Which of the following factors supported you in applying knowledge/skills, tools, or resource support gained from this program?
*Check all that apply.*
☐ My level of commitment was high
☐ Work environment systems/processes supported application of knowledge/skills
☐ I had enough time to apply the learning
☐ Strong management support
☐ Support from peers, team members
☐ The timing of this project was right
☐ Other (please specify):

16. What additional benefits would you attribute to this program?
_____
_____

17. Do you think your participation in this program represented a good investment of time for the company?
Yes ☐        No ☐
If no, please explain:_____
_____
_____
_____

**Figure 4.4.** (*Continued*)

18. Would you recommend the Development Discussion Planning approach of career development to others?

Yes ☐        No ☐

If no, why not? If yes, what groups and why? _____

_____

_____

19. What specific suggestions do you have for improving this program or approach?

_____

_____

**Other Comments:**

**Figure 4.4.** (*Continued*)

**Table 4.1.    Application Data from Participants**

| Issue | Rating |
| --- | --- |
| Frequency of application of knowledge/skills | 4.4 |
| Effectiveness in applying knowledge/skills | 4.4 |
| Criticality of applied knowledge/skills to job success | 4.2 |
| Effectiveness of manager in Development Discussion planning process | 3.9 |

*Source:* Rating Scale: 1 = Lowest 5 = Highest

Table 4.2. Level 3 Data: Reported Behavioral Changes Due to Program Participation (Q – 4)

| | No Change | Little Change | Some Change | Significant Change | Very Significant Change | No Opportunity to Apply |
|---|---|---|---|---|---|---|
| A. Communicating with my manager about performance priorities | 0 | 0 | 9% | 70% | 21% | 0 |
| B. Maintaining focus on short-term performance priorities | 0 | 0 | 18% | 67% | 15% | 0 |
| C. Maintaining focus on long-term performance priorities | 0 | 0 | 5% | 76% | 19% | 0 |
| D. Communicate with my manager about barriers in achieving performance priorities | 0 | 0 | 35% | 55% | 10% | 0 |
| E. Communicating with my manager about Job Gaps | 0 | 8% | 20% | 67% | 5% | 0 |
| F. Implement a Development Action plan to close Skill Gaps | 0 | 10% | 10% | 65% | 15% | 0 |
| G. Making good use of internal systems, groups, and/or resources for improved job effectiveness | 0 | 10% | 41% | 38% | 11% | 0 |
| H. Enlisting management support in identifying development options | 0 | 6% | 30% | 55% | 8% | 0 |
| I. Soliciting management support for pursuit of career development goals | 0 | 4% | 38% | 56% | 2% | 0 |
| J. Implement a Development Action plan to enhance current career opportunities | 0 | 0 | 3% | 22% | 75% | 0 |

managers, some limitations with environmental resources (i.e., cross-functional project assignments and/or rotational opportunities) due to unexpected policy or personnel restrictions, and conflicting priorities based on rapidly changing product cycles. Enabling factors included visible support from senior management, resource support provided by career development program materials/tools/assessments/inventories, and improved development incentives associated with revised HR processes (job rotations, mid-year and annual performance reviews, bonus plans) that were clearly aligned with employees' execution of Development Planning actions.

## Level 4: Impact

The intended impact outcomes of the Career Development initiative were increased operational capacity, increased labor efficiency, increased bench strength, and an enhanced work climate for employee engagement, attraction, and retention. Level 4 data was collected through participant/manager input provided in both the Development Discussion Action Plan and the sixty-day Impact Questionnaires. Key areas addressed in the Impact Questionnaire included the following:

- Success with program objectives
- Relevance to job
- Usefulness of the skills/knowledge provided
- Knowledge/skills increase
- Actions taken
- Accomplishments linked to program participation
- Supervisor support
- Business measures linked to program participation

- Recommended improvements

- Enablers/barriers to implementing targeted skills/knowledge

Participants also estimated the business impact of the performance associated with their approved development plans. To ensure strong response, the questionnaire was administered during a sixty-minute follow-up session, scheduled two months after program participation. Management expected employees to attend and were on paid company time. Despite every attempt to collect follow-up data from all pilot participants, dynamic factory conditions and volatile business demands associated with frequent product change-overs created some issues with data collection. A 69 percent response rate was achieved with the Impact Questionnaire. Using a conservative approach, improvement results were noted only for those participants who provided improvement data.

Business results substantiate that employees who applied structured Development Discussion practices significantly impacted targeted measures of labor efficiency and productivity.

## Isolation and Data Conversion

Since many factors influence performance improvement, the evaluation strategy included the use of participant estimates as a method for isolating the direct impact of the Career Development solution on targeted business measures. The effectiveness of this approach rests on the assumption that participants are capable of estimating how much a performance improvement measure is related to application of learned skills/knowledge. In this case, participants were considered credible sources of data to senior management.

*Data conversion.* Once the isolation factors were determined, the Level 4 impact data was converted to monetary value. Table 4.3 provides a sample of the monetary values that participants assigned

Table 4.3. Participant Estimates of Business Impact

| Participant Number (N = 35) | Business Unit of Measure | Monthly Improvement Value (A) × | Confidence Estimate (B) × | % Change Due to Program (C) × | Total Adjusted Monthly Benefit (D) = | Annualized Program Benefit (E) × 12 |
|---|---|---|---|---|---|---|
| 1 | Efficiency (Project Downtime) | $3,000 | 80% | 60% | $1,440 | $17,280 |
| 2 | Productivity (Time Savings) | $1,875 | 60% | 45% | $506.25 | $6,075 |
| 3 | Productivity (Time Savings) | $2,500 | 35% | 50% | $437.50 | $5,250 |
| 4 | Productivity (Rework) | $1,500 | 60% | 45% | $405 | $4,860 |
| 6 | Efficiency (Cycle Time) | $2,050 | 75% | 60% | $922.50 | $11,070 |
| 7 | Efficiency (Project Mgmt.) | $2,500 | 50% | 50% | $625 | $7,500 |
| 8 | Productivity (Time Savings) | $2,750 | 80% | 60% | $1,320 | $15,840 |
| 9 | Efficiency (Cross-Communications) | $1,800 | 60% | 50% | $540 | $6,480 |
| 10 | Productivity (Rework) | $2,200 | 45% | 60% | $594 | $7,128 |
| | Total for the Items Above | | | | | $81,483 |
| | Total for the Other 25 Items | | | | | $200,517 |
| | Total Annualized Benefit **Directly** Attributable to Training | | | | | $282,000 |

to identified business benefits (Column A). In accordance with Phillips' ROI Methodology, these values were then adjusted to account for potential error (Column B) and other influences (Column C). For purposes of this case study, only data from the first ten participants is shown, with the remaining improvement values from the other participant responses shown in the overall total. Specifically, the adjusted values in Column D were totaled and annualized (Column E) for all thirty-five participants who supplied questionnaire data. These values were then used as cost-benefit data and compared to program costs in the final ROI analysis and calculation. The data conversion process was conservative, with the assumption that unresponsive participants had realized no improvement.

**Solution Costs.** Following the data conversion to capture cost benefits, cost categories were determined. As shown in Table 4.4, costs were fully loaded and included costs associated

**Table 4.4.  Fully Loaded Program Costs**

| Item | Calculation | Cost |
|---|---|---|
| Material costs | $350 per person × 50 | $17,500 |
| Needs assessment | | $ 2,100 |
| Design/development | Customization of vendor-based program | $ 2,390 |
| Facilitation | | $ 3,690 |
| Refreshments | | $ 3,300 |
| Participant time | $225 per day × 1.32 (benefit factor) × 2 days* × 50 | $29,700 |
| Management time | $320 per day × 1.32 (benefit factor) × 1 day* × 50 | $21,120 |
| Evaluation costs | | $ 3,500 |
| | **Total Costs** | $83,300 |

*Participant and management time includes average salaries multiplied by a benefits factor of 32 percent. Participant time includes workshop participation as well as pre-work, briefing, and follow-up time. Management time includes pre-work, briefing, and follow-up time.

with needs analysis, pilot program design/development, delivery, and evaluation. Labor costs included time incurred from HRD staff, facilitators, managers, and trainees, respectively, during various aspects of solution assessment, design, implementation, and evaluation. The evaluation costs included costs to conduct the impact study, such as data collection, data analysis, and the development of the management report.

## Level 5. ROI

The ROI formula for investments in human resource development is calculated as it would be for other investments: earnings divided by investments. To calculate the ROI of this initiative, program costs were compared to program benefits using the following formula:

$$\text{ROI}(\%) = \frac{\text{Net Program Benefits}}{\text{Program Costs} \times 100}$$

$$\frac{\text{Net Benefits Attributable to Program (\$282,000)} - \text{Program Costs (\$83,300)}}{\text{Program Costs (\$83,300)} \times 100} = \text{ROI}\% = 239\% \text{ ROI}$$

The ROI value suggests that for every dollar invested in the program, the investment dollar was returned and another $1.36 was generated.

A benefit/cost ratio (BCR), the ratio of total monetary benefits divided by the total costs, yielded the following results:

$$\text{BCR} = \frac{\text{Benefits}}{\text{Costs}}$$

$$\text{BCR} = \frac{\$282,000}{\$83,300} = 3.39 : 1$$

The BCR value suggests that for every dollar invested in this initiative, $3.39 was returned.

**Table 4.5.  Intangible Benefits Identified by Participants and Managers**

| Participants | Managers |
|---|---|
| 1. Improved relationship with immediate manager | 1. Improved clarity of roles, responsibilities, priorities |
| 2. Increased perception that employer cares about my career growth | 2. Better awareness of how changing business conditions influence performance expectations |
| 3. Increased confidence in job role | 3. Improved communications with associates |
| 4. Improved ability to adapt to changing business conditions | 4. Improved use of Development Planning |
| 5. Improved ability to view performance priorities in relation to "big picture" | 5. Improved job satisfaction for associates |
| 6. Anticipated plan to stay with employer for next twelve months | 6. Improved teamwork |

**Intangible Benefits.** Other important outcomes of interest to senior management included intangible benefits. Participant/manager input about intangible benefits was captured in both the Development Action Plans and Impact Questionnaires. Table 4.5 shows the intangible benefits linked directly to the program but not converted to monetary values.

These results suggest that the Career Development initiative successfully met targeted objectives of enhancing employees' awareness and ability to meet performance priorities, along with their perceptions about the company's interest in their professional growth and development. Senior management was especially pleased with results showing that pilot participants reported an intent to stay with the company for another twelve months, given the rising difficulties in retaining top technical/professional talent due to perceived limitations in career pathing and heightened "poaching" of high performers by industry competitors.

## Communication Strategy

Communication of results was vital given the high visibility of this initiative. In addition, effective communication ensured that the HRD function was perceived as a viable business partner with a focus on helping stakeholders define results-oriented, value-added solutions. From the onset, stakeholders were advised of program progress and implementation issues. Specifically, senior management participated in gap analysis, solution planning, and the process of aligning solution objectives with desired business results. As noted in the transfer strategy, senior management served as steering committee members and participated in participant/manager briefings to communicate the purpose and importance of the project. Subject-matter experts, participants, and line managers provided technical expertise in defining business measures and were also a key resource in helping define the relevancy of the instructional design and identifying environmental issues that may enable or impede on-the-job application of learned skills and knowledge.

Once the pilot study was completed, a one-hour briefing, with corresponding PowerPoint slides, was presented to executive sponsors, participants, and their managers. Agenda items included:

- The program background and purpose

- Program design

- Need for evaluation

- Evaluation approach

- Evaluation results

- Barriers/enablers

- Conclusions and recommendations

Given the organization's previous experience with the ROI Methodology, including its guiding principles and six data categories, an action plan of the impact study was provided, as well (see Figure 4.5). Results were also communicated in the company's internal website. Communication of project success was defined by tangible results that showed improvement in targeted business measures of labor efficiency. Evaluation results showed a link between improved productivity and labor efficiency and the solution's focus on aligning employees' critical skills and developmental opportunities with prioritized job tasks. Stakeholders also communicated satisfaction with the intangible benefits associated with this effort.

## Lessons Learned

A broad-based performance improvement solution will achieve greater success when key stakeholders are involved and visible in the process from the beginning and when impact and performance objectives are clearly aligned with strategic business needs. This study also shows how the ROI evaluation process can be implemented with minimal resources since much of the responsibility for critical steps—providing data, isolating program effects, and converting data to monetary value—was assumed by participants.

Despite evidence of a proactive, integrated, cost-effective evaluation approach with engaged stakeholders who had previous experience with the ROI Methodology used, few evaluation efforts will have a seamless, trouble-free implementation process. Lessons learned during this particular project, included the following:

- Project management activities and business partner communications could have been enhanced by improved risk analysis and risk management. For instance, risk management planning may have helped mitigate

Name _____ Instructor Signature _____ Follow-Up Date _____ to _____

**Objective** To apply skills and knowledge gained from career development program **Evaluation Period** _____

**Improvement Measures:** Productivity; Efficiency; Rework; Communication; Response Time; Other

| Action Steps | Analysis |
|---|---|
| As a result of this program, what specific actions will you apply based on what you have learned? | What specific unit of measure will change as a result of your actions? (see above) |
| 1. Conduct development discussion with manager, within thirty days of program completion. | 1. What is the unit of measure? Efficiency |
| 2. Enlist support from my manager to apply skills and talents towards cross-functional job rotation or project assignment with engineering group, within sixty days. | 2. As a result of the anticipated changes, please **estimate** the monetary benefits to your line or department **over a one-month period.** $768 |
| 3. Initiate follow-up with development discussions and recommended actions to close skill gaps, bi-weekly, or as determined. | 3. What is the basis of this estimate? (How did you arrive at this value?) $32 per hour x 6 hrs a week x 4 weeks a month = $768 month Based on salary and average time spent on project rework a week due to issues with product change-overs, material supply |
| | 4. What level of confidence do you place on the above information? (100% = Certainty and 0% = No Confidence) 85% |
| | 5. What percentage of the changes above was the **direct result** of applying skills learned in the career development program? 60% (0% to 100%) |
| | 6. What other influences, besides training, might have influenced these improvements? Project management software |
| **Intangible Benefits:** | What barriers, if any, may prevent you from applying what you have learned? |
| *Improved cooperation with manager. Better focus on performance priorities and the "big picture." Improved visibility to upper management— allows me to be more strategic in promoting my skills and talents for career mobility and job satisfaction.* | *Lack of follow-up due to work volume, conflicting priorities from corporate, moving targets* |

**Comments:** _____

**Figure 4.5. Sample Action Plan for Career Development Initiative**

Adapted from J. Phillips, *Return on Investment in Training and Performance Improvement Programs.* (1997).

frequent "fire-fighting" issues and implementation, scheduling delays that occurred due to volatile production demands in a dynamic manufacturing environment.

- Ensure that all necessary infrastructures are in place to support a comprehensive talent management, career development strategy. In this case, many job rotation processes, incentive plan policies, and action learning project assignments were not readily approved or available for participants' immediate benefit or application.

- Good leaders affect every aspect of solutions aimed at capacity building and attraction/retention of top talent. People don't quit companies, they quit bosses. Ensure that managers selected to serve as development coaches and project advisors are competent, capable, and appropriately motivated and rewarded to fulfill the role and that their developmental responsibilities and accountabilities have been clearly defined.

## Questions for Discussion

1. How would you critique the evaluation strategy and data collection methods used in this case study?

2. How can the outcomes of human resource initiatives that focus on "soft-skill" development be properly aligned with your organization's strategic direction?

3. What other impact measures might you have included in this study?

4. How would you ensure the right mix of participants and stakeholders when piloting a career development initiative?

## References

Broad, M. L., & Newstrom, J. W. (1992). *Transfer of training: Action-packed strategies to ensure high payoff from training investments.* Reading, MA: Addison-Wesley.

Burkett, H. (2002). Evaluation: Was your HPI project worth the effort? In G. M. Piskurich (Ed.), *HPI essentials.* Alexandria, VA: American Society for Training and Development.

Burkett, H. (2002). Leveraging employee know-how with structured how-to training. In R. Jacobs (Ed.), *Action: Implementing on-the-job learning.* Alexandria, VA: American Society for Training and Development.

Burkett, H. (2006). Evaluating a career development initiative. In D. L. Kirkpatrick, *Evaluating training programs* (3rd ed.). San Francisco, CA: Berrett-Koehler.

Phillips, J., Phillips, P., Stone, R., & Burkett, H. (2006). *The ROI fieldbook: Strategies for implementing ROI in HR and training.* Burlington, MA: Elsevier, Butterworth Heinemann.

Phillips, J. J., & Stone, R. D. (2002). *How to measure training results: A practical guide to tracking the six key indicators.* New York: McGraw-Hill.

Phillips, P., & Burkett, H. (2001). Managing evaluation shortcuts. *Info-line.* 0111. Alexandria, VA: American Society for Training and Development.

## About the Author

**Holly Burkett**, MA, SPHR, CPT, is principal of Evaluation Works and a certified ROI professional with over twenty years' experience assisting public and private sector clients measure the business value of WLP efforts. Editor of ISPI's *Performance Improvement Journal*, she is a frequent conference presenter, workshop leader, and author on performance measurement issues. She recently co-authored *The ROI Fieldbook* with Jack and Patti Phillips and Ron Stone. She can be reached at burketth@earthlink.net.

# 5

# Measuring ROI in a Sales Training Programme

## An International Hotel Company

Peter Haigh, edited by Jane Massy

## Abstract

In August 2004 Le Meridien Hotels introduced a training programme for its hotels' conference coordinators to implement a
series of customer promises, which were part of a marketing campaign to increase conference sales and achieve the budgeted goal
for the year. The training programme rolled out in four European cities and included directors of sales and international sales
representatives, as well as the conference coordinators, who had
been designated as meeting champions for their respective hotels.
Research prior to the training highlighted poor rollout of the customer promises. Post-training implementation had improved, as
had customer loyalty and satisfaction, coupled with improved sales.

## Background

Le Meridien Hotels and Resorts is an international hotel company
with 130 hotels in more than fifty countries. It has recently been
acquired by Starwood Hotels and Resorts. During a business review
the company projected a rooms' revenue shortfall for the remainder

Note: This case was prepared to serve as a basis for discussion rather than an illustration of either effective or ineffective administrative and management practices.

of the year compared to budget. Although the company has hotels in more than fifty countries, the European region generates the majority of its revenue, and within Europe there are a small handful of hotels that are critical to the success of the company. For most of the European hotels, their rooms' revenue comes from a combination of market segments. The major ones are individual leisure, individual corporate, conference and incentive, and in some cases, airline crews.

## Focus on the Conference Market

It was agreed that the conference and incentive market was the most appropriate to target for short-term results. The corporate segment is contracted on an annual basis, and many hotels were experiencing a shortfall in this segment due to restrictions on travel and a downgrading of hotels selected for some corporate accounts. Similarly, in the leisure segments, it was much more difficult to forecast future results due to changes in the clients' booking behavior and the increasingly competitive marketplace in many cities. Hence, the conference and incentive market was selected as the focus for growth to make up the projected shortfall.

## Role of the Regional Sales Offices

It was decided to concentrate the efforts of the Regional Sales Offices (RSOs) on a small number of hotels that could benefit most from this initiative, either because of their facilities and location or because of their need for business from this market segment. Since the focus for this exercise was only intended to be over the August to December period, it was referred to as the "Sprint" initiative. The hotels were asked to produce a short PowerPoint presentation to highlight their facilities and to compare their hotels with their main competitors in this market segment. Each hotel then held a web-based conference call with the main producing RSOs for their hotel, using the PowerPoint presentation to highlight the relevant points. The RSOs were able to use the same presentation when reviewing the hotels with their clients. Each hotel introduced a regular conference call with the major producing RSOs to review the status of each conference booking lead and to follow up on any initiatives for that hotel in a particular marketplace.

## Internet Promotion

In addition, all the European hotels were encouraged to participate in a rate promotion on the Le Meridien website for conference business. The hotels were asked to provide their best rates for the following six-month period and to include bed, breakfast, and an eight-hour delegate rate. To track the success of this campaign, the hotels were asked to allocate a specific rate code in the reservation system for any bookings generated from this promotion.

A list of Customer Promises for the meeting planner or conference organizer was developed to encourage loyalty. These promises included:

- Twenty-four hour or next business day response to RFPs (Request for Proposal)

- Use of the Standard Proposal Template by each hotel

- Meetings director (on-site client contact) appointed for every event, to be the key contact person for the client representing all areas of the hotel

- Online floor plans and specifications

- Online planning tools

- Post-event evaluation meeting

- Reward programme for the meeting planner

## Appointment of Meetings Champions

To help with the rollout of this programme each hotel nominated a meetings champion from their group sales department. The meetings champion was tasked with building the profile of Le Meridien meetings and events at his or her hotel and to work with the group sales team to understand and deliver the customer promises on a consistent basis. An online training programme was developed for the meetings champions to help them implement the programme at their hotels. Figure 5.1 shows the timeline of this project.

The initiative to drive conference and incentive business was extended as the hotels continued to under-perform. None of the hotels were coding any group booking under the specific rate code for this business. It was therefore difficult to assess the effectiveness of the Internet campaign. The feedback from the hotels was that the clients felt the package offered did not meet their needs and they wanted to amend the package to suit their specific needs. Following consultation with the hotels, it was decided to amend the package promoted on the Internet. The original offer was for

|  | A | S | O | N | D | J | F | M | A | M | J | J | A | S |
|---|---|---|---|---|---|---|---|---|---|---|---|---|---|---|
| 1st Planning Mtg | ▓ |  |  |  |  |  |  |  |  |  |  |  |  |  |
| Sprint Initiative |  | ▓ | ▓ | ▓ | ▓ |  |  |  |  |  |  |  |  |  |
| Meetings Champions Appointed |  |  |  | ▓ |  |  |  |  |  |  |  |  |  |  |
| Web Promotion 1 |  |  | ▓ | ▓ | ▓ |  |  |  |  |  |  |  |  |  |
| Web Promotion 2 |  |  |  |  |  | ▓ | ▓ | ▓ | ▓ |  |  |  |  |  |
| Tracking Research |  |  |  |  |  |  |  |  | ▓ |  |  |  |  |  |
| Training Approved |  |  |  |  |  |  |  |  |  | ▓ |  |  |  |  |
| Pilot Training Class |  |  |  |  |  |  |  |  |  |  |  | ▓ |  |  |
| Three Training Classes |  |  |  |  |  |  |  |  |  |  |  |  | ▓ | ▓ |

Figure 5.1. Project Timeline

overnight accommodation, breakfast, and an eight-hour delegate rate inclusive of lunch, meeting room, and coffee breaks. This was amended to a room-only rate. However, with the promotional period extending over several months, the hotels were reluctant to offer their best available rate since it might not be valid for the whole period. The hotels also believed that some meeting planners would use this promotional rate as the starting point for negotiating a better rate for their clients.

It also became apparent in talking with the meetings champions in the hotels that they had not been effective in reinforcing the customer promises. The hotels had been asked to appoint someone to this role without a clear indication of the responsibilities and duties for the programme to be implemented successfully. In some hotels, the meetings champions were not empowered to carry out the roles expected of them.

It was apparent that something needed to be done to get the programme on track and to ensure that all hotels were delivering the customer promises.

The immediate reaction was to design and roll out a training programme for the meetings champions. Following discussions about the objectives for this training, it was agreed to determine initially the skills and knowledge level of the meetings champions and the issues facing them in their hotel. A research questionnaire was therefore developed. It was also agreed between the Training Department, Marketing, and the European Regional Team that it would be useful to evaluate the ROI on this training, and to adopt the Phillips ROI Methodology. The following data collection plan was prepared in planning the evaluation. (See Exhibit 5.1.)

### Pre-Training Evaluation Research

The research was needed to understand current knowledge levels of the Meetings and Events Programme. The research questionnaire was distributed to the meetings champions in each of the forty-four European hotels; twenty-two responded.

# FOR USE DURING WORKSHOP
## DATA COLLECTION PLAN

Programme/Project:      Responsibility: MEETINGS CHAMPION      PETER HAIGH      Date:

| Level | Broad Programme Objective(s) | Measures | Data Collection Method/Instruments | Data Sources | Timing | Responsibilities |
|---|---|---|---|---|---|---|
| **1** | **SATISFACTION/PLANNED ACTION** Feedback from participants on pilot test (Paris 23/24 July) about the programme and their planned actions once they return to their hotels | Post-training evaluation. End-of-day feedback conduct training at hotel. Implement meeting planner promises consistently | Questionnaire | Course attendees | Complete before leaving the training room 24 July | PH/Jl |
| **2** | **LEARNING** Meridien Meetings Programme | Pre-training Questionnaire results Understanding of meeting planner promises and their responsibility to implement at hotels | Questionnaire | Meetings champions at each hotel | May | Mkt dept. JL |
| | Roll Out to Meetings Champions | Pilot training programmes | Post-training questionnaire | Course participants | Paris July | PH/JL |

| | | | | | |
|---|---|---|---|---|---|
| **3** | **APPLICATION/IMPLEMENTATION** | Time log for leads | Monthly reports | Group sales files | Monthly | Meetings champions/DOS |
| | Respond to enquiries within twenty-four hours | | | | | |
| | Use of standard proposal template | Spot check on client files | Hotel visits | Client files | Monthly | DOS |
| | Post-event evaluation | Post-event forms | DOS checks | Client files | Monthly | DOS |
| | Rewards signups | Customer feedback | Monthly loyalty member sign ups | Moments database | Monthly | Marketing department |
| **4** | **BUSINESS IMPACT** | Monthly/year-on-year comparisons | Monthly revenue reports. Room nights and revenue | Property management systems | Monthly | DOS |
| | Improve conference sales | | | | | |
| | Improve conversion ratios | Booking pace Reports/ conversion logs | Monthly reports | Group sales booking systems | Monthly | DOS |
| | Increase number of Rewards members | Membership logs by hotel | Number of members by hotel | Moments database | Monthly | Marketing department |
| **5** | ROI | Comments: | | | | |
| | | Determine whether the training of the Meetings Champions had a positive business impact | | | | |

**Exhibit 5.1. Data Collection Plan**

When asked about their level of understanding of the customer promises, the majority answered Excellent/Good, although some did admit that their knowledge of the rewards programme was low (Figure 5.2).

The respondents were asked "In what areas would your hotel most benefit with extra training?" (Figure 5.3). The overwhelming response was that they were completely proficient and that no help was required. The respondents also felt that their knowledge of the use of the Standard Proposal Template was Excellent/Good, although when asked, only fourteen of the twenty-two hotels were actually using it.

**Training Programme**

Despite the meetings champions' overwhelming confidence in their understanding and implementation of the various elements of the meetings programme, it was still felt appropriate at Head Office to conduct a two-day training programme for the meetings champions to reinforce the specific elements of the meetings programme, especially those where the implementation appeared to be lowest. To ensure the meetings champions received the necessary support at their hotel to implement the various elements of the programme, their director of sales was also invited to participate in the training.

|  | Excellent/Good | Moderate | Low |
|---|---|---|---|
| 24-Hour Response | 100% |  |  |
| Worldwide Meetings and Events Desk | 50% | 50% |  |
| On-Site Meetings Director | 64% | 32% | 4% |
| Facility Search, Floor Plans, and Specs | 82% | 18% |  |
| Online Planning Tools | 53% | 38% | 9% |
| Moment of Truth | 87% | 9% | 4% |
| Reward Programme | 64% | 23% | 13% |

**Figure 5.2. Knowledge Levels**

| | Completely Proficient | Processes in Place, But Need More Focus | Low Level of Expertise, Need Guidelines Training |
|---|---|---|---|
| Preparing Proposals | 64% | 36% | |
| Sales Processes and Negotiating | 36% | 59% | 5% |
| Liaising with the RSOs | 46% | 41% | 13% |
| Client Management During the Event | 68% | 32% | |
| Internal Communication Regarding Client Needs | 55% | 41% | 4% |
| Post-Event Billing | 68% | 23% | 8% |
| Post-Event Evaluation | 41% | 55% | 4% |
| Reward Programme for Meeting Planners | 14% | 32% | 54% |

**Figure 5.3. Percentage of Benefits Projected from Extra Training**

Since a portion of the group leads for each hotel is generated through the regional sales office network, representatives from the RSOs were also invited. Printed materials covering all aspects of the programme were produced for distribution to each participant at the training event.

Although 59 percent of the respondents identified sales processes and negotiating as subjects for which more focus was needed, it was not the purpose of this proposed training to cover these areas, as other company training programmes were more appropriate. This information was passed on to the training department.

The pilot training class was held over two days in Paris in July. The combination of the meetings champions, directors of sales, and RSO personnel fostered healthy discussions about the delivery of the Meetings Promises at each hotel as each element of the programme was covered. In addition, each participant was asked to look at the website of a competitor to compare it to the Le Meridien site. This helped attendees appreciate how a client might search for meeting space and the challenges they might find when doing so. The training also included a session titled Major Trends in the Meetings Industry, which allowed the participants to understand some of the changes that are taking place and how these could impact the way they might work in the future.

Following the successful pilot class, further training sessions took place in The Hague, Cologne, and Sardinia to cover the other hotels in the European region. In total, twenty-seven directors of sales, thirty-six meetings champions, and four regional sales office representatives participated in the training across the four classes.

### Level 1 (Reaction and Satisfaction) and Level 2 (Learning)

Each group of attendees completed a questionnaire to assess the learning at the end of the two days to gauge their reaction and satisfaction with the training. One hundred percent of the attendees across all four classes agreed that the training met their expectations in terms of content and information. When asked, "Can you take back some learning from this conference and apply it at your hotel?" comments included:

- "Previously unclear, highlighted competitors and need for action"

- "Good ideas and best practices to share"

- "Clarification of the processes and need to cooperate better with RSOs"

The rewards programme was the one aspect of the Meetings and Events Programme that the participants felt that they were more confident about. They realized that the programme was not as difficult to implement as expected. There was also considerable discussion about the standard proposal template, which had been designed to include color borders and pictures of the hotel. The feedback from many of the hotels was that some of their clients' computers could not accept it because of the graphics and it did not present well when faxed. The marketing department agreed to simplify the format and provide different versions for online and offline delivery. All the participants appreciated the time to share ideas and concerns with the RSOs. Rarely do the groups sales coordinators at the hotels have face-to-face discussions with the RSO personnel, and several misunderstandings and misconceptions were resolved, resulting in a better relationship between the hotels and the RSOs and an appreciation from the RSOs of the competitive environment in which the hotels operate.

The attendees also completed an action plan. The meetings champions tended to focus on one particular aspect of the meetings programme, such as the rewards programme or twenty-four-hour response measurement. The directors of sales were more concerned with ensuring the whole programme was implemented, involving operations and finance as well as the group sales department, and setting up training programmes to cascade the information throughout the hotel. (See Exhibit 5.2 for a sample Action Plan.)

Following the training, there has been an improvement in the group lead conversion ratio at many of the hotels; the standard proposal template has been adapted to be more readable and acceptable to the client when e-mailed; and the Internet promotions for meeting planners have been simplified.

| Programme/Project: | MEETING CHAMPIONS | Responsibility: | PETER HAIGH | Date: | | | |
|---|---|---|---|---|---|---|---|

PURPOSE OF THIS EVALUATION: TO IMPROVE CONFERENCE AND INCENTIVE SALES AT THE EUROPEAN HOTELS

| Data Items (Usually Level 4) | Methods for Isolating the Effects of the Programme/Process | Methods of Converting Data to Monetary Values | Cost Categories | Intangible Benefits | Communication Targets for Final Report | Other Influences/Issues During Application | Comments |
|---|---|---|---|---|---|---|---|
| Improve conference sales | Participants estimate | Monthly revenue reports | Facilitation fees; Programme materials; Meals/refreshments/transport | Customer satisfaction; Customer loyalty | Programme participants; Directors of Sales | Several process improvement issues raised during training; proposal template; rewards collateral | Participants responsible for training colleagues at hotel; Needs to ensure training takes place |
| Improve group lead conversion ratios | Trend line analysis | Monthly Delphi reports | Facilities; Participants/salaries/benefits | Better relationships with RSOs | Hotel GM's Regional Marketing Director VP Marketing | Meetings website; Tracking of payment to trigger rewards | |
| Increase number of reward members | Trend line analysis | Monthly marketing reports | | Improved relationship between sales and operations employee satisfaction | | Points being credited | |

**Exhibit 5.2. ROI Analysis Plan**

## Level 3 (Application and Implementation) and Level 4 (Business Impact)

Three to four months after the completion of the training classes, a further questionnaire was distributed to the meetings champions and the directors of sales. The purpose of this questionnaire was to determine whether the participants were applying what they had learned and whether there had been any business impact as a result. Only seven of thirty-six of the meetings champions and fourteen of twenty-seven directors of sales responded. Several of the meetings champions had left the company, one hotel had been sold, and the two Sardinian properties that had provided the majority of the participants for that class had closed for the winter with the dispersal of most of the staff.

As a starting point, it was important to discover to what extent the hotels were delivering on the Meeting Promises prior to the training, in other words, to establish the baseline for improvement. The responses for the directors of sales are reported in Table 5.1. Next they were asked, "Since the training, what would you estimate your level of delivery on the Meeting Promises?" Results are reported in Table 5.2.

Results show an encouraging improvement in twenty-four-hour response, use of the standard proposal template, and post-event evaluation but a slower than expected change in the enrollment in the rewards programme.

**Table 5.1.  Percentage of Hotels Delivering on Meeting Promises**

| % of the Time | 100% | 80% | 60% | Less Than 40% | Less Than 20% |
|---|---|---|---|---|---|
| 24-Hour Response | 43% | 36% | 3% | | |
| Dedicated Contact | 71% | 29% | | | |
| Use of Std Proposal Template | 29% | 21% | 7% | | 43% |
| Enrolment in Rewards Program | 7% | 7% | 14% | 22% | 50% |
| Post-Event Evaluation | 14% | 36% | 29% | 7% | 14% |

Table 5.2.    Level of Delivery on Meeting Promises

| % of the Time | 100% | 80% | 60% | Less Than 40% | Less Than 20% |
|---|---|---|---|---|---|
| 24-Hour Response | 54% | 46% | | | |
| Dedicated Contact | 85% | 15% | | | |
| Use of Std Proposal Template | 62% | 8% | 15% | | 15% |
| Enrolment in Rewards Program | 15% | 40% | 15% | 8% | 22% |
| Post-Event Evaluation | 38% | 62% | | | |

Table 5.3.    Pre-Training Responses

| % of the Time | 100% | 80% | 60% | Less Than 40% | Less Than 20% |
|---|---|---|---|---|---|
| 24-Hour Response | 29% | 42% | 29% | | |
| Dedicated Contact | 43% | 29% | 14% | 14% | |
| Use of Std Proposal Template | 43% | 14% | | 14% | 29% |
| Enrollment in Rewards Programme | 29% | | 29% | 13% | 29% |
| Post-Event Evaluation | 29% | 29% | 14% | 14% | 14% |

The meetings champions were asked the same questions. Although the number of respondents is low, these figures can be taken as being indicative of the changes taking place at the hotels. Pre- and post-training responses are shown in Tables 5.3 and 5.4.

Again, a marked improvement in twenty-four-hour response, use of the standard proposal template, and enrollment in the rewards programme with some improvement in the post-event evaluation. Interestingly, the meetings champions were much more positive about the improvements in the twenty-four-hour response and the enrollment in the rewards programme, areas where on a day-to-day basis they would be much closer to reality.

## Twenty-Four-Hour Response

The twenty-four-hour response is monitored in different ways at the hotels, depending on the size of the hotel and the software

**Table 5.4.  Post-Training Responses**

| % of the Time | 100% | 80% | 60% | Less Than 40% | Less Than 20% |
|---|---|---|---|---|---|
| 24-Hour Response | 71% | 29% | | | |
| Dedicated Contact | 43% | 43% | 14% | | |
| Use of Std Proposal Template | 72% | 14% | 14% | | |
| Enrollment in Rewards Program | 72% | 14% | | 14% | |
| Post-Event Evaluation | 29% | 57% | | 14% | |

system used. In the smaller hotels, a time log is used to monitor and track the turnaround of group leads. In the larger hotels, software systems such as Delphi or Fidelio are used for recording all group leads. These systems track each lead and record the rooms and space reserved. Reports are produced showing the status of leads, when they were entered into the system, and when each contact is made with the client. This system is therefore used to help the hotels to monitor whether they are responding within twenty-four hours. With the emphasis placed on this promise within the hotels to satisfy customer demand and the ability to track performance, both the meeting champions and the directors of sales are conscious of the results in this area.

### Dedicated Contact

In the smaller hotels, the groups coordinator (and also usually the designated meetings champion) acts as the direct contact for the clients during their meetings in the hotel. In the larger hotels, each confirmed booking is passed from the group sales department to the convention department, where a dedicated contact is assigned. Based on the above estimates, the directors of sales consider that this is happening more of the time than the meetings champions do.

### Use of Standard Proposal Template

As referenced above, there was extensive discussion at each of the training classes about the layout and design of the standard proposal template. Based on the feedback of the attendees, the marketing department at head office redesigned the template. With these changes, the usage estimates indicated above show a marked improvement, with 62 percent of the directors of sales estimating its use 100 percent of the time. However, the meetings champions who are involved on a day-to-day basis are more confident, with 72 percent estimating its use 100 percent of the time.

### Enrollment of Meeting Planners into the Rewards Programme

With full training on this aspect of the programme, the meeting champions are obviously much more confident about selling the rewards programme and in estimating its promotion 100 percent of the time. However, the directors of sales seem less confident, with only 15 percent estimating its promotion 100 percent of the time. One hotel, which deals with mainly small local companies, admitted that the rewards programme was not promoted since their customers did not use other Le Meridien hotels and they were already loyal to the one hotel. One director of sales commented:

> "Only the enrollment of the meeting planners programme is still on the slow side, as people are confused having heard of the changes with Starwood ... and would rather wait."

### Post-Event Evaluation

Post-event evaluation is estimated to be happening more often since the training. Sixty-two percent of the directors of sales estimated that it happens 80 percent of the time, compared with 57 percent of the meetings champions. With a higher proportion of repeat business in the smaller hotels and strong personal relationships, a formal post-event evaluation is not considered essential. Nonetheless, in the major convention hotels, with larger annual conferences, an evaluation is an essential tool to review the performance of the hotel staff and facilities so that future business can be solicited with confidence.

The directors of sales are responsible for measuring their teams' performance against each of these Promises, and where available, Delphi is able to produce reports tracking many of these activities. Where Delphi is not available, then other tools are used as referenced by one of the directors of sales:

> "Weekly meeting with group sales and sales team. Every day daily report. I personally welcome each meeting planner and make sure to have feedback on their departure or post-event by phone. Check evaluation sheet when returned. Feedback of group sales and event coordinators."

When asked to estimate the impact of the training in improving their teams' performance in executing the various elements of the Meetings and Events Programme, the directors of sales believed that no more than 50 percent could be attributed to the training, with many asserting that no improvement was due to the training. There was nothing specifically "new" in the training that the hotels should not have been doing already. The training acted as reinforcement and as a refresher of the business processes that are integral to the smooth running of a sales and catering department. The following two comments are representative:

> "Most contents of the Le Meridien Meetings Promises were already known by the staff before the training. The biggest impact resulted not only on the contents but more on the awareness and importance of the programme and promises."
>
> "Some of the techniques we already had, but it is always important to review and improve our knowledge.

It was very important to learn more about the reward programme."

However, one hotel was very positive about the impact of the training in improving their processes:

"The hotel never implemented any of the Le Meridien meetings standards before. After the training we better understood the reasons behind the programme and, having assigned the champion role to a more appropriate person within the team, we had more clear directions, coaching, and supervision about the process in general."

Most of the training attendees had gone back and trained their colleagues on the Meeting Promises, which helped with the implementation of the programme. It had been stressed during the training classes that the processes that were being covered were sound business practices, irrespective of the hotel management company.

The participants were asked to identify any intangible benefits resulting from the training. The most common response was the improved relationship with the RSOs. Also identified were the changes made to the standard proposal template that had resulted from the discussions during the training, which were much appreciated by the clients. There was also a general feeling that there was improved team spirit in the hotels as a result of the training on the Meeting Promises, as referenced by one respondent:

"Understanding and handling the programme led to 'speaking one voice'—initiated by the sales people, who sold the programme and fulfilled by our Banquet Operations staff."

When asked to determine the business impact of the training, the majority of the respondents were unable to respond. When challenged, many responded that it was difficult to isolate the impact of the training from the other factors influencing demand in their marketplace. Sixty-five percent of the directors of sales and 85 percent of the meetings champions did not believe there was any business impact as a result of the training or were unable to measure it. The two Sardinian hotels closed shortly after the training, and the Barcelona hotel is undergoing major refurbishment and has limited meeting space available to sell. However, one director of sales did comment:

> "Despite the fact that we have not increased business-wise, what I have noticed is that our clients are very complimentary on the speed of response, professionalism in terms of response (business knowledge), and confidence to place business in our properties."

## Costs

Following the ROI Methodology, full costs were included. The accompanying ROI analysis plan was prepared in planning the final stages of the evaluation (shown in Exhibit 5.2).

The full costs for the training are outlined in Table 5.5.

## Business Impact

The room revenue in each market segment is tracked monthly. Table 5.6 shows the European regional figures. They have been broken down into four time periods to allow for comparison. The critical periods are September to December of the first year compared with the second (see Table 5.6), since these periods relate to the beginning of the Sprint Initiative and the period immediately after the training for the meetings champions.

The increase in sales in the September to December period immediately after the meeting champions training is £875,252, compared with the same period in the previous year.

Table 5.5.   Training Costs

|  | Salary/ Benefits | Travel | Accom. | DDR* | Dinner | Total |
|---|---|---|---|---|---|---|
| Paris | 9048 | 2612 | 2000 | 2520 | 798 | 16978 |
| Cologne | 6864 | 2370 | 1442 | 1888 | 640 | 13204 |
| Hague | 5304 | 4275 | 3025 | 1320 | 540 | 14464 |
| Sardinia | 6864 | 2260 | 1242 | 2470 | 950 | 13786 |
| Facilitator prep time | 13255 |  |  |  |  | 13255 |
| Course Materials |  |  |  |  |  | 2500 |
| Evaluation Costs incl. Labor and materials | 3780 |  |  |  |  | 3780 |
| Total |  |  |  |  |  | £77967 |

*DDR = Daily Delegate Rate

The courses were comprised of the following attendees:

Paris: ten directors of sales, nine Meeting Champions, and three RSOs

Cologne: seven directors of sales, eight Meeting Champions, and one RSO

The Hague: five directors of sales, seven Meeting Champions, and one RSO

Sardinia: five directors of sales, twelve Meeting Champions, and one RSO

There were two facilitators at each training class, and their costs have been included for each location.

Although many of the directors of sales were unable to estimate the business impact of the training, those who could estimated only 30 percent of any improvement could be attributed to the training, with a 90 percent confidence level. Taking these estimates we can surmise the following ROI:

$$875,252 \times 30\% = 262,576 \times 90\% \text{ confidence} = 236,318$$

$$\frac{236,318 - 77,967}{236,318} = \frac{158,351}{77,967} = 2.03 \times 100 = 203\% \text{ ROI}$$

Other measurement criteria included the increase in enrollment for the rewards programme.

**Table 5.6.    European Regional Figures for Rooms' Revenue**

| Period | Conference Segment Revenue £s (Non-Comp*) | Conference Segment Revenue £s (Comp*) |
|---|---|---|
| January –August, year 1 | 40,972,385 | 40,926,835 |
| September –December, year 1 | 24,980,081 | 24,901,355 |
| January –August, year 2 | 45,490,434 (+11.02%) | 44,839,229 (+9.6%) |
| September –December, year2 | 26,777,057 (+7.2%) | 25,776,607 (+3.5%) |

*Non-Comp = non-comparative (in terms of hotels being compared between the two years). Comp = comparative Le Meridien Stuttgart opened in November 04 and contributed £78,726 in the first year and £1,526,730 in the next year. Le Meridien in The Hague closed for renovation in May and re-opened in October. Between January and May their conference sales were £45,550 and between October and December £124,925. Therefore the Comp. Column, with these two hotels extracted, is a fairer comparison of performance of the region over the various time periods.

## Intangibles

One intangible from this training was the realization from the hotels that they needed to do a better job in selling their property to the RSOs. The standard format, which was developed as a PowerPoint presentation, was recognized as a powerful selling tool and helped the RSOs expand their knowledge of not only the hotel but also the competition. Prior to the training, regular review calls had been arranged between the major convention hotels and their primary RSOs. Following the training, the camaraderie between the hotels and the RSOs was strengthened and those regular review conference calls became more consensual than adversarial.

## Other Benefits

The exercise of reviewing competitive hotel companies' websites for ease of use in booking meetings highlighted some opportunities for Le Meridien hotels to improve their own offerings and functionality of the site. The availability of group rates and display of the rooms were two areas where it was agreed there was room for improvement.

Another benefit for the attendees was the opportunity for them to experience being meeting attendees in one of their own hotels and appreciate the interruptions—intentional or unintentional—that can occur during the course of an event.

### Barriers and Enablers

Unfortunately, some hotels were unable to send any attendees, either because of sickness, pressure of business, or budget constraints. It was particularly unfortunate that, although the second training class was held in The Hague to show off the newly opened Hotel Des Indes, there were no attendees from any of the Dutch hotels. The time from concept to delivery of the training took longer than expected due in part to the uncertainty within the company. Nonetheless, the full support of the marketing department was critical in rolling out the initial Meeting Promises programme and then being involved in every stage of the design and delivery of the training programme once it was apparent that it was not being fully implemented at the hotel level.

## Communication Strategy

By the time the results were compiled and analyzed, most of the head office Le Meridien stakeholders had left the company, including the CEO who initiated the project; the VP of marketing; and the European regional vice president. The senior vice president for Starwood Hotels responsible for transition of Meridien into Starwood approved the final report for publication.

## Lessons Learned

This programme showed the importance of a thorough pre-event evaluation to determine the knowledge level of the participants so that an appropriate training program could be developed. Initially, there was little understanding of the role and responsibilities expected of the meetings champions, and some hotels appointed someone who did not have the authority to implement the Customer Promise program. This was highlighted during the pre-training research and prompted the directors of sales being invited to attend the training programmes. With differing sales and catering systems being used across the portfolio of hotels, it was not easy to monitor consistently the performance of the respective sales teams.

## Conclusion

While it has proved difficult to estimate the impact of the training from the comments above, even with the small amount of data available and using a conservative approach, it is possible to show a positive ROI. It is also evident that there have been some intangible benefits in terms of improved customer loyalty, team spirit, and better relationships between the hotels and the RSOs. In addition, the meetings champions have a much better understanding of the need to maintain the promises with their clients. As referenced above, the rollout of this Meeting and Events Programme was put on hold, following the training in Europe, pending the conclusion of the takeover of the company by Starwood Hotels and Resorts.

*Questions for Discussion*

1. Was this training program an appropriate meeting for an ROI study? Why or why not?

2. How could have additional Level 2 learning results been captured?

3. Should the adjusted revenues (as used in this case study) or the profit on these revenues have been used to calculate the ROI on this program? If a profit margin of 30 percent is used, a profit of 70, 895 (236, 318 × .3) translates into − 9 percent.

4. How would you change the objectives for this training program?

## About the Authors

**Peter Haigh** is the former regional director of sales operations, Europe, Le Meridien Hotels and Resorts. The training classes referenced above were conducted by Peter Haigh and Janine Lakiss, formerly marketing manager, Le Meridien Hotels and Resorts. Janine was also responsible for designing and producing the Meetings Champions Support Pack, which was an integral part of the training material. Josephine Le Yannou, regional trainer, Europe for Le Meridien Hotels and Resorts, contributed to the design of the training course content and programme. The help and support of ROI Institute in the preparation and review of this study has been much appreciated.

**Jane Massy** is CEO of abdi ltd, which represents ROI Institute in the UK. Jane has extensive experience evaluating projects in both the private and public sectors.

# 6

# Measuring ROI in Coaching for New-Employee Retention

## A Global Media Company

Lisa Ann Edwards and Christina Lounsberry

## Abstract

This case illustrates how a pilot study generated a return on investment for a coaching program targeted to new hires. By pinpointing a turnover problem with new employees who voluntarily terminate their employment prior to their first-year anniversary, this study focuses on how the specific causes of turnover were determined, how the solution was matched to the special causes, and how a calculation of the actual impact of the turnover reduction was developed. The strength in this case lies in its ability to gain support for a strategic accountability approach in an organization that did not initially see the benefit of this method.

## Background

Ruche Media Company (RMC) is a global media company with twenty-four offices located around the world. The corporate headquarters of this $260 million organization is based in a major

Note: This case was prepared to serve as a basis for discussion rather than an illustration of either effective or ineffective administrative and management practices. All names, dates, places, and data may have been disguised at the request of the author or organization.

metropolitan city in North America. Most of the 1,100 employees are based at the corporate headquarters, while the remaining workforce is located in sales offices in major metropolitan cities throughout the world. As with many organizations, RMC has faced industry consolidation problems, competitive pricing pressures, and employee turnover. RMC's annual voluntary turnover rate was 22 percent worldwide compared to an industry average of 19 percent, or 9 percent for companies listed in *Fortune* magazine's 100 Great Places to Work. Although management was not concerned with addressing the turnover problem, it suspected it was causing operational problems, taking up much staff and manager time, and creating disruptive situations with customers. This pilot study represents a way to build support for addressing retention in an organization that needs to see turnover as a real business issue and better understand the value in a methodical, strategic approach that links the solution to business impact and ROI.

## Measuring and Monitoring Turnover at RMC

RMC monitored turnover by various categories and defined them as either voluntary or involuntary separations. Voluntary separations included career, dissatisfaction with pay/benefits/policies, dissatisfaction with working conditions, and personal reasons. Involuntary separations included reductions in workforce, disciplinary action, and termination for failure to meet performance expectations. No one terminated his or her employment as a result of a disability or because he or she retired during the period reviewed, so these categories were not considered in the analysis.

After creating a common definition of turnover, RMC analyzed the turnover rates by various demographics such as location, business group, and years of service. Through this analysis, it was discovered that turnover was highest among employees who were employed for less than one year at RMC in the corporate office. In fact, RMC discovered that turnover in the corporate office was

30 percent, and 12 percent of all new-hires departed prior to their one-year anniversary.

## Develop Fully Loaded Costs of Turnover

After reviewing where turnover was the greatest, RMC then calculated the turnover costs. Table 6.1 contains a list of turnover cost ranges as a percent of annual wage or salary as captured from dozens of impact studies (Phillips & Connell, 2003). The data are arranged by job category, ranging from non-skilled, entry-level positions to middle managers. The ranges listed represent the cost of turnover as a percent of annual wage/salary and are rounded off

**Table 6.1.  Turnover Costs Summary**

| Type/Category | Turnover Cost Ranges as a Percent of Annual Wage/Salary |
|---|---|
| Entry Level—Hourly, Non Skilled (e.g., Fast-Food Worker) | 30–50% |
| Service/Production Workers—Hourly (e.g., Courier) | 40–70% |
| Skilled Hourly (e.g., Machinist) | 75–100% |
| Clerical/Administrative (e.g., Scheduler) | 50–80% |
| Professional (e.g., Sales Representative, Nurse, Accountant) | 75–125% |
| Technical (e.g., Computer Technician) | 100–150% |
| Engineers (e.g., Chemical Engineer) | 200–300% |
| Specialists (e.g., Computer Software Designer) | 200–400% |
| Supervisor/Team Leaders (e.g., Section Supervisor) | 100–150% |
| Middle Managers (e.g., Department Managers) | 125–200% |

*Source*: Phillips and Connell, 2003.

for ease of use and communication. The costs represented in these studies are fully loaded and include the exit cost of the previous employee, recruiting, selection, orientation, initial training, wages and salaries while in training, lost productivity, quality problems, customer dissatisfaction, loss of expertise/knowledge, supervisor's time for turnover, and temporary replacement costs. The data in this table reflects studies in industry and trade magazines as well as practitioner publications, academic research, and independent studies conducted by professional organizations and associations.

In order to obtain an average cost that could be used per turnover, RMC calculated the cost of turnover for each individual who left the organization during a twelve-month period by multiplying that individual's wage/salary by the median percent of annual wage/salary for the job category appropriate for that individual. The cost of each turnover during that period was then totaled and divided by the total number of individuals during that period to arrive at an average turnover cost of $116,927.09 per employee. Using this average cost of turnover, the total cost of turnover company-wide was calculated at $28.3 million; $8.7 million in the corporate office and $2.8 million for first-year employees in the corporate office. More importantly, $116,927.09 became the commonly agreed-on average cost of one turnover.

## Determining the Cause of Turnover

Two basic techniques were used to pinpoint the actual cause of turnover. First, a review of the turnover causes as recorded in the Human Resource Information System (HRIS) database indicated that 46 percent of those individuals leaving prior to their first-year anniversary listed "career" as the reason they were leaving the organization. It was surprising that an individual who had not yet met his or her first-year anniversary would leave for career reasons, and so RMC reviewed the exit interview forms as the second technique to pinpoint the actual cause of turnover. It was believed that a review of the exit interviews would illuminate any hidden

**Table 6.2.    Stated Reasons of Voluntary Separation from First-Year RMC Employees**

1. General chaos, confusion, and disorganization
2. Unclear job expectations
3. Unsure what responsibilities were from one day to the next
4. Doing a different job than hired for

causes of the turnover that would better explain why individuals were leaving for career reasons prior to their first-year anniversary. Table 6.2 shows the most frequently mentioned causes of turnover as uncovered and recorded during the exit interview.

Since this program was a pilot study and involved a relatively small number of participants, it was decided that it was unnecessary to do a more thorough investigation of the cause of turnover. Ideally, RMC would have conducted focus groups with new-hires and utilized the Nominal Group Technique to gain a more comprehensive understanding of the cause of turnover; however, given the size of the study, it was decided that step was unnecessary.

# Solution: New-Hire Coaching Pilot Study

Recognizing that not all of the causes of turnover could be addressed immediately, a solution was designed to help new-hires navigate the stated chaos, confusion, and disorganization frequently mentioned and recorded in the exit interviews. RMC created a New-Hire Coaching Pilot Study called The Inside Track. The Inside Track was designed to ensure a new-hire's success, retain the new-hire through to the first-year anniversary, improve new-hire commitment, and to better understand challenges new-hires face.

## Participant Selection

The program was intended for new-hires located in the corporate office who had joined the company within the last two months of the start date of the pilot study. E-mails marketing the new program were sent to a group of new-hires, who were later invited to an information session to learn more about the program before committing to it. Participants were informed that this was a pilot study to improve new-hire on-boarding and ensure success, and the importance of staying in the program for the duration of the program was communicated to the participants during the information session. More than 90 percent of participants who attended the information sessions enrolled in the program, making a total of thirteen participants enrolled in the program. Of those participants, two individuals dropped out within the first two weeks of enrolling in the program. One of those participants decided not to participate as he did not feel that he needed the program. That individual is still at RMC. The other participant dropped out due to termination—however, it was later discovered that the individual should not have been included in the program at the start, as the individual's manager was in the process of exiting the employee from the organization, and the individual's tenure far exceeded the selection criteria of the program.

**Program Design**

Participants attended a one-hour group coaching session each month for four consecutive months. They were also able to participate in a maximum of eight individual coaching sessions with a professional, internal coach. At the start of the study, participants completed a pre-assessment survey that was designed to measure their level of engagement and commitment to the organization, and all participants took the survey at the conclusion of the study as well. The final survey also asked for Level 1 data, including the participants' reaction to the program and specific open-ended questions related to their perception of the impact of the study.

*Group Coaching*

Participants were invited to a one-hour monthly group coaching session for four consecutive months. Each session utilized an appreciative inquiry approach, and sessions were designed around the fundamental belief that the power to be successful in a new job lies within the individual.

The topic of Session I was on strengths, how new-hires were using their strengths in their jobs, and how their new roles mapped to the hopes and dreams they had for themselves prior to beginning their work at RMC. Session II was designed to help new-hires understand their development level within the framework of a learning model and how to ask for what they needed from their managers based on their development level within the framework of that learning model. Session III concerned successful career management strategies and helping new-hires to prepare for their performance evaluation later in the year. Finally, Session IV covered career development tactics and a discussion about how to avoid common career derailers.

*Individual Coaching*

All participants had the opportunity to participate in a maximum of eight individual coaching sessions. All participants were required to define a coachable issue and work with a professionally trained, internal coach. Research by Posner and Schmidt (1993) has shown that people who have clarity about their personal values have higher levels of commitment to the organization than those who do not, regardless of the organization's values. With this understanding, the context of the coaching work included the whole person and sometimes addressed personal values and personal mission, as well as the cycle of renewal of adult development, especially as it related to the individual's new role at RMC. Again, the fundamental assumption underlying the coaching philosophy and style was that the power for career success lies within the individual.

## Measuring Success

There were four primary objectives of this program:

1. Ensure new-hire's success,
2. Improve new-hire engagement and commitment,

3. Better understand challenges new-hires face, and

4. Retain new-hires through to their first-year anniversaries

### Ensure New Hire's Success

Success of the solution for new-hire success was measured by asking for the participants' reaction to and satisfaction with the program. Measurement at this level provided input from the participants on their reactions to the solution, their perspectives of the different elements of the program, and whether they accomplished the goal they set for themselves at the start of the program. Using the post-assessment survey to collect this information, data was collected on a 5-point scale. As expected, the results were positive, averaging a 5.0 composite rating. Figure 6.1 represents participants' responses to the five questions related to participants' reactions to and satisfaction with the program.

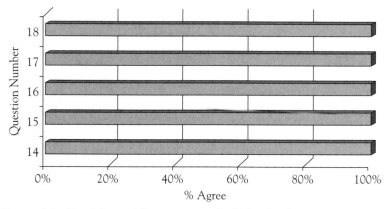

**Figure 6.1. Participants' Reactions to the Pilot Study**
   Q14. Overall, I am satisfied with The Inside Track (New-Hire Coaching Pilot Study) program.
   Q15. Overall, this program was relevant in helping me to be successful in my job.
   Q16. Overall, this program was a good use of my time.
   Q17. I have used the information from the program and insight gained from the coaching in my job.
   Q18. I would recommend this program to other new-hires.

In addition to asking participants' reaction to the program, the post-assessment survey also provided participants the opportunity to re-state their goal from the start of the coaching program and indicate whether they accomplished their goal by the end of the program. Table 6.3 lists participants' goals at the start of the program and outcome at the conclusion of the program.

### Improve New-Hire Engagement and Commitment

In addition to participants' reactions, RMC also measured participants' level of engagement and commitment to the organization before and after the program. Overall, there was an 11 percent improvement on all items related to engagement. Further, each of the items used in the survey is believed to be correlated to specific bottom-line measurables such as retention, profitability, productivity, and customer satisfaction. Figure 6.2 represents participants' agreement to questions as related to retention, profitability, productivity, and customer satisfaction at the start of the program and at the conclusion of the program.

### Better Understand Challenges New-Hires Face

Another objective of this study was to better understand the challenges that new-hires face and why they might choose to leave RMC prior to their first-year anniversary. To gather this data, the internal coach recorded notes at the end of each coaching session and was able to extract common themes heard from participants about the various challenges and barriers they faced at RMC. Table 6.4 lists the most common challenges faced by new-hires that emerged out of the individual coaching sessions.

### Retain New-Hires Through to First-Year Anniversary

Finally, a fourth objective of this study was to retain new-hires throughout their first year. Voluntary turnover of first-year

Table 6.3.    Participants' Goals and Outcomes

| Participant # | Stated Goal: What Was Your Stated Goal When You Started This Program? | Outcome: Do You Believe You Made Progress in Reaching Your Goals? |
|---|---|---|
| 1 | Career development | Definitely |
| 2 | Focus on goals and responsibilities | I was able to work on a plan of attack for addressing areas that need change and how I can be instrumental in that process. |
| 3 | I wanted to learn effective methods for voicing my ideas and opinions and understand the management philosophy at RMC. | I'm getting there, have been given the proper tools and techniques. |
| 4 | Learning RMC business operations developing leadership capabilities | Yes |
| 5 | Managing employees | Yes |
| 6 | To learn more about RMC as a whole | Yes |
| 7 | How to obtain training | Yes |
| 8 | Improving the working relationship with my manager and clarifying my role and responsibilities | Yes |
| 9 | Career focus, organizational skills, work/life balance, time management | Yes |
| 10 | Mostly items from my personal life | Yes |
| 11 | Time management and stress management | Absolutely |

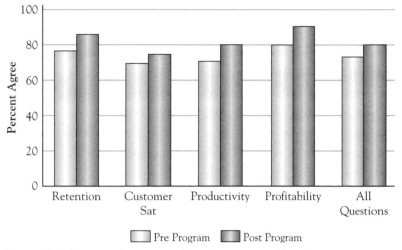

**Figure 6.2. Percent Agreement Pre-Program vs. Post-Program**

**Table 6.4.  Common Challenges Faced by New-Hires**

1. Manager unavailable for direction and support
2. Available manager, but poor direction and support
3. Chaotic, disorganized workflow
4. Lack of training for tools specific to the job

employees at RMC is 12 percent. Given this statistic, it would be normal for one individual to terminate employment prior to his or her first-year anniversary. Instead, not one individual terminated employment prior to his or her first-year anniversary. As a result, RMC saved $116,927.09. Interestingly, at the conclusion of the study, three participants confided to the coach that had the program not been in place to support them throughout their first year, they would likely have voluntarily terminated their employment. While this was an interesting insight, RMC chose a conservative approach to evaluating the program and only acknowledged a savings of one turnover.

## ROI Analysis

### Solution Benefit

It was agreed that the solution benefit would be 50 percent of the average cost of one turnover. RMC acknowledged that there might be other factors influencing retention in addition to this program. While it might have been ideal to run a control group or to ask the participants for their evaluations of the effect of this program on their decisions to stay with the organization for the full year, it was agreed that one-half of the impact, or $58,463.55, would be utilized to calculate ROI.

### Project Cost

Table 6.5 represents the cost of the program.

### Calculating ROI

In effect, the ROI was calculated as follows:

$$\text{ROI} = \text{Net Solution Benefits/Solution Cost}$$
$$= \frac{\$58,463.55 - \$16,665.13}{\$16,665.13} \times 100 = 251\% \text{ ROI}$$

In terms of ROI, for every $1 RMC invested, $2.51 was returned after the costs were captured. These results are excellent. However,

**Table 6.5.   Cost of Program**

| Cost Category | Cost |
| --- | --- |
| ***Internal Coach's Salary and Benefits*** | |
| Group Coaching | $450.00 |
| Individual Coaching | $3,898.13 |
| Materials | $55.00 |
| Facilities | $7,730.00 |
| ***Participants' Salary and Benefits*** | |
| Group Coaching | $1,760.00 |
| Individual Coaching | $2,772.00 |
| **Total** | **$16,665.13** |

ROI is only one measure and should be considered in consideration with other measures. It should be remembered that this is an estimate that is developed utilizing a conservative approach, and it probably underestimates the actual return from this project.

As a result of this study, the recommendation was made that this program be adopted for full implementation.

## Lessons Learned

This study is a good example of how to implement a pilot study in an organization that may not yet be ready to take on a full ROI study. By conducting a smaller study and demonstrating to management how an ROI study may be useful, individuals may be able to garner greater support for conducting a full-scale ROI study in the future.

Had the organization been in greater support of an ROI study, several elements would have been conducted differently. For example, the cause of turnover would have been more thoroughly investigated. While the program was effective in reducing turnover, it is likely that there are other causes and perhaps better solutions that would have had a more significant and broader impact. Additionally, isolating the effects of the program could have been calculated by asking for participants' estimation of the impact, or better yet, running a control group that receives the pre- and post-assessment, but not the solution.

In conclusion, this pilot study positively demonstrated the impact of coaching on new-hire retention, and the organization was satisfied with the result.

## Communication Strategy

Because this pilot study only had support for the solution, and not the ROI aspect of the study, it was a challenge to communicate the study to a senior-level and broader audience. The approach of the study helped to defend the analysis and make the results more believable and credible at the middle-management level. The results were presented to the vice president of human resources as well as two directors of human resources in the following sequence:

1. Brief review of the project and its objectives

2. Overview of the methodology

3. Assumptions used in the analysis

4. Reaction and satisfaction measures

5. Engagement and commitment measures

6. Business impact

7. ROI

8. Recommendations

This information was presented in a one-hour meeting that provided an opportunity to present the methodology and results. This meeting had two purposes:

1. Present the methodology, assumptions, solution, and results

2. Gain support to implement the solution on a broader scale

The project was considered a success.

## Questions for Discussion

1. Can the value of this program be forecast? If so, how?

2. Are there other costs that should be included? Explain.

3. Should learning any application data be involved? Explain.

4. Are the ROI values realistic? Explain.

5. Is this study credible? Explain.

*Reference*

Phillips, J.J., & Connell, A.O. (2003). *Managing employee retention*, Boston, MA: Elsevier.

Posner, B.Z., & Schmidt, W. H. (1993). Values congruence and differences between the interplay of personal and organizational value systems. *Journal of Business Ethics, 12*, 171–177.

## About the Authors

**Lisa Ann Edwards** is the director, Global Learning & Development, with a global media company and is the founder of Bloom Consulting, Inc., a consulting firm specializing in employee engagement and retention. She holds a master's degree in psychology and a coaching certification from The Hudson Institute. She may be contacted at: Lisa@BloomWhereYouArePlanted.com.

**Christina Lounsberry** is a learning and development specialist with a global media company and is an experienced facilitator, classroom instructor, and human resources specialist.

# 7

# Measuring ROI in Operational and Quality Training

## A Plastics Manufacturing Company for the Prepared Foods Industry

Kirk Smith

## Abstract

A plastics thermoforming company had quality and operational issues that it wanted to address with training. A collaboration between the company, a community college, and a skill development provider helped achieve a very high ROI in just a few weeks by improving and making visible the thinking of a handful of employees. Conducting an ROI impact study was an important goal for all three parties.

## Background

### Need for Program

Plastics Manufacturing Company (PMC) is an international organization that makes plastic trays for the prepared foods industry. It uses proprietary resins and processes in a thermoforming operation to produce trays for frozen foods, case ready meats, bakery, institutional, and ready meals. Customers include most of the name brands in North America and Europe. One of the plants, in the southeastern United States, was having operational and quality problems that it wanted to address with training.

PMC had qualified for funding for training through its state's New and Expanding Industry Training program. This economic and workforce development program is administered and delivered through the state's community college system and provides training, at no cost, to organizations that qualify due to being new to the area or are growing their workforce at a specified minimum rate. PMC sought to take advantage of the situation and arranged a meeting with the local community college's workforce development department. Representatives of PMC and the community college met to discuss the performance needs that could be satisfied with training. The primary issues were in quality and overall equipment effectiveness (OEE). The scrap losses and equipment utilization deviated from the desired levels of the company, and improvement was desired. PMC felt that if it could improve these rates even incrementally, it could have a significant impact on profitability.

The meeting was facilitated by the community college's corporate learning director. In attendance from PMC were managers from operations, quality, engineering, and human resources development. Using a situation appraisal process, the business, performance, knowledge/skill, and preference needs were determined. The business objectives were to improve the scrap rate from the current 5 percent to 2 percent and to improve OEE from the current 65 percent to 75 percent. The job performance objectives were to improve assessing trouble situations and the speed and quality of finding the root cause of deviations. The knowledge/skill objectives were to improve the troubleshooting and decision-making capabilities of operators, engineering, and quality personnel. The preference of PMC was to conduct a five-day instructor-led training session for twenty key employees in operations, engineering, and quality.

The state's community college system had recently formed a partnership with Kepner-Tregoe (KT), a Princeton, New Jersey-based skill development and consulting firm that specializes in transferring and implementing those critical thinking skills needed by PMC. The community college system had started the certification process for five KT Program Leaders (instructors) for their Analytic Troubleshooting (ATS) workshop. The stringent certification process includes attending a five-day pre-exposure workshop, a two-week train-the-trainer session called a Leader Development Institute (LDI), and a check-out teach monitored by an experienced KT consultant. The session planned for PMC would be the check-out teaches for two of the PL candidates.

The ATS program for PMC would be a five-day program. The first four days would include instruction, practice, and application of KT's four rational thinking processes; situation appraisal, problem analysis, decision analysis, and potential problem/opportunity analysis. After each concept briefing taught by the PL, the participants practice, in small groups, their newfound knowledge and skills with case studies and real application. During the case practice and application, the PLs coach each group when they need help with the processes. The fifth day was reserved for the groups to present their progress on real job application work to senior management.

## Need for Evaluation

Conducting a return on investment (ROI) evaluation was important for all three parties involved: PMC, the community college system, and KT. PMC wanted to ensure that the skill development effort was worth the time involved by the participants and that it did improve the business objectives that were of importance to them. The community college system wanted to make sure that they received a good return on the money they invested—both the investment required to certify the Program Leaders and to provide the training to PMC. They also wanted to make sure they were meeting the needs of their client. KT, the learning provider, had an almost fifty-year history of showing positive, measurable results and wanted to be able to show that their core thinking technologies made a difference in organizations. In fact, one of KT's core values is that it provides positive measurable workshop results.

## Evaluation Methodology

It was decided by the community college's corporate learning director to conduct the evaluation using the Phillips ROI Methodology. Using the four primary stages of evaluation planning, data collection, data analysis, and reporting results, most of the discrete steps within each phase would be conducted and documented. The first step in evaluation planning, developing the objectives of the solution, had already been accomplished. The next step was to develop the evaluation plans and baseline data.

ROI Institute's Data Collection Plan template was used to capture the information that spelled out what data was to be collected, what measures and data were to be used, the method of collection, sources of data, timing of the collection, and who was responsible. This was done for each of the four learning levels and the fifth level, ROI. It is shown in Figure 7.1.

The ROI strategy targeted the Level 4 business need objectives of reducing PMC's scrap rate and increasing its OEE. To help ensure that the effects of the workshop were isolated from other factors that could have caused an improvement in these measures, a method of isolating the effects had to be decided. Through discussions between the community college representatives, the PLs, and PMC management, it was decided that the participants and their managers/supervisors would estimate how much improvement was due to the training. This would be done in individual interviews and facilitated focus groups to obtain a consensus. To convert the percentage improvements in the objectives to monetary value, PMC had very accurate standard costs for each percentage improvement.

**Program:** PMC ATS   **Responsibility:** Corporate Learning Director        **Date:** _____

| Level | Objective(s) | Measures/Data | Data Collection Method | Data Sources | Timing | Responsibilities |
|---|---|---|---|---|---|---|
| 1 | **Reaction/Satisfaction** Average evaluation score of at least 4.5 out of 5.0 | Instructor courseware action plan course structure | Survey | Participants | At end of session | PLs |
| 2 | **Learning** Learn the steps of the analytic thinking processes. | Exhibiting the knowledge in case study practice and real application during the class. | Observation by PLs | PLs | During session | PLs |
| 3 | **Application/Implementation** Use the KT problem analysis and decision analysis processes in real situations on the job | Use at least 75 percent of time when needed | Interviews and focus groups | Participants and managers | Five weeks after session | PLs and PMC management |
| 4 | **Business Impact** Reduce scrap rate from 5 to 2 percent Increase OEE from 65 to 75 percent | Within six months | PMC's operational information system | PMC management | Five weeks Four months Six months | PLs and PMC management |
| 5 | **ROI** Target of 50 percent | **Comments:** _____ | | | | |

Figure 7.1.  Data Collection Plan

To be as conservative as possible in the evaluation, all costs associated with the program were to be included in the ROI calculation. Costs, such as participant time away from their jobs, were fully loaded to include employer provided employee benefit programs. Participants' salaries used in calculations were increased by 40 percent to account for this. The cost categories included:

- Vendor (KT) costs

- Travel costs

- Participants' time

- Managers' time

- Meals during workshop

- Administrative time (PMC and community college)

- Evaluation costs

The ROI Analysis Plan is shown in Figure 7.2.

## Evaluation Results

### Reaction

At the conclusion of the program, the participants completed a paper evaluation with typical Level 1 (Reaction) feedback about the course, instructor, courseware, and environment. Each participant also completed an action plan for applying the new knowledge and skills that was to be followed for five weeks by the PLs. The average overall score based on a 5-point scale was 4.61, with no individual category falling below a score of 4.35. This was considered successful. However, since the ultimate goal was to measure the ROI of the program, the Level 1 data was not considered vital to the successful outcome.

| Data Items (Usually Level 4) | Methods for Isolating the Effects of the Program/Process | Methods of Converting Data to Monetary Values | Cost Categories | Intangible Benefits | Communication Targets for Final Report | Other Influences/Issues During Application | Comments |
|---|---|---|---|---|---|---|---|
| Reduce scrap rate from 5 to 2 percent | Participant and manager estimates | Standard values | Vendor costs | Common language | Plant Mgr. | Time pressure | |
| Increase OEE from 65 to 75 percent | Participant and manager estimates | Standard values | Travel costs | Improved cross-functional teamwork | Plant Eng. | Inertia | |
| | | | Participants' time | | Quality Dir. | Highly motivated champion in Plant Engineer | |
| | | | Managers' time | Improved communication | | | |
| | | | Meals during session | | | | |
| | | | Admin time | | | | |
| | | | Evaluation costs | | | | |

Figure 7.2. ROI Analysis Plan

177

## Learning

Level 2 (Learning) results were not measured by a written assessment or by the participants' estimates of how much they learned. Throughout the program, the PLs and KT observer discussed, before and after each day, each participant's contribution during class discussions, case practice, and most important, during real job application. As in most learning programs, there are those who advance and learn more quickly than others and there are those who lag behind. If the PLs and KT observer felt that someone was not "getting it," extra coaching was provided during the person's real job application work. Very little remediation was needed in this program. The learning levels of each participant were considered adequate to apply and implement successfully on the job. Again, because the ultimate evaluation goal of the program was ROI, this method of learning level measurement was considered adequate.

## Application and Impact

The intention of the evaluation, according to the data collection plan, was to follow up with the participants and their managers/supervisors approximately five weeks after the end of the session. Because of an unexpected, albeit very positive, situation, we were able to gather Level 3 (Application) and Level 4 (Business Impact) data concurrently and ahead of schedule. Approximately three weeks after the training session, the plant engineer for the PMC facility called the community college's corporate learning director to announce that a problem-solving team of training participants had solved a significant quality problem that they had started working on during the session's real job application segments. It was a quality problem that had plagued the company for eight years.

As you may recall, PMC's thermoforming operation produces trays for the prepared foods industry. One of the common quality problems that contributed to a higher than desired scrap rate and lower than desired OEE was "angel hair," a condition that creates very thin strands of plastic around the edges of the cuts in the sheets of plastic near the end of the continuous processing extrusion line. Because neither PMC's customers nor their customers' customers want strands of plastic around trays that are made to hold food, those trays had to be scrapped and reworked back into the process. They had tried many times over eight years to solve the problem. Often the angel hair would go away for a while, only to recur after a short time. It was very frustrating and costly for PMC. Using the unique problem-solving methodology learned in the training session, a team of participants led by the plant engineer found the root cause of angel hair and were able to stop it. Part of the KT problem analysis methodology involves describing a deviation (angel hair on trays) by asking, answering, and documenting a series of questions in four dimensions: what, where, when, and extent. Part of what makes KT's methodology unique is that not only do you ask questions in those four dimensions about what "is" happening, but also what could be but "is not." The "is" and "is not" questions are asked in pairs throughout the four dimensions to help frame the deviation and give it boundaries. According to the plant engineer, it was persistence in finding the answers to these pairs of questions that led to the root cause and the solution. The angel hair had been caused all this time by improper machine tolerances in the cutting tools.

The plant engineer then calculated that solving the angel hair problem would save PMC more than $1.3 million per year. The calculation was done using standard values related to the reduction in scrap rate and increase in OEE based on production runs conducted after the adjustment was made to machine clearance. In one major application on the job by a handful of training participants, Level 3 (Application) and Level 4 (Business Impact) were confirmed. We did not have to use the planned data collection methods of individual interviews and focus groups. The results were confirmed by members of senior management at the site. The plant engineer also wrote a paper about the case for a graduate course he was taking in quality management. To be thorough, the members of the problem-solving team were asked to estimate how large a part the training played in solving the problem. Unanimously, they said that without learning the "is" and "is not" questions, they would not have solved the problem—100 percent. Normally, extreme data items should not be used in ROI calculations, but given the proximity in time, team agreement, and use of the new methodology, it was agreed to let it stand as is. To save time and resources, further collection of Level 3 and 4 data was considered unnecessary given the scope of the initial findings. Other improvements or benefits for the year due to the training were considered to be zero.

Although the results were obtained quickly, a barrier still needed to be overcome. The problem-solving team was an ad hoc team from different departments within PMC. They had to plan their analysis sessions around their normal job duties. This was overcome by a stronger enabler. The leadership and persistence of the plant engineer and the willingness of the other team members should not be underestimated in the part played in achieving the ultimate results.

## ROI Calculation

The calculation of the ROI was next. We already knew the benefits: $1.3 million. Even though PMC stated that it would be an annual savings, to be conservative we only considered the first year's benefits in the calculations. The costs were as follows:

| | |
|---|---|
| Vendor costs | $20,000 |
| Travel costs | $1,900 |
| Participants' time | $29,166 |
| Managers' time | $3,166 |
| Administrative time | $500 |
| Meals during training | $500 |
| Evaluation costs | $1,500 |
| **Total** | **$56,732** |

Even though PMC did not have to pay the vendor or travel costs, they were included because they were paid by the community college system; and ultimately the taxpayers of the state.

### ROI Formula and Calculation

$$\text{ROI} = [(\text{Total Benefits} - \text{Total Costs}) \div \text{Total Costs}] \times 100$$
$$\text{ROI} = [(1{,}300{,}000 - 56{,}732) \div 56{,}732] \times 100$$
$$\text{ROI} = 2{,}191\%$$

### Intangible Benefits

In other discussions with participants and the management of PMC, there were several intangible benefits worth mentioning. These are benefits that were purposely not converted to monetary values or were difficult or impossible to convert. Both participants and managers felt strongly that having a common language and methodology improved communication and teamwork at the site. Knowing this helped to make senior management confident that other significant monetary benefits would be forthcoming at PMC. Specifically, the plant manager said that one of the greatest benefits he saw was that people are asking him questions they never asked before.

## Communication Strategy

The final step was to present the results to senior management at PMC. In attendance were the plant manager and the managers of quality, operations, and human resources. The presentation was made by the plant engineer. Word had already leaked about the success, and the presentation was more of a formality than initially informing. However, showing the specific methodology helped bring credibility to the findings, and the response was overwhelmingly positive. Because of the success of the first program, rollout of the KT program to other parts of the organization was planned.

A report was also sent to KT, the skill development provider. Each year KT awards recognition to the best use of its rational thinking processes, the International Rational Process Achievement Awards. The PMC "angel hair" team and the community college PLs who conducted the training and application coaching were one of the recipients of the award for that year.

## Lessons Learned

As one of my first ROI evaluations, there was a lot to learn. Front-end planning is critical to a successful evaluation. Always start with business need objectives or an ROI target first. Then work backward through the learning levels from there. A training program has to be about results. If it is just an intellectual exercise, it is likely wasting a lot of peoples' time and resources. The data collection and ROI analysis plans help save a lot of time and effort. Knowing up-front what data you need, where to get it, and who is responsible for it reduces anxiety throughout the process. It is also important to keep the channels of communication open after the conclusion of the program. It is too easy for people to get wrapped up in their workday world and lose sight of the objectives.

*Questions for Discussion*

1. How do you develop internal customer champions like the plant engineer at PMC?

2. How would you check the accuracy of the standard values you are using to convert to monetary values?

3. If the results had not been obtained so quickly or had not been reported back to you, how would you have structured the interviews and focus groups?

4. What if you are called in to do the evaluation after the fact and have not completed a data collection plan or ROI analysis plan? What would you do first?

5. If you had two ways to convert to monetary value, standard values or a manager's input, which would you use?

6. Are there any challenges to communicating an ROI of 2191 percent? Explain.

7. Is this case credible? Explain.

*Resources*

Kirkpatrick, D.L. (1998). *Evaluating programs: The four levels* (2nd ed.). San Francisco, CA: Berrett-Koehler.

Phillips, J.J. (2003). *Return on investment in training and performance improvement programs* (2nd ed.). Boston, MA: Butterworth-Heinemann.

**About the Author**

**Kirk Smith**, CPT, PMP, is a senior consultant with Kepner-Tregoe, based in the Atlanta, Georgia, area. He is a Certified ROI Professional and is currently pursuing a Ph.D. in technology management from Indiana State University. He received his bachelor's degree in industrial engineering from Georgia Tech and his master's of science degree in industrial technology from East Carolina University. He is also an adjunct faculty member at Western Carolina University, where he teaches a course in organization performance.

# 8

# Measuring ROI in a Professional Development Day
## A Technical College

Jennifer Janecek Hartman and Leah Woodke

## Abstract

This case study evaluates a program offered by the Distance & Continuing Education Department of the United Tribes Technical College (UTTC). This professional day was designed to maximize the use of funding to efficiently reach a maximum number of people with a given number of goals. Because of the success of this professional day, it is now established on a yearly calendar for three days dedicated to professional development. This study shows the application of the ROI Methodology in a simple way. It uses simple action plans to capture data at Levels 3 and 4, with questionnaires used to capture data at Levels 1 and 2. The cost of the simplicity is that sometimes the accuracy is questioned. That is a typical tradeoff. This study generated a negative ROI of −15.2 percent, with important intangible measures, application data, as well as reaction and learning data.

---

Note: This case was prepared to serve as a basis for discussion rather than an illustration of either effective or ineffective administrative and management practices.

## Background

The Distance & Continuing Education department (DCE) has collaborated with the Professional Development Committee to maximize the use of the Bush funds to efficiently reach the maximum number of people in a greater number of goal areas of the grant. UTTC has now dedicated three days of its yearly calendar to professional development. The Professional Development Day (PDD) is a regular contract day when classes are cancelled and faculty and staff members are invited to meet for a learning opportunity.

Faculty and staff members are asked to submit proposals for presentations, thereby tapping into the expertise and resources located on campus. Some outside presenters are invited to present as well. The United Tribes Rural Systemic Initiative, funded by the National Science Foundation, sponsored some of the speakers for the March PDD. The topics of the presentations were derived from the training needs identified by faculty and outlined in the goals of the Bush grant. Twenty-nine sessions were offered on PDD in March. It was conducted in a conference format whereby participants chose sessions that interested them. The DCE tracked attendance in each session and conducted Level 1 and 2 evaluations of each session. Then participants evaluated the overall PDD at Level 3 using Action Plans. CEUs were awarded to those participants who apply. This report evaluates the PDD activity in terms of Levels 4 and 5.

### Purpose of Evaluation

The Professional Development Day is a fairly new program to the College. The overall view of the program by participants and many of the administrators of the College is that it is a valuable activity, is cost-effective, and is an enjoyable way to learn and grow together. The costs of the day are shared by different departments and funding sources. The PDD impacts many departments across campus. The College also invests time in this program. A full school day is set aside for the event three times each year. Since most people on campus view the event favorably, this training program has a low political temperature attached to it. In addition, the two people who are conducting the ROI study are precisely the people who plan, coordinate, and execute the events. The question at the heart of this study is whether the Professional Development Day events are worth the investment.

## Evaluation Methodology

The ROI process for this study included steps to address each of the five levels of evaluation, as well as the intangible benefits. The first step was to collect reaction data for each session provided at the PDD, held March 13, 2006. (See Exhibit 8.1.) As one means of measuring how much learning occurred as a result of the PDD, participants were asked to complete a survey about the overall day, which included questions about how much they learned that day. (See Exhibit 8.2.) Participants completed Action Plans as a means of recording how they used what they learned from that day. The Action Plan included a means for participants to record the improvement measure, current and target performance levels, action steps, and a section for analysis of their improvement measures. It also provided a means for isolating the effects of the program and identifying intangible benefits of the PDD activities. The Action Plan is available in Exhibit 8.3. The researchers used the Action Plans to determine the business impact of the PDD and calculate the ROI.

## Evaluation Results

### Reaction Data (Level 1)

Over the course of the day, seventy-two people participated in the PDD. Most people participated less than the full day. Individual session evaluations were positive. Participants were asked to

Session Title:_____

Session Time:_____

Please indicate your response to the following question using the scale:

> 1 = Strongly Disagree
> 2 = Disagree
> 3 = Neither Agree nor Disagree
> 4 = Agree
> 5 = Strongly Agree

1. The information presented is relevant to my work.
   ❑ 1        ❑ 2        ❑ 3        ❑ 4        ❑ 5

2. The presentation contained valuable information.
   ❑ 1        ❑ 2        ❑ 3        ❑ 4        ❑ 5

3. I plan to use the information I learned in this presentation.
   ❑ 1        ❑ 2        ❑ 3        ❑ 4        ❑ 5

4. The presentation provided me with new information.
   ❑ 1        ❑ 2        ❑ 3        ❑ 4        ❑ 5

5. The presenter was effective.
   ❑ 1        ❑ 2        ❑ 3        ❑ 4        ❑ 5

6. I would recommend this presentation to others.
   ❑ 1        ❑ 2        ❑ 3        ❑ 4        ❑ 5

What was the most important thing you learned in this session?

**Exhibit 8.1. Professional Development Day Session Evaluation**

evaluate each session regarding presenter's knowledge, activities, and effectiveness. Each participant was asked to complete a session evaluation at the end of each session he or she attended. The return rate on the session evaluations was approximately 96 percent. The overall mean score was 4.2 on a 5-point scale, which translates to an overall 92.5 percent. Figure 8.1 displays the mean scores from each question for the Level 1 (Reaction/Satisfaction) questions from all of the session evaluations.

United Tribes Technical College

Thank you for taking the time to complete this evaluation. Answer the questions as honestly and completely as you are able. Include your name only if you are comfortable in doing so. This form is intended to be anonymous.

What Dean/Division are you under?
- ❑ President's Office
- ❑ Student & Campus Services
- ❑ Vocational & Academics
- ❑ Intertribal Programs
- ❑ Childhood Services
- ❑ Finance & Business Services
- ❑ I am a student who is not employed at UTTC

1. The session choices available throughout the day were relevant to my work?
   Strongly Disagree........ Disagree........ No Opinion........ Agree........ Strongly Agree........
   ❑            ❑            ❑            ❑            ❑

2. The length of the sessions (75 minutes) was adequate and appropriate.
   Strongly Disagree........ Disagree........ No Opinion........ Agree........ Strongly Agree........
   ❑            ❑            ❑            ❑            ❑

3. How do you rate the pace of the sessions?
   Poor..................... Fair..................... Good..................... Excellent.....................
   ❑            ❑            ❑            ❑

4. How do you rate the session choices provided?
   Poor..................... Fair..................... Good..................... Excellent.....................
   ❑            ❑            ❑            ❑

5. What was the most valuable aspect of the Professional Development Day?


6. What is one way the Professional Development Day can be improved?


7. Please provide any other comments you would like to make below:


**Thank you for your time.**

# Exhibit 8.2. All Staff Professional Development Day Evaluation

| Name: | | Follow-Up Date | 4/14/06 |
|---|---|---|---|
| Objective | | | |

Improvement Measure: _____

Current Performance _____

Target Performance _____

| Action Steps | Analysis |
|---|---|
| 1. _____ _____ | A. What is the unit of measure? _____ |
| | B. What is the value (cost) of one unit? $ _____ |
| | C. How did you arrive at this value? _____ _____ _____ |
| 2. _____ _____ | |
| 3. _____ _____ | D. How much did the measure change during the evaluation period? (monthly value) _____ |
| 4. _____ _____ | E. What percent of this change was actually caused by this program? _____ % |
| | F. What level of confidence do you place on the above information? (100% = Certainty and 0% - No Confidence) _____ % |

Intangible Benefits: _____

## Exhibit 8.3. Action Plan

Adapted from Phillips, P.P. (2002). The bottom line on ROI: Basics, benefits, & barriers to measuring training & performance improvement. In J.J. Phillips (Ed.), *The bottom line on ROI*. Silver Spring, MD: Society for Performance Improvement.

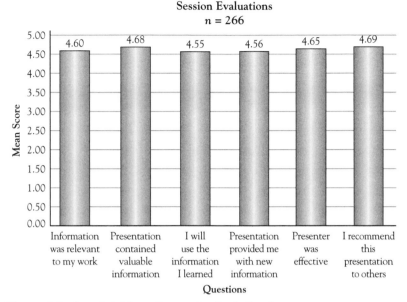

Figure 8.1. Level 1 Mean Scores for Each Session

## Learning Data (Level 2)

The session evaluation responses regarding the learning of skills, knowledge, or attitude changes related to the sessions were gathered through the last question on the session evaluations: "What is the most important thing you learned in this session?" The top three most important indicated were de-escalation techniques, technology topics, and Native American topics. (See Figure 8.2.)

## Application Data (Level 3)

Level 3 information was gathered from self-reporting on the action plans. Of the twenty-seven action plans that were turned in, twenty-six were used in the Level 3 analysis. Participants reported changes in behavior, specific application, and/or implementation of their learning in five different areas: FERPA, Using Technology, Stress Management, De-Escalation Strategies, and Native American Topics. The percent change, the percent attributed to the

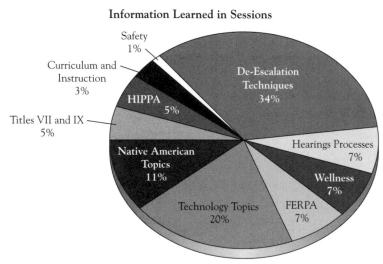

**Information Learned in Sessions**

Safety 1%

Curriculum and Instruction 3%

De-Escalation Techniques 34%

HIPPA 5%

Titles VII and IX 5%

Native American Topics 11%

Hearings Processes 7%

Wellness 7%

Technology Topics 20%

FERPA 7%

**Figure 8.2. Level 2 (Learning)**

program, and the participant confidence levels were calculated to ascertain a median change attributed to the program. The outliers were removed, and a 30 percent average change attributed to the program was reported.

**Barriers to Success**

The following barriers to success were determined:

- A general feeling of not being listened to by faculty and staff

- Scheduling conflicts

- Not all can participate due to the nature of their work (shift nature or their work is integral to the College's daily operations)

- Funding, as the program is grant-based. Sometimes funds are restricted, as well as limited

## Enablers to Success

The following enablers to success were determined:

- Support from most administrators

- Faculty generally enjoy the day for its collegiality and opportunities to learn together

- There is assessment going on at the basic levels of evaluation

- Support is provided across departments at the College

## Business Impact Data (Level 4)

Of the seventy-two people who attended the PDD, approximately fifty attended the last session of the day, in which the action plans were distributed and explained. Each of the participants who received action plans set his or her own objectives and identified improvement measures, target performance, and action steps. One month later, all participants were invited to another session in which the researchers helped them with the analysis portion of their action plans. Twenty-seven participants completed the activity with the researcher.

The PDD included several different sessions on various topics. Each person chose topics of individual interest. Some of the outcomes, by their nature, were not easily converted to monetary value. The assumption was that each participant would be in the best position to assign a monetary value and/or intangible benefit to the outcomes from the PDD. Each person would also gain something different from the PDD based on personal needs or interests, depending on his or her current level of expertise in the area. In most cases, average salary values, rather than individual salary values, were used to calculate monetary values toward the measure of change. When participants were vague about how much time they based their change on, the activity was not included.

After analyzing the action plans and calculating the participants' reports, monetary values were assigned. Seventeen of the action plans submitted were deemed complete for analysis at Level 4. The others were not included in the calculations of monetary values. They were included in the discussion of intangible benefits. Standard values of employee time based on average class salaries as well as workman's compensation values from outside experts were used to calculate monetary values where appropriate.

### Isolating the Effects of the Program

It is important to isolate the effects of the program. Using participant estimates in this case makes sense due to the individualized nature of the training program. Participants were asked to estimate the percent change that occurred, to estimate the percent that the program was responsible for the change, and then to estimate the level of confidence they had on the information they provided.

### Converting Data to Monetary Value

Data was converted to monetary value only if it was logical to do so. Respondents' reports on action plans were used as a basis for converting the data to monetary value (shown in Table 8.1). Only those action plans that were complete were used for the analysis and data conversion. In the end, only seventeen of the twenty-seven action plans returned were used for analysis. Table 8.1 shows the total savings, the standard value for the basis, the improvement factor, the percent of the results allocated to the program, the confidence in the allocation, and the total adjusted value. Typically, standard values were used. Employee time was converted to monetary value using standard average salary amounts. It would not be prudent to use individual salaries in the culture of this institution. Salaries are private matters. The improvement factor represents an adjustment made to reflect the value of the change. For example, one of the staff members completed an action plan regarding the use of Outlook to schedule meetings and appointments as well as daily "to-to" lists after attending a session on how to use Outlook more efficiently. The staff member indicated that s/he saved one hour per day or five hours per week. Based on the average staff per hour rate of $27.16, the raw savings was calculated at $6,518.40. The staff member indicated on the action plan 95 percent of the time saved is used productively (improvement factor), that the percent of change attributed to the program was 95 percent and his/her confidence placed on the estimates given was 80 percent. The final benefit calculation was $4,706.28 ($6,518.40 × 95% × 95% × 80%).

In another example, external experts provided data regarding the average cost of a workman's compensation medical claim. This amount was used as a standard cost of one unit in the cases where respondents indicated that stress management or de-escalation were the objectives and units of measure in the action plans. For example, according to the North Dakota Workman's Compensation Bureau, the average workman's compensation claim is valued at $800. One participant indicated that s/he experienced two conflict de-escalation events within the evaluation period, averting a potential workman's compensation claim each time. For this participant, the measure changed 200 percent, since two conflicts were averted. The percent of change attributed to the program was 50 percent and his/her confidence placed on the estimates given was 80 percent. The final benefit calculation was $640 ($800 × 200% × 50% × 80%).

**Table 8.1.** Converting Data to Monetary Values

| Value | Standard | Improvement Factor | % Program | % Confidence | Total |
|---|---|---|---|---|---|
| $ 1,567.12 | Faculty Salary | 50% | 100% | 90% | $ 705.20 |
| $ 329.92 | Faculty Salary | 10% | 90% | 95% | $ 28.21 |
| $ 853.86 | Faculty Salary | 400% | 100% | 95% | $ 3,244.67 |
| $ 195.89 | Faculty Salary | 75% | 25% | 100% | $ 36.73 |
| $ 303.68 | Administration Salary | 50% | 70% | 50% | $ 53.14 |
| $ 434.34 | Faculty Salary | 10% | 100% | 100% | $ 43.43 |
| $ 6,518.40 | Administration Salary | 95% | 95% | 80% | $ 4,706.28 |
| $ 587.67 | Faculty Salary | 33% | 100% | 100% | $ 193.93 |
| $ 1,078.56 | Faculty Salary | 100% | 100% | 95% | $ 1,024.63 |
| $ 1,600.00 | Workman's Comp | N/A | N/A | N/A | $ 1,600.00 |
| $ 195.89 | Faculty Salary | 100% | 10% | 25% | $ 4.90 |
| $ 800.00 | Workman's Comp | 100% | 100% | 50% | $ 400.00 |
| $ 800.00 | Workman's Comp | 200% | 50% | 80% | $ 640.00 |
| $ 800.00 | Workman's Comp | 50% | 50% | 50% | $ 100.00 |
| $ 800.00 | Workman's Comp | 0% | 0% | 0% | $ — |
| $ 9,402.72 | Faculty Salary | 20% | 10% | 50% | $ 94.03 |
| $ 9,402.72 | Faculty Salary | 40% | 50% | 50% | $ 940.27 |
| $ 800.00 | Workman's Comp | 50% | 80% | 100% | $ 320.00 |
| | | | | **Total Benefits** | **$ 12,535.42** |

**Table 8.2.  PDD Budget, March 2006**

| Professional Development Day Budget, Monday, March 13, 2006 | |
|---|---:|
| Total Food and Drinks | $  1,259.00 |
| Total Trainers | $  3,000.00 |
| Total Participant Salaries (72 participants) | $  5,600.00 |
| Total Supplies | $  3,042.00 |
| Total Administrative Costs | $  1,875.00 |
| Total Budget | $ 14,776.00 |

## Costs of the Program

The costs associated with the program are included in Table 8.2. Fully loaded costs included all participants' salaries for the day, all supplies, food, CEUs, presenter fees, and printing required to implement the program and evaluations. The total cost for the program was $14,776.00.

## Return on Investment (Level 5)

A return on investment of 0.9 percent means that, for every dollar spent, the college lost $0.10 in benefits after recouping the dollar investment. The ROI is calculated by dividing the net program benefits (Benefits minus Costs) by program costs and multiplying by 100 to get the percentage. ROI is always reported as a percentage. The benefits were calculated to be $12,535.42. The costs were $14,776.00. Net benefits were −$2,240.58. The calculation is:

$$\frac{\$12,535.42 - \$14,776.00}{\$14,776.00} \times 100 = -15.2\%$$

## Intangible Benefits

Several intangible benefits were reported by respondents. The comments made on the action plans included:

- Student privacy practices were enhanced.

- Time is now saved by using Outlook calendar.

- There is a greater accessibility of students to instructors and vice versa via e-mail.

- There is reduced stress due to scheduling using Outlook tasks and calendar features.

- There is less stress due to efficient use of e-mail.

- It is nice to finally decide on something "I" think might work.

- Safety and security are priceless.

Comments reported on the overall evaluations at the end of the day were positive. Some of the common comments were:

- Appreciation for the collegiality of the day

- De-escalation techniques were perceived as valuable

- Training on technology (Outlook and Staying Organized Online)

- Discussion on racism topics was perceived as valuable

## Credibility of the Study

This ROI study is credible because it followed the twelve guiding principles used in the ROI Methodology. It included data reported from all levels of evaluation, Levels 1 through 5. The lower levels of data supported the higher levels of data. The sources were credible. Participants were the most qualified to report on their own learning and their own progress. The data used for calculations were not inflated. In fact, the most conservative estimates were used and the costs were fully loaded. The effects were isolated through respondent estimates of use, program effect, and confidence in the data they reported. If no improvement data was supplied, none was assumed. All outlier data were discarded and not used in the calculations. The ROI is relevant for a one-year period, no longer than that. The analysis was based on a month-long effect and extrapolated to a year for staff and to 9.5 months for faculty, since that best reflects their work year. A 9.5-month effect is more conservative than a year for faculty. Those benefits that were not convertible to monetary value were reported as intangible benefits. The results of this ROI were communicated to all stakeholders.

## Communication Strategy

Results of the ROI study on PDD were reported to all stakeholders. First, results were shared with the Administration of the College. A one-page summary was provided to the president, the vice presidents, and other key administrative officials. After the results were shared using a PowerPoint presentation, the administration was given the full report. The faculty and other PDD participants were invited to a general all-hands meeting to hear the results of the study, at which they received the one-page summary of the results. Finally, the researchers shared the results at the next PDD held in September 2006.

## Lessons Learned

The PDD is funded by a variety of grant sources, mostly Bush Foundation-Faculty Development monies. One would expect a 0 percent return on investment for grant activities. Even though the study found a −15.16 percent ROI, the College believes this is a worthwhile activity. Although the benefits do not translate into income for the College, the literature suggests that quality professional development programs strengthen a learning community.

The rather low return rate on the action plans, combined with the extremely conservative estimation of benefits, suggests that the ROI reported may be too conservative.

If we change our assumption, the ROI becomes positive. The salaries of the staff for the time involved in training were included in the costs. This is consistent with the standards of the ROI Methodology. If another assumption was made and the salaries were not included, then the ROI is positive. The new cost would be $9,179.20, and thus the ROI becomes a positive 37 percent, as shown in this calculation:

$$\frac{\$12,535.42 - \$9,179.20}{\$9,179.20} \times 100 = 36.6\%$$

This provides another scenario. However, the standard is used to reflect the conservative approach. Management can quickly see the sensitivity of adding the fully loaded costs.

The current model for the PDD program includes utilizing internal as well as external expertise. Using internal experts for presentations enables the College to build confidence in current employees while providing a means to share information and skills as a means to build human capacity. The use of external experts enhances the expertise available at the College and brings fresh and new perspectives to the PDD participants.

The PDD is causing a positive change. Respondents reported an average 64 percent overall change in behavior, attitudes, and skills. Respondents indicated that the PDD was an average of 56 percent responsible for the changes. The confidence level that they had in their response was an average of 61 percent. It appears that the PDD caused a significant change in participant behavior or performance.

It was determined that the College should continue to provide professional development through the PDD format. The benefits far outweigh the costs of the program, especially when including intangible benefits. There has been discussion about having a student-run PDD for students at the College. Based on the results of the faculty/staff PDD, it is likely that, with high student participation, the results will be similar.

## Questions for Discussion

1. Critique the overall approach to the evaluation.
2. What could be done to enhance the participation rate in the action plan process?
3. Is it clear how the monetary values were arrived at? If not, what should be done to arrive at a better understanding of the value?
4. Should the participants' salaries be included in the fully loaded cost? Are there any other costs that should be included to be fully loaded following Guiding Principle 10?
5. Discuss the issue of simplicity versus accuracy as it relates to credibility and acceptance of studies.

## About the Authors

**Jennifer Janecek Hartman** has spent twenty-one years in the field of education. She earned a B.S. degree in elementary education with specializations in science and reading. She holds a master's in gifted and talented education from the University of Connecticut. She has a Ph.D. in education with a focus on human performance improvement from Capella University. Dr. Janecek Hartman is the director of the UTPASS project at United Tribes Technical College, which established a new Tribal Environmental Science (TES) degree program at UTTC. The TES program emphasizes student support and success strategies. She also coordinates collaborations with regional and national organizations and institutions. In addition, Dr. Janecek Hartman has served in leadership capacities with local, state, and national educational organizations. Dr. Janecek Hartman is responsible for coordinating various continuing education and professional development activities at the college.

**Leah Woodke** has worked in the field of education for twenty-one years and has served in various roles at United Tribes Technical College for the past eleven years. She was the chair of the Early Childhood Education Department and the director of the Child Development Center and currently serves as the director of distance and continuing education at UTTC. Dr. Woodke earned a B.S. degree in elementary education with a concentration in remedial reading. She holds an M.Ed. in educational leadership from the University of Central Florida and a Ph.D. in education with a focus on instructional design for online learning from Capella University. Dr. Woodke has been instrumental in UTTC receiving accreditation approval to offer five degree programs online. As the director of distance and continuing education, she works closely with Dr. Janecek Hartman to manage various continuing education and professional development activities at the college.

# 9

# Measuring ROI in Sales Training in a Nonprofit Business

## An Information Technology Company

Lisa Sallstrom

## Abstract

In the last decade, the IT market experienced drastic changes. Industry monopolies, guaranteed revenue streams, and open checkbooks have been replaced by overseas outsourcing, complex sales approaches, and bottom-line profitability. New sales skills need to be developed to successfully sell business solutions to companies obsessed with minimum margins and declining shareholder value. This case study demonstrates how the ROI Methodology was used to determine the results of a training initiative designed to teach *Conceptual Selling*® and *Strategic Selling*® approaches to a global sales staff.

## Background

For twenty-five years, the Computing Technology Industry Association (CompTIA) has served as the voice of the world's information

---

Note: This case was prepared to serve as a basis for discussion rather than an illustration of either effective or ineffective administrative and management practices.

*Conceptual Selling*® and *Strategic Selling*® are registered trademarks of Miller Heiman, Inc.®

technology (IT) industry. The Association represents the business interests of more than twenty thousand member companies world-wide and is committed to advancing the long-term success and growth of the IT industry. It is dedicated to helping organizations maximize the benefits received from investments in technology. The Association also assists individuals in obtaining the skills and credentials needed for productive careers in IT. CompTIA's major source of operating income is revenue generated from the sale of its technical certifications. With the dotcom bust, the decline in IT jobs, and deterioration in IT business profitability, CompTIA's revenue stream from traditional markets mirrored the IT industry decline.

To address the situation, a new sales strategy was created. It included new sales positions, new vertical markets to pursue (outside of the traditional IT market), and a new sales approach, including a company-wide sales vision, go-to-market strategy, and process. To ensure consistency of the approach across both the U.S. and international sales teams, an agreement was reached between the U.S. vice president of sales and the international vice president of sales to introduce the Miller Heiman® *Conceptual Selling®* and *Strategic Selling®* methodologies during a three-day, consolidated training program in the U.S. for all international and U.S. account managers, business development managers, and sales directors. This training was planned during the annual face-to-face sales meeting to avoid incurring travel expenses for a separate training session.

A Level 5 (ROI) evaluation was needed to justify the largest training expense ever incurred by the organization. This was a substantial risk and investment made by the executive staff, with expectations of significant results. Furthermore, the efforts of learning from and completing a Level 5 evaluation would be integrated in the go-to-market sales strategy to be used when consulting with member companies interested in understanding the ROI of similar career and skill development programs in CompTIA's product suite. Finally, ROI results of the initial program would be used to justify further training on additional elements of the Miller Heiman® sales approach.

## Evaluation Methodology

The decision to conduct an ROI evaluation on this project was made after the program had been delivered. Therefore, the advantages of pre-program evaluation planning were missed. These include communicating the expectations for providing data and the focus on achieving results throughout the project. Also, the forecasting step was not completed. The evaluation plan was defined as a post-project implementation, based on known executive-level requirements at that time.

In terms of data collection, shown in Table 9.1, Level 1 (Reaction and Planned Action) data on participant feedback were collected upon completion of the class. This information was helpful in understanding the value of this approach and its applicability as a sales strategy in the different vertical markets and territories represented by a diverse, global sales team. The information was also used as instructor feedback on overall training effectiveness. Level 2 (Learning) data were collected via an online assessment exam, which was delivered during the last hour of class to identify effectiveness of the learning process. A score of 85 percent was required to pass the exam, at which time successful candidates would receive a certification of completion. All participants successfully met this objective, with exam records forwarded to their managers for storage in their personnel files. Level 3 (Application and Implementation) data were collected on application effectiveness through adherence to new processes developed and management observation. Weekly meetings were instituted to review pipeline reports, and occasional blue and green sheet team reviews were held with forms stored on a newly created shared drive. Business development manager job requirements were updated with new process expectations, and ongoing on-the-job observations were conducted. Business impact

## Table 9.1. Data Collection Plan

Evaluation Purpose: Level 5—ROI  **Responsibility:** <u>Lisa Sallstrom</u>
**Program:** Miller Heiman® Sales Training

| Level | Broad Program Objective(s) | Measures | Data Collection Method/Instruments | Data Sources | Timing | Responsibilities |
|---|---|---|---|---|---|---|
| 1 | REACTION<br>• Positive employee reaction to training | >4 out of five-scale survey | Feedback Survey | Participants | Two months after class delivery | Management |
| 2 | LEARNING<br>• Employee understanding of *Conceptual Selling*® and *Strategic Selling*® process | Score >85% on post-class assessment | Exam Records | Participants | Immediately following the last day of training | Employees/ Management |
| 3 | APPLICATION/ IMPLEMENTATION<br>1. Blue/Green Sheet implementation<br>2. Pipeline reviews<br>3. Lead creation and tracking in CRM<br>4. Commissions paid only on data in CRM | 1. any > $10K opportunity<br>2. Weekly<br>3. Daily<br>4. Quarterly<br>5. As Required<br>6. As Required | 1. Sample review and follow-up questionnaire<br>2. Verification of meetings in Outlook<br>3. Sample review<br>4. Payroll records<br>5. Blue Sheet availability | 1. Sheet logs<br>2. Outlook calendar<br>3. Company records– CRM<br>4. HR/ Accounting | 1. Per criteria<br>2. Weekly<br>3. Daily<br>4. Quarterly<br>5. As required<br>6. Per criteria | Program coordinator |

| | | | |
|---|---|---|---|
| 5. Blue Sheet requirement prior to SWATT team execution | | | |
| 6. Management involvement in initial significant opportunity meeting to ensure skills are applied | | | |
| | 6. On-the-job observations | 5. Sheet logs | |
| | | 6. Supervisors | |
| **4 BUSINESS IMPACT** | | | |
| • Achieve membership and voucher revenue goals for 2006 | -Profit/revenue results from accounting | -Business performance monitoring | -Profit and loss statement |
| • Two new vertical penetrations | -Participant questionnaire | -CRM | -Participants |
| • Increased member engagement: | -Number of verticals based on opportunities logged in CRM | -IMIS | -Participants |
|   • Sponsorships | -Increased number of logged activities on customer report card | | -6 months post-program |
|   • Downloads | | | -6 months post-program |
|   • Committee participation | | | -6 months post-program |
|   • Certification success stories | | | Program coordinator |
| **5 ROI** | | | |
| Target ROI | Baseline Data: | | |
| | Comments: | | |

data for Level 4 were gathered from several reliable sources, including the profit and revenue results from finance and activities logged by participants in the new customer relationship management system. To quantify the revenue impact of the program and to isolate its effects, a questionnaire was distributed to participants of the training. This was determined to be a credible source of program impact. Overall response of the questionnaire exceeded expectations with 80 percent completion. With participant results being reported for a nine-month period, results were extrapolated to twelve months, following Guiding Principle 9 in the ROI Methodology. Participants were asked to provide a level of confidence for all estimates, which was used to adjust net business impact improvements to ensure the most conservative reporting of data. When converting the data to monetary values for final ROI calculations, no improvement data was factored in from the individuals who did not respond to the questionnaire. Program costs, with regard to employee time spent in the class, were converted to a fully loaded hourly rate, as illustrated in the cost estimation table (Table 9.2).

**Data Collection Instruments**

A class survey (shown in Figure 9.1) was used for data collection at Level 1 (Reaction/Satisfaction). This form was administered and complied by Miller Heiman® and used both by CompTIA to determine employee satisfaction and by the training provider to determine effectiveness of their delivery and identify any opportunities for improvement.

To collect Level 2 (Learning) data, a sales assessment report output was used (shown in Figure 9.2). By the nature of our business, CompTIA promotes test-taking (via certifications) as a method for proving knowledge assimilation. Creating an online assessment was a natural extension designed to identify the effectiveness of this particular learning event and continues to be an available resource for ongoing use in the future as a way to access new employee skills after hire.

**Figure 9.1. Miller Heiman® Class Survey Example for Level 1**

Figure 9.3 shows the participant questionnaire used to collect Level 4 (Business Impact) data. Because a major product change was introduced during this interval yielding erratic monthly revenue results, trend line analysis and forecasting methods were not credible. To isolate the effects of the solution while adjusting for potential error, direct feedback from participants was the preferred, and most credible, method for obtaining business impact results.

210

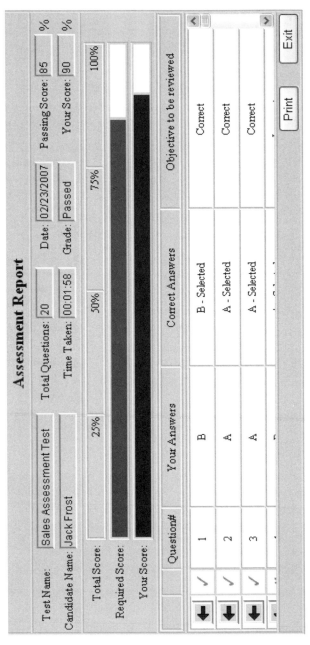

Figure 9.2. Level 2 (Learning) Example of Sales Assessment Report Output

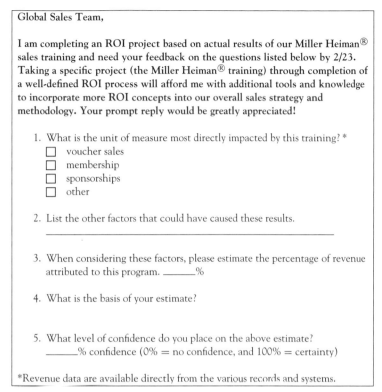

Global Sales Team,

I am completing an ROI project based on actual results of our Miller Heiman®
sales training and need your feedback on the questions listed below by 2/23.
Taking a specific project (the Miller Heiman® training) through completion of
a well-defined ROI process will afford me with additional tools and knowledge
to incorporate more ROI concepts into our overall sales strategy and
methodology. Your prompt reply would be greatly appreciated!

1. What is the unit of measure most directly impacted by this training? *
   ☐ voucher sales
   ☐ membership
   ☐ sponsorships
   ☐ other

2. List the other factors that could have caused these results.
   _____

3. When considering these factors, please estimate the percentage of revenue
   attributed to this program. _____%

4. What is the basis of your estimate?


5. What level of confidence do you place on the above estimate?
   _____% confidence (0% = no confidence, and 100% = certainty)

*Revenue data are available directly from the various records and systems.

**Figure 9.3. Level 4 (Business Impact) Example from Participant Questionnaire**

## ROI Analysis Plan

Though several intangible benefits were realized as a result of the
solution, the executive team's main focus was on profit from the
revenue which were the key data elements to figuring the ROI.
Figure 9.4 shows the detailed ROI Analysis Plan.


# Evaluation Results

Level 1 results yielded an Overall Effectiveness of Instructor rating
of 4.4 out of a 5-point scale. The Overall Effectiveness of Content
rated a 4.83 on the 5-point scale, while the Overall Satisfaction
rated a 4.79. At Level 2, all participants eventually passed the

**Program:** Miller Heiman® Sales Training     **Responsibility:** Lisa Sallstrom

| Data Items (Usually) Level 4 | Methods for Isolating the Effects of the Program/ Process | Methods of Converting Data to Monetary Values | | Cost Categories | Intangible Benefits | Communication Targets for Final Report | Other Influences/ Issues During Application | Comments |
|---|---|---|---|---|---|---|---|---|
| Revenue | - Expert estimates discounted based on % of confidence | - Standard Value for Profit | | - Program fee<br>- Lodging<br>- Participants' loaded salaries<br>- Meals | Increased member satisfaction and involvement in committees, programs, and events | Executive Management<br><br>Sales Team | Major Product Revision on CompTIA A+<br><br>Staff Turnover | |

**Figure 9.4. ROI Analysis Plan**

assessment. There was no restriction on the number of times an individual could take the exam. Level 3 results showed that 100 percent of SWATT opportunities were initiated with a Blue Sheet. Weekly sales pipeline meetings were scheduled throughout the year. Commissions were paid out based on CRM reports, which are also used to direct the weekly pipeline meetings, and management involvement included updated job expectations to ensure process compliance.

At Level 4, membership revenue goals were missed by 4 percent. However, voucher sales goals were exceeded at 140 percent of the budget forecast. Based on new opportunities logged for CRM, accounts in the finance, healthcare, manufacturing, and government sectors were tracked, yielding four new vertical penetrations. Additionally, member engagement increased, while event participation also increased (breakaway, services section). The number of requests for CompTIA involvement at member events increased, as did sponsorship levels. This resulted in positive informal feedback. Based on questionnaire results from participants, the amount of revenue attributed to the program averaged 23 percent (confidence level factored in).

Cost estimations for Level 5 calculation are shown in Table 9.2, and represent a fully loaded profile.

Expert estimates from the questionnaire reported that 23.3 percent of revenue was attributed to the program. Consequently, the increase in revenue attributed to sales skill improvements was $627,300 (discounted based on confidence level), over a nine-month period. When extrapolating for a twelve-month annual return, the total revenue increase was $836,400. Assuming a profit margin of 15 percent yields a profit of $125,460. Revenue must be converted to profit to use in the ROI formula.

Benefit/Cost Ratio (BCR) = Program Benefits/Program Costs

**Table 9.2.  Cost Estimation**

| | |
|---|---|
| 1. Facilities rental incurred as training was delivered on-site | $1,500 ($500 per day, three days) |
| 2. Cost for Miller Heiman® training | $42,000 |
| 3. Three lunches for twenty-one people at $10/head | $630 |
| 4. Three dinners for eleven international staff members at $25/head | $990 |
| 5. No airfare was factored into costs as the training was planned during the annual face-to-face sales meeting | $0 |
| 6. Staff time for two, seven-hour days (one of the three training days was a Sunday) at a loaded rate of $100/hour for twenty-one people | $29,400 |
| 7. Four hotel nights for eleven international staff members at a corporate rate of $130/night | $5,720 |
| 8. Evaluation (time and materials) | $3,000 |
| **TOTAL:** | **$83,240** |

$$BCR = \$125,460/\$83,240 = 1.50$$

$$ROI\% = \frac{\$125,460 - \$83,240}{\$83,240} \times 100 = 50\%$$

The intangible benefits of the program, as identified by participants of the training, included:

- Greater customer engagement with a variety of CompTIA committees and programs through improved relationship management

- Quicker turnaround of purchases

- Identification of more up-sell opportunities with a single client

- It is a good process for building long and sustainable business relationships

## Communication Strategy

An executive summary was prepared and shared with the vice president of international sales and vice president of U.S. sales. They were both pleased to see quantitative results against the program, thereby determining that the implementation risk proved successful in returning positive business impacts. Agreement was reached to expand the program to include a third Miller Heiman® module, Large Account Management Process<sup>SM</sup> (LAMP®), delivered to the same team of sales personnel sixteen months after the initial training program.

## Lessons Learned

Ensuring ongoing application and implementation of learned skills proved to be the most challenging aspect of the project. It was difficult to get a remote, self-directed team of sales staff to consistently follow a process-driven sales model with required written forms. In addition to active management enforcement, and observations, infrastructure was built to track adherence, that is, new job expectations socialized and a new shared drive location created to store documents and ensure compliance.

Furthermore, after the initial training, it was also observed that several other internal departments touched the customer in various "sales" roles. Recognizing that all organizational touch-points must have a consistent customer methodology and terminology, an abbreviated Miller Heiman® offering was delivered to the additional support staff, thereby leveling the understanding of customer

---

LAMP® is a registered trademark of Miller Heiman, Inc.®

*Large Account Management Process*<sup>SM</sup> is a service mark brand of Miller Heiman, Inc.®

management. A cross-organizational sales model was communicated and adopted, including a process for account management ownership with expectations for interacting with customers on multiple CompTIA engagement opportunities.

## Questions for Discussion

1. How credible is the ROI value?

2. What would you have done differently to improve the application of the training program?

3. Why is it important to plan the ROI study before the program is implemented?

4. Would you have converted any of the intangible benefits noted in this study to monetary values? Please explain.

5. Why is it important to engage others outside of the targeted department in this program rollout, and how could that impact the overall success of program implementation?

## About the Author

**Lisa Sallstrom** is an IT industry executive with more than twenty years of for-profit and nonprofit corporate experience in program, product, and project management, customer service, and sales. Her current position at CompTIA focuses on business development through demonstration of value. Ms. Sallstrom holds two bachelor's degrees (in computer science and music performance), a master's degree in computer science, and a professional project management certification in CompTIA Project+. She can be reached at LSallstrom@comptia.org

# 10

# Measuring ROI in RxSource:
# An Electronic Documentation Tool
## A Pharmacy Benefit Management Company

## Nathan Faylor, Isabelle Maisse, and Kristen Neal

## Abstract

Within CVS Caremark Pharmacy Operations, one of the important tasks was to determine how to best deliver content and information to employees. During an initial assessment it was noted that pharmacy employees primarily used paper manuals and reference materials. Additionally, most communication of process changes within the pharmacies was distributed by way of paper memos that each employee would then store with paper manuals in three-ring binders. The creation of an electronic repository and communication system held promise to increase speed and accuracy of information dissemination. It also promised to provide a more reliable means of ensuring employees were referencing current and relevant information. This study provides the results of this project with six types of data.

## Background

CVS Caremark, one of the nation's leading pharmacy benefit management companies, provides comprehensive prescription benefit

---

Note: This case was prepared to serve as a basis for discussion rather than an illustration of either effective or ineffective administrative and management practices.

217

management services to more than two thousand health plans, including corporations, managed care organizations, insurance companies, unions, and government entities. CVS Caremark operates a national retail pharmacy network with more than 60,000 participating pharmacies, as well as eleven mail service pharmacies.

The Operations Training Department collaborated with the IT e-Business team and an outside vendor to design and create an online document repository and communication tool to provide relevant, accurate, consistent, and timely information to all Pharmacy Operations employees. The application, named RxSource, is available from the company intranet. RxSource contains various sections that house announcements, training materials, job aids, and reference documents. Each time a document is updated, it replaces the previous version so employees are only accessing the latest information. Employees are able to search across or within the various sections by using keywords. This allows them to locate needed information more efficiently than manually paging through notebooks of previous memos and manuals.

Additional functionality was created to track acknowledgement of particularly important or urgent materials. Each employee must log in to the system. Supervisors and managers are able to run reports to confirm that their employees have seen information related to specific changes or updates. The login also allows an employee to control what content they have presented to them during site navigation and searching. An employee can change his or her personal settings to filter RxSource content by site and by department. They can also subscribe to frequently used content in order to be notified of recently updated documents that are directly related to their work.

Once the RxSource repository was built, the Training Department began the task of collecting and loading materials in preparation for implementation of the tool. Each location contributed content through their trainers. Once a sufficient amount of content was loaded, trainers began holding workshops to teach employees how to use RxSource. It was implemented in seven pharmacies. Each location adapted to the new system at varying rates. Some locations adjusted to the change quickly and began contributing documents on their own. Other locations took longer to adapt to the electronic format, having preferred the manual forms of paper distribution.

## Case Study Overview

The study, described in the following pages, attempted to measure the return on investment for the RxSource project. This case study contains several sections. The first section describes the methodology used to examine the project. Next, this report provides a summary of the data collected and analyzed. Barriers are then presented that affected both the rollout of RxSource as well as the completion of this ROI study. The case study then describes any additional benefits realized as a result of the RxSource implementation. Based on this information and other data collected, an ROI was calculated following accepted guidelines and conventions of the Phillips ROI Methodology. This study concludes with a discussion and interpretation of these results and findings.

## Summary of Findings

Overall, the benefits reported and the ROI calculated for the RxSource implementation were positive. The study was designed to assess the value of RxSource from several perspectives. First, surveys were designed to provide insight to employee information search practices. Questions were also included in the surveys to inquire of employees and their managers about perceived productivity improvements. Second, business data were collected in an attempt to determine whether overall metrics of productivity and quality were affected. Last, analysis of document printing activity was conducted to determine financial benefits resulting from online availability of documentation. Based on these data, a twelve-month ROI of 1,196 percent was calculated for the project after considering all costs and benefits associated with the project.

Several intangible (non-monetary) benefits were also identified during the study and are discussed within this case study. RxSource created access and visibility to process documentation across sites. Cross-site visibility allowed for the identification of specific documented variances in processes across the seven mail order facilities. This resulted in heightened awareness that led to the need for standardization and prompted a restructuring and refinement of the SOP Steering Committee process. The combination of RxSource and the SOP committee structure has provided resources needed to more fully pursue standard processes and virtual pharmacy capabilities. RxSource has also provided a means of reducing version control issues. Prior to RxSource, employees were responsible to ensure they were referencing the latest version of any document. RxSource has significantly reduced the risk of outdated documents by only presenting the most current document online. Now, employees are certain they are viewing the most current approved document when they use RxSource.

## Evaluation Methodology

This section describes the approach used to conduct this study. It includes descriptions of the methods used, data sources, and instruments employed for data collection. This return on investment study for RxSource was conducted using the Phillips ROI process model (see Figure 10.1). The steps used included collecting data before and after RxSource was implemented, analyzing the data, isolating the effects of RxSource on any data trends, converting the data to monetary value, calculating the ROI, and identifying the intangible benefits of RxSource.

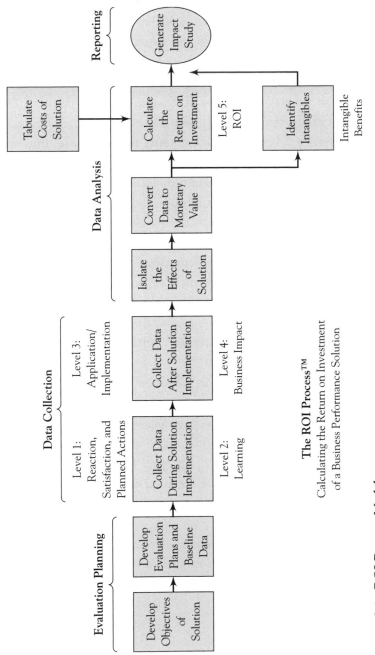

**Figure 10.1. ROI Process Model**

*Source:* ROI Institute, Inc.

## Data Collection Methods

The data collection targeted five levels of evaluation and their objectives. Each is described here and summarized in Table 10.1, which represents the data collection plan.

**Level 1 (Reaction/Satisfaction) and Level 2 (Learning)** were measured via a survey given to RxSource users at the end of their initial training class before using the tool in their respective work settings. Level 1 measurements included intention to use RxSource, relevance to job function, and importance to job success. The Level 2 measurement included the ability to use RxSource in finding necessary information to perform their main job function. The users were asked to rate their own ability to use RxSource.

**Level 3 (Application/Implementation)** was measured via a questionnaire given to RxSource users approximately six months after they began using the tool and via the RxSource hit counter. The hit counter was measured every thirty days for six months. The data reflected the frequency with which employees used RxSource to find information.

**Level 4 (Business Impact)** was measured using business reports and user estimates. Measurements focused on productivity (e.g., prescription entry and prescription verification rate), quality (e.g., internal errors and external complaints), and cost of materials. Production and quality rates were reported for departments most affected by RxSource. Surveys were used to estimate improvements to production and quality specifically attributable to the implementation of RxSource.

**Level 5 (Return on Investment)** can be calculated by converting business metrics and results from prior levels of evaluation into monetary values, then compare the monetary benefits to the cost of the project.

**Table 10.1. Data Collection Plan**

| Level | Objective(s) | Measures/Data | Data Collection Method | Data Sources | Timing |
|---|---|---|---|---|---|
| 1 | Reaction/Satisfaction<br>• Intention to use<br>• Relevance<br>• Importance to success | 4 on a 5-point rating scale | Survey | Participants | End of class |
| 2 | Learning<br>• Ability to use tool to find needed information | 4 on a 5-point rating scale | Self-assessment of ability to perform key functions | Participants | End of class |
| 3 | Application/Implementation<br>• Employees regularly use tool to find information | Frequency of use as reported by employees<br>Regularity of Use (Hit counter) | Questionnaire<br>RxSource reports | Participants<br>Ops Training | Six months<br>Every thirty days for six months |
| 4 | Business Impact<br>• Productivity<br>• Quality<br>• Materials cost | Quality Rates; Production rates<br>Estimates of improvements attributable to RxSource<br>Changes in info searches<br>Documents loaded to RxSource | Company reports<br>Survey<br>Questionnaire<br>Reports | Quality; Managers<br>Supervisors<br>Participants<br>Ops Training | Every thirty days for six months<br>Six months<br>Zero and six months<br>Six months |
| 5 | ROI | Calculation based on monetary values of costs and benefits identified through methods above. | | | |

## Survey Participants and Locations

Participant surveys were distributed to all technicians and pharmacists using the front-end prescription processing application and RxSource. They were distributed immediately after each workshop and six months after implementation at the users' facilities. Leader surveys were distributed to all front-end managers and supervisors who oversee RxSource users. The surveys were distributed in all seven mail order facilities.

## Instruments for Data Collection

Participant and leader surveys were used for most of the data collection. Questions on each survey were selected to obtain specific types of information for purposes of this study as listed below.

### *Pre-RxSource Participant Survey (see Exhibit 10.1)*

- Demographic Information: role, department, hours in a work week and tenure

- Resource Information: method of research, frequency of the need to research, and length of time it takes to find the necessary information

### *RxSource Participant Follow-Up Survey (see Exhibit 10.2)*

- Demographic Information: role, department, hours in a work week, and tenure

- Resource Information: method of research, frequency of the need to research, length of time it takes to find the necessary information, and length of time using RxSource

- Learning Effectiveness: success of the training

- Job Impact: successful use of RxSource and importance of RxSource to the job

- Barriers and Enablers: reasons for using or not using RxSource

- Business Results: improvement in job performance related to RxSource

- Return on Investment: value of RxSource to the company

- Feedback: open-ended questions requesting pros and cons of RxSource.

*RxSource Leader Survey (see Exhibit 10.3)*

- Demographic Information: role, department, and tenure

- Job Impact: change in the amount of time spent answering procedural questions for employees as a result of the employees using RxSource

- Business Results: improvement in employees' job performance related to RxSource

- Return on Investment: value of RxSource to the company

- Feedback: open-ended questions requesting pros and cons of RxSource

## Data Analysis

This section discusses the data obtained for this ROI study as described in our Data Collection Plan (see Table 10.1) and methods for isolating data results. This section will then describe each level of evaluation and report associated findings. The last portions

---

---

**CAREMARK**
*It all starts with care*                                    RxSource Survey

---

Thank you for taking a moment to complete this survey. Your responses will help us to measure the impact of the new RxSource tool. Please provide candid and honest answers to the items below. Your responses will remain anonymous.

**DEMOGRAPHIC INFORMATION**

1. Survey date        _____

2. Location:
   □ PHX      □ BHM      □ MAR
   □ SAT      □ WBP      □ MTP
   □ AFW

3. What is your role?
   □ Pharmacist          □ Representative
   □ Technician          □ Mgr/Supervisor
   □ Clerk               □ Team Lead
   □ Other
   If *other* please specify:
   _____

4. What is your primary department?
   □ Translation         □ Rx Entry
   □ PTV                 □ Rx Review
   □ DPC                 □ MD Calls
   □ Interventions       □ Patient Services
   □ PRU                 □ Ask A
   □ Changeback             Pharmacist
   □ Clinical            □ Clinical
     Counseling            Consulting
   □ NewRx               □ Filling
   □ Dispensing          □ Materials
   □ Shipping
   If *other* please specify:
   _____

5. On average, how many hours a week do you work? _____

6. How long have you been in your current position?
   □ 0-6 months          □ 1-4 years
   □ 7-12 months         □ 5+ years

**RESOURCE INFORMATION**

7. When looking up information to help do your job (i.e. Translation/Dispensing Guidelines, CCM manual, memos, etc) do you use:
   □ an electronic      □ a written
     document on            document
     the network       □ both

8. On average, how many times a day do you reference or look up Caremark procedural information (i.e. Translation/Dispensing Guidelines, CCM manual, memos, etc)

9. On average, how long does it take you to locate the information you seek? Please provide your response in minutes or seconds.
   _____ minutes      or      _____ seconds

10. On average, how many times a day do you reference or look up non-Caremark procedural information (i.e. ICD-9, MPR, Facts & Comparison, etc)?

11. On average, how long does it take you to locate the information you seek? Please provide your response in minutes or seconds.
    _____ minutes      or      _____ seconds

12. On average, how many times a week are you unable to locate needed information?

---

*Thank you for completing this questionnaire.*
*If this questionnaire is being completed during a class, please hand it to the trainer before leaving.*
*If this questionnaire is being completed outside of class, please leave it on a trainer's desk*
*or send via interoffice mail to Nathan Faylor (Mail Code: SAT).*

Operations Training

**Exhibit 10.1. Pre-RxSource User Survey**

Y

## RxSource Follow Up Survey

Thank you for taking a moment to complete this survey. Your responses will help us to measure the benefits of the new RxSource tool. Please provide candid and honest answers to the items below. Your responses will remain anonymous.

### Demographic Information

1. Survey date _____

2. Location:
   - ❑ PHX     ❑ BHM     ❑ MAR
   - ❑ SAT     ❑ WBP     ❑ MTP
   - ❑ AFW

3. What is your role?
   - ❑ Pharmacist          ❑ Representative
   - ❑ Technician          ❑ Mgr/Supervisor
   - ❑ Clerk               ❑ Team Lead
   - ❑ Other
   - If *other* please specify: _____

4. What is your primary department?
   - ❑ Translation         ❑ Rx Entry
   - ❑ PTV                 ❑ Rx Review
   - ❑ DPC                 ❑ MD Calls
   - ❑ Interventions       ❑ Patient Services
   - ❑ PRU                 ❑ Ask A Pharmacist
   - ❑ Changeback          ❑ Clinical Consulting
   - ❑ Clinical Counseling ❑ Filling
   - ❑ NewRx               ❑ Materials
   - ❑ Dispensing
   - ❑ Shipping
   - If *other* please specify: _____

5. On average, how many hours a week do you work?
   _____

6. How long have you been in your current position?
   - ❑ 0-6 months          ❑ 1-4 years
   - ❑ 7-12 months         ❑ 5+ years

### Resource Information

7. When looking up information to help do your job (i.e. Translation/Dispensing Guidelines, CCM manual, memos, etc) do you use:
   - ❑ an electronic       ❑ a written document
     document on the       ❑ both
     network

8. On average, how many times a day do you reference or look up non-Caremark procedural information (i.e. ICD-9, MPR, Facts & Comparison, etc)?
   _____

9. On average, how long does it take you to locate the information you seek? Please provide your response in minutes or seconds.
   _____ minutes  *or*  _____ seconds

10. How long have you been using RxSource?
    - ❑ Less than1 month    ❑ 4 months
    - ❑ 1 month             ❑ 5 months
    - ❑ 2 months            ❑ 6 months
    - ❑ 3 months            ❑ More than 6 months

11. On average, how many times a day do you reference or look up Caremark procedural information (i.e. Translation/Dispensing Guidelines, CCM manual, memos, etc) **in RxSource**?
    _____

12. On average, how long does it take you to locate the information you seek **in RxSource**? Please provide your response in minutes or seconds.
    _____ minutes  *or*  _____ seconds

13. On average, how many times a week are you unable to locate needed information **in RxSource**?
    _____

**Exhibit 10.2.  Follow-Up Survey**

of this section will discuss monetary costs and benefits along with any intangible benefits experienced, as well as any barriers encountered in measuring the ROI of the RxSource project. Table 10.2 reports the intended methods of analyzing data collected for this project.

**Learning Effectiveness**

Strongly Agree  StronglyDisagree
7  6  5  4  3  2  1  n/a
○ ○ ○ ○ ○ ○ ○ ○

14.  The RxSource training
adequately prepared me to use
the tool.

**Job Impact**

Strongly Agree  Strongly Disagree
7  6  5  4  3  2  1  n/a
○ ○ ○ ○ ○ ○ ○ ○

15.  I have been able to successfully
use RxSource to perform my job.

16.  On a scale of 1 (not at all) to 7    Not at All        Extremely Critical
(extremely critical), how critical is    7  6  5  4  3  2  1  n/a
using RxSource to your job              ○ ○ ○ ○ ○ ○ ○ ○
success.

17.  I was able to use RxSource within:
○ 1 week
○ 2-4 weeks
○ 5-6 weeks
○ I have not used RxSource yet, but I plan to in the future
○ I do not expect to use RxSource

**Barriers and Enablers**

18.  If you have NOT been able to use RxSource, why not? (check
all that apply)
□   RxSource is not useful/practical
□   prevented or discouraged from using
□   no opportunity to use RxSource
□   have not needed to use RxSource
□   not comfortable using RxSource
□   other higher priorities
□   other (please specify) _____
19.  Which of the following enables you to use RxSource? (check all
that apply)
□   have opportunity to use RxSource
□   receive management support
□   have support from colleagues and peers
□   have sufficient knowledge and understanding of RxSource
□   RxSource is useful/practical
□   am comfortable using RxSource
□   other (please specify) _____

**Business Results**

Strongly Agree  Strongly Disagree
7  6  5  4  3  2  1  n/a
○ ○ ○ ○ ○ ○ ○ ○

20.  RxSource has improved my job
performance.

21.  Given all factors,including RxSource, estimate how much your
job performance has improved since you began using
RxSource.
□ 0%  □ 10%  □ 20% □ 30%  □ 40%  □ 50% □ 60% □ 70%
□ 80%  □ 90% □ 100%
22.  Basedon your response to the question 21, estimate how
much of the improvement was a direct result of RxSource.For
example if you feel that half of your improvement was a direct
result of RxSource, mark 50% here.
□ 0%  □ 10%  □ 20% □ 30%  □ 40%  □ 50% □ 60% □ 70%
□ 80% □ 90% □ 100%
23.  RxSource had a significant impact on: (check all that apply)
□ increasing quality  □  increasing productivity
□ increasing employee satisfaction
□ decreasing costs   □  increasing customer satisfaction
□ decreasing turn around time   □   increasing issue resolution

**Return onInvestment**

Strongly Agree  StronglyDisagree
7  6  5  4  3  2  1  n/a
○ ○ ○ ○ ○ ○ ○ ○

24.  RxSource is a worthwhile
investment for my job function.

Strongly Agree  Strongly Disagree
7  6  5  4  3  2  1  n/a
○ ○ ○ ○ ○ ○ ○ ○

25.  RxSource is a worthwhile
investment for Caremark.

**Feedback**

26.  What information do you most commonly look for in RxSource?
_____
_____
_____

27.  What features of RxSource do you find mostuseful?
_____
_____
_____

28.  How can we improve RxSource to make it more relevant to your
job?
_____
_____
_____

**Thank you for completing our survey.**

Please give this completed survey to a trainer or send it via interoffice mail to Nathan Faylor (Mail Code: SAT).

**Exhibit 10.2.  (Continued)**

## Isolating the Effects

There were several competing factors that could have influenced any changes to business metrics during the period RxSource was implemented. Those factors included:

- Upgrades to the current pharmacy prescription processing system occurring on a bi-monthly basis

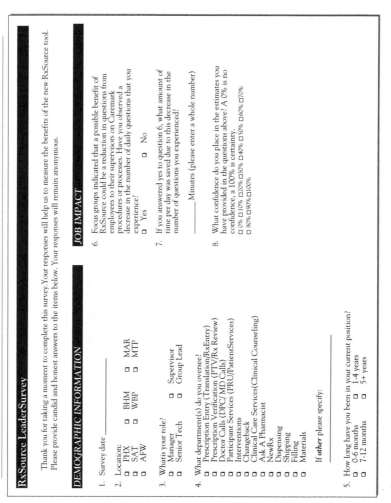

## RxSource LeaderSurvey

Thank you for taking a moment to complete this survey. Your responses will help us to measure the benefits of the new RxSource tool. Please provide candid and honest answers to the items below. Your responses will remain anonymous.

### DEMOGRAPHIC INFORMATION

1. Survey date _____

2. Location:
   - □ PHX      □ BHM      □ MAR
   - □ SAT      □ WBP      □ MTP
   - □ AFW

3. Whatis your role?
   - □ Manager        □ Supervisor
   - □ Senior Tech    □ Group Lead

4. What department(s) do you oversee?
   - □ Prescription Entry (Translation/RxEntry)
   - □ Prescription Verification (PTV/Rx Review)
   - □ Doctor Calls (DPC/ MD Calls)
   - □ Participant Services (PRU/PatientServices)
   - □ Interventions
   - □ Changeback
   - □ Clinical Care Services(Clinical Counseling)
   - □ Ask A Pharmacist
   - □ NewRx
   - □ Dispensing
   - □ Shipping
   - □ Filling
   - □ Materials

   If *other* please specify:

5. How long have you been in your current position?
   - □ 0-6 months     □ 1-4 years
   - □ 7-12 months    □ 5+ years

### JOB IMPACT

6. Focus groups indicated that a possible benefit of RxSource could be a reduction in questions from employees to their supervisors on Caremark procedures or processes. Have you observed a decrease in the number of daily questions that you experience?
   - □ Yes      □ No

7. If you answered yes to question 6, what amount of time per day was saved due to this decrease in the number of questions you experienced?

   _____ Minutes (please enter a whole number)

8. What confidence do you place in the estimates you have provided in the questions above? A 0% is no confidence, a 100% is certainty.
   - □ 0% □10% □20% □30% □40% □50% □60% □70%
   - □ 80% □90% □100%

## Exhibit 10.3. Leader Survey

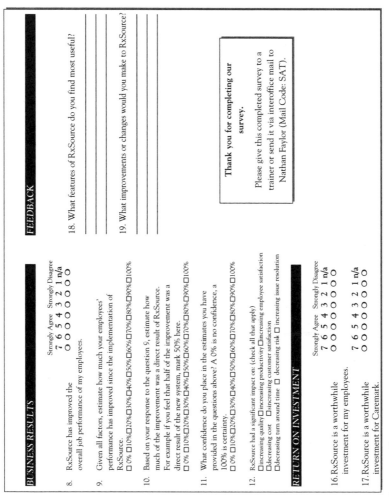

**BUSINESS RESULTS**

Strongly Agree    Strongly Disagree
7 6 5 4 3 2 1 n/a
○ ○ ○ ○ ○ ○ ○ ○

8. RxSource has improved the overall job performance of my employees.

9. Given all factors, estimate how much your employees' performance has improved since the implementation of RxSource.
☐ 0% ☐10%☐20%☐30%☐40%☐50%☐60%☐70%☐80%☐90%☐100%

10. Based on your response to the question 9, estimate how much of the improvement was a direct result of RxSource. For example if you feel that half of the improvement was a direct result of the new system, mark 50% here.
☐ 0% ☐10%☐20%☐30%☐40%☐50%☐60%☐70%☐80%☐90%☐100%

11. What confidence do you place in the estimates you have provided in the questions above? A 0% is no confidence, a 100% is certainty.
☐ 0% ☐10%☐20%☐30%☐40%☐50%☐60%☐70%☐80%☐90%☐100%

12. RxSource had a significant impact on: (check all that apply)
☐increasing quality ☐increasing productivity ☐increasing employee satisfaction
☐decreasing cost ☐increasing customer satisfaction
☐decreasing turn around time ☐ decreasing risk ☐ increasing issue resolution

**RETURN ON INVESTMENT**

Strongly Agree    Strongly Disagree
7 6 5 4 3 2 1 n/a
○ ○ ○ ○ ○ ○ ○ ○

16. RxSource is a worthwhile investment for my employees.

Strongly Agree    Strongly Disagree
7 6 5 4 3 2 1 n/a
○ ○ ○ ○ ○ ○ ○ ○

17. RxSource is a worthwhile investment for Caremark.

**FEEDBACK**

18. What features of RxSource do you find most useful?

19. What improvements or changes would you make to RxSource?

**Thank you for completing our survey.**

Please give this completed survey to a trainer or send it via interoffice mail to Nathan Faylor (Mail Code: SAT).

Exhibit 10.3. (*Continued*)

**Table 10.2. Data Analysis Plan**

| Data Items (Usually Level 4) | Methods for Isolating the Effects of the Program/Process | Methods of Converting Data to Monetary Values | Cost Categories | Intangible Benefits | Communication Targets for Final Report | Other Influences/ Issues During Application |
|---|---|---|---|---|---|---|
| **Productivity** | Trend line/ Participant's and supervisor's estimate | Standard Measures | Tool development/ Training development/Training delivery | Improved communication/Employee satisfaction/ Improved convenience for users | Report/ Presentation to Executive sponsors (GMs)/Summary to directors and managers | Other productivity improvements due to: code pushes/ system enhancements; new procedures; changes in current procedures |
| **Quality** | Trend line/ Participant's and supervisor's estimate | Standard Measures | | | | |
| **Materials Costs** | Estimated number of printed copies had RxSource documents been printed/Number of new hire employees who would have needed printed manuals | Cost of document printing (includes materials and labor costs) | | | | |

- System, process, and cultural changes were being made on an ongoing basis to support the merger of Caremark and AdvancePCS

- Employee turnover and ramp-up associated with new business and the company integration

- Seasonal related changes in the mail order prescription business associated to the addition of several new clients in the first and third quarters of every year

- General changes to process and procedures to support pharmacy priorities and customer needs

A few strategies were used in order to determine the amount of performance improvement directly related to the implementation and use of the RxSource tool. The following were used for this particular study.

**Trend lines:** Prescription entry and verification rates pre- and post-implementation were collected to determine if a trend could be identified.

**Participants' estimate:** Four hundred fifty-four pre-assessment surveys and 201 follow-up surveys were collected. Surveys asked employees to estimate the amount of improvement that they had experienced since the implementation of RxSource. Surveys also asked employees to estimate the amount of that improvement that was directly associated with their use of RxSource.

**Supervisors' estimate of employee improvement:** We collected eleven surveys from the supervisors to determine their estimate of percent improvement of their direct reports following the implementation of RxSource.

**Estimates of materials cost savings:** RxSource had a direct impact on materials cost avoidance. These costs were based on historical pricing of outsourced document printing.

## Evaluation Results

### Respondent Demographics

Table 10.3 displays the response rate on the pre-assessment and follow-up surveys. The response rate on the follow-up surveys was significantly less than that of the pre-assessment. The response rate also differed between pre-assessment and follow-up surveys within the mail order facilities. All survey results reported throughout the remainder of this document are based on the total number of returned surveys and will not be separated by mail order facility.

### Level 1 (Reaction)

Table 10.4 reports employee responses to survey questions related to their initial reaction to RxSource and the associated training delivered during its implementation.

### Level 2 (Learning)

Table 10.5 reports employee responses to survey questions related to their perceptions of learning achieved as a result of the training delivered during the RxSource implementation.

Table 10.3.    Response by Site and Survey

|  | F | G | A | B | C | D | E | Total |
|---|---|---|---|---|---|---|---|---|
| Participant Pre-Assessment | 2 | 27 | 88 | 151 | 158 | 13 | 0 | **439** |
| Participant Follow-Up | 17 |  | 3 |  | 63 | 109 | 17 | **209** |
| Supervisor Follow-Up |  | 1 |  | 1 | 2 | 6 | 1 | **11** |

Table 10.4.    Level 1 Results

|  | Facilitator | Courseware | Environment |
|---|---|---|---|
| Average (10 pt. scale) | 9.20 | 9.07 | 8.80 |
| % Satisfied/Very Satisfied | 88.50% | 87.12% | 82.00% |

**Table 10.5.    Level 2 Results**

|  | Learning Effectiveness |
|---|---|
| Average | 9.01 |
| % who perceive they experienced significant knowledge and skills gains | 87.23% |

### Level 3 (Application/Implementation)

Application and implementation was measured from two perspectives. Implementation was measured by researching employee use of the RxSource intranet site. Application consisted of measures reported through the employee and supervisor surveys, which were reflective of employee job improvement or change.

*Employee Usage*

The implementation of RxSource began in April and finished in December of year 1. Figures 10.2 and 10.3 report the growing use and traffic experienced on the RxSource site since its implementation. During the last six months of data (excluding May, which experienced a data reporting system error), an average of

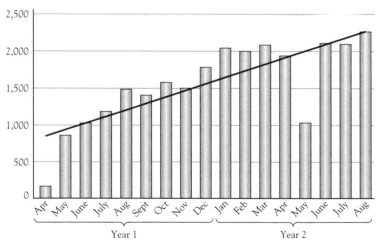

**Figure 10.2. Unique Visitors to RxSource**

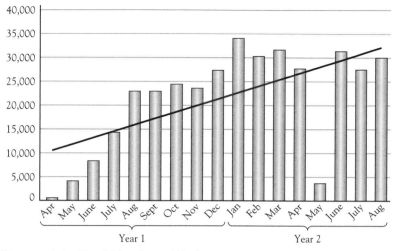

**Figure 10.3. Total Number of RxSource Visits**

2,070 employees used RxSource each month. During the same period, those employees accounted for an average 29,460 visits to RxSource per month.

*Employee Job Improvement*

Using accepted principles of estimation, isolation, and error adjustment, data collected from 208 employee follow-up surveys were used to calculate approximate improvement gained from employee use of RxSource. Table 10.6 reports the line-item averages and overall results for employee job improvement. Results indicate perceived job improvement of 3 percent.

Supervisors were also surveyed after employees had adequate time to use the new RxSource system. Eleven out of a possible seventy-eight supervisors responded to the survey. Although the response rate is not enough to be statistically meaningful at the .05 level of significance, their estimates of employee improvement are in general agreement with employee estimates. As compared to employee estimates of 3 percent improvement, supervisors estimated an improvement of 4.6 percent. Table 10.7 reports the

**Table 10.6.  Employee Perceptions of Job Improvement (n = 208)**

|  | Average Response |
|---|---|
| Total percent improvement in performance since RxSource was implemented | 22.4% |
| RxSource's contribution to improved performance | 20.6% |
| Percent improvement due to RxSource (20.6% of 22.4%) | 4.61% |
| Adjustment factor for confidence in estimations | 65.0% |
| Adjusted percent improvement due to RxSource (65% of 4.61%) | **3.00%** |

**Table 10.7.  Supervisor Perceptions of Job Improvement (n = 11)**

|  | Average Response |
|---|---|
| Total percent improvement in performance since RxSource was implemented | 34.0% |
| RxSource's contribution to improved performance | 21.0% |
| Percent improvement due to RxSource (21.0% of 34.0%) | 7.14% |
| Adjustment factor for confidence in estimations | 65.0% |
| Adjusted percent improvement due to RxSource (65% of 7.14%) | **4.6%** |

line-item averages and overall results for job improvement as estimated by the supervisors.

Data was also collected before and after implementation to assess any changes in the amount of time that employees spend searching for information. Previous to using RxSource, employees searched binders of printed memos for procedural updates and clarification. One of the key factors in justifying the creation of

RxSource was the potential for electronic searches and overall reduced search times. Table 10.8 displays reported differences.

RxSource was intended to decrease the amount of time spent searching for information. The data results in Table 10.8 indicate that there was an overall increase to search times. While this finding is troublesome, there are some additional considerations that may explain the result.

As noted at the beginning of this section, the response rate for the follow-up survey was far less than the response rate of the initial pre-assessment (see Table 10.3). Additionally, the distribution across respondent locations varied greatly between the two surveys. It is therefore likely that different samples of employees filled out the follow-up survey than those who initially completed the pre-assessment. If true, this variance would greatly reduce the validity of this comparison.

Time spent looking up non-Caremark information was outside the scope of the RxSource project. The measurement was included in both surveys as a control item by which to validate other items within the survey. Because RxSource did not include any features or functionality to address non-Caremark information,

**Table 10.8.  Comparison of Reported Search Times in Employee Pre-Assessment and Follow-Up Surveys**

| Survey Question | Pre-Assessment | Follow-Up Survey | Difference |
|---|---|---|---|
| Time spent looking up non-Caremark information **per day** | 9.14 min | 12.90 min | +41.14% (3.76 minutes) |
| Time spent looking up Caremark procedural information **per day** | 13.73 min | 19.49 min | +41.95% (5.76 minutes) |
| Number of times **per week** unable to locate needed information | 2.10 | 3.27 | +1.17 |

nothing should have changed. There was, however, a 41.14 percent increase in the times provided by employees. This may give further support to the discussion of survey respondents above. Interestingly, time spent searching Caremark-specific materials increased an almost identical rate of 41.95 percent. If the non-Caremark search time item is a valid control measurement then this may indicate that there was negligible change (positive or negative) to actual search times.

Last, the data may not accurately reflect decreases in searching efficiency alone. During the months following the implementation, it was observed that employees were having some difficulty using the complete search features of RxSource. Using only singular search terms returned large numbers of results. Where before each employee had a customized method for flagging and searching paper documents, they now needed to learn how to search the system using combinations of filters and specific terms to narrow search results. Some employees learned this quickly, since it is patterned after common Internet search engines. Others struggled for a prolonged period to adapt to the searching capabilities. Additionally, RxSource was implemented at the beginning of a period of significant change and standardization. As documents from various locations were loaded, opportunities arose for consolidation and revision. As such, items within RxSource were constantly changing, which may have created some difficulty for employees to find what they were looking for.

In addition to the job performance change calculation reported above, surveys also collected information regarding which factors enabled or prevented employees to successfully use RxSource. Tables 10.9 and 10.10 report data collected to those enablers and barriers.

### Level 4 (Business Impact)

In addition to knowing how a project affected individual employee performance (Level 3), it is also important to assess how the project

**Table 10.9.  Enablers to Using RxSource**

Survey Question: Which of the following enables you to use RxSource?
(Check all that apply.)

| Item | % Selected |
|------|------------|
| Have opportunity to use RxSource | 47% |
| Receive management support | 21% |
| Have support from colleagues and peers | 23% |
| Have sufficient knowledge and understanding of RxSource | 35% |
| RxSource is useful/practical | 36% |
| Am comfortable using RxSource | 34% |

**Table 10.10.  Barriers to Using RxSource**

Survey Question: If you have NOT been able to use RxSource, why not?
(Check all that apply.)

| Item | % Selected |
|------|------------|
| RxSource is not useful/practical | 14% |
| Prevented or discouraged from using | 6% |
| No opportunity to use RxSource | 5% |
| Have not needed to use RxSource | 6% |
| Not comfortable using RxSource | 8% |
| Other higher priorities | 1% |

affected overall business results. Data collection plans called for collection and analysis of quality and productivity trends, as well as analysis of documents that could be published online rather than through printed means.

**Quality:** Figures 10.4, 10.5, 10.6, and 10.7 depict external complaint and internal error rates, respectively. The first graph in each set provides the data, and the second graph shows the trend line for that data. An arrow denotes the date RxSource was implemented for each specific mail order facility. Data indicate the implementation of RxSource did not change the error trend

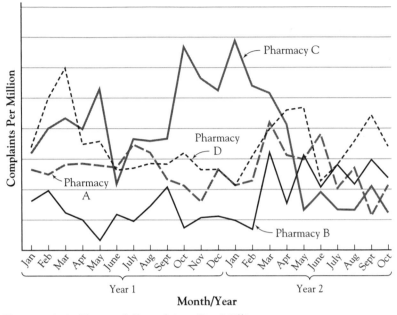

**Figure 10.4. External Complaints Per Million**

(positively or negatively) for any of the four facilities. Those trending upward or downward continued to do so post-RxSource.

**Productivity:** Figures 10.8, 10.9, 10.10, and 10.11 depict prescription entry and prescription verification rates, respectively. The first graph in each set provides the data, and the second graph shows the trend line for that data. An arrow denotes the date RxSource was implemented for each specific mail order facility. Productivity data was only available for three pharmacies in this study. Data indicate the implementation of RxSource did not change the rate trend (positively or negatively) for any of the three facilities. Those trending upward or downward continued to do so post-RxSource.

**Materials Printing Avoidance**—Two main benefits were expected as they relate to materials cost. One of the benefits is the reduction of printed training materials. Prior to RxSource, training manuals ranged from ten to seven hundred pages per class. The other opportunity for avoiding materials printing cost included

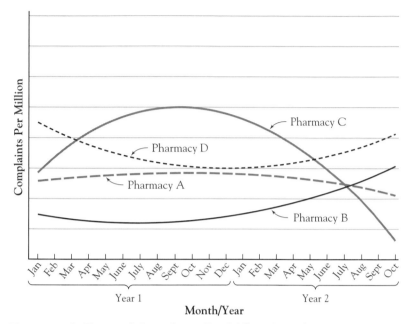

**Figure 10.5. External Complaints Per Million Trend Line**

documents used for communication in business departments (memos, process updates, etc.) that could now be published via RxSource. Costs associated with the reduction in these two activities will be discussed in the Data Conversion section.

The number of employees who would have required printed training manuals and the cost of each manual were used to determine the cost avoidance associated with training information loaded into RxSource. An RxSource report provided the number of informational documents loaded into RxSource that would have been printed for each employee needing the information. The report detailed the work instructions, job aids, reference charts, and announcements loaded into RxSource, the intended audience, and content summary. The number of documents, average page count for each document type, and number of employees that each document would have been distributed to was used to determine the number of document pages that would have been printed

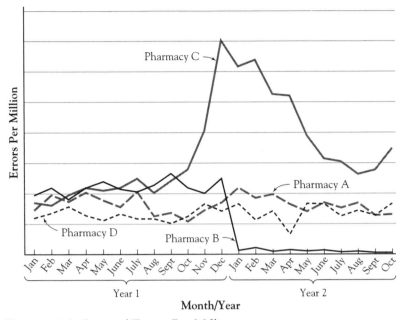

Figure 10.6. Internal Errors Per Million

Table 10.11.   Materials Not Requiring Printing

|  | # Pages |
| --- | --- |
| Training Manuals | 54,023 |
| Work Instructions/Memos | 4,895,397 |

had RxSource not been implemented. Table 10.11 summarizes the number of pages for which printing was not required.

**Other Affected Business Metrics**—Follow-up surveys also asked individuals to indicate key business metrics that RxSource likely affected. These results are indicative of the alignment between the project and key focus areas within the company. Responses reported in Table 10.12 provide insight to how employees perceive the ability of RxSource to affect those measurements and results.

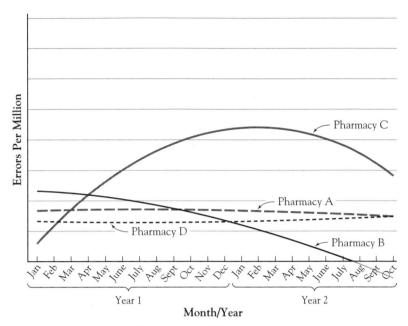

**Figure 10.7. Internal Errors Per Million Trend Line**

**Table 10.12.  Business Alignment**
Survey Question: RxSource had a significant impact on:
(Check all that apply.)

| Item | % Selected |
|---|---|
| Increasing quality | 44% |
| Increasing issue resolution | 29% |
| Increasing productivity | 24% |
| Decreasing turn around time | 18% |
| Increasing employee satisfaction | 11% |
| Increasing customer satisfaction | 10% |
| Decreasing costs | 9% |

## Data Conversion

Table 10.13 presents a summary of the cost to develop the RxSource system. These costs were incurred prior to and during the time of implementation to develop, build, test, and train RxSource.

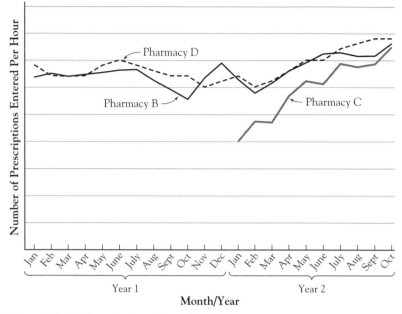

**Figure 10.8.  Prescription Entry Rate**

**Table 10.13.    Project Costs**

|  | Unit/Value | Cost |
|---|---|---|
| **System Development** | | |
| Consultant charges | Invoiced fee for system development | $56,000 |
| Employee time and benefits | 1919.5 hours @ $41.32/hr | $79,314 |
| **Training/Implementation** | | |
| Trainer salaries and benefits (1.25 hr training and preparation) | 50 classes @ $32.52/hr | $2,032 |
| Trainee salary and benefits (1-hr training) | 1012 @ $29.59/hr | $29,945 |
| | Total | $167,291 |

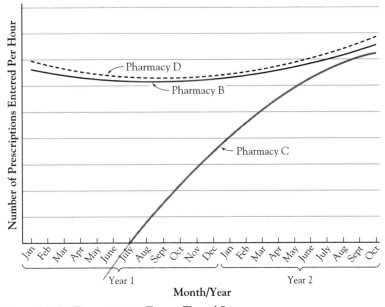

**Figure 10.9. Prescription Entry Trend Line**

The data reported below represent benefits that were realized for one year following the implementation of RxSource (October 1, year 1, to September 30, year 2). Financial benefits included reduction of printing costs for classes where online resources could be used and for business communication that could be distributed electronically. Employee estimates of performance improvement (see Table 10.14) were also calculated for one year. The value of the performance improvement is based on average salary and benefits. The actual measure of productivity and quality improvement converted to money would have provided a more accurate accounting of benefits. Considering concepts of utility analysis, monetary value was based on salary plus benefits and the performance contribution to the job associated with RxSource.

Realizing RxSource would not have completely eliminated printing in mail order pharmacies, the number of pages calculated from the RxSource reports was reduced by 25 percent. The cost per

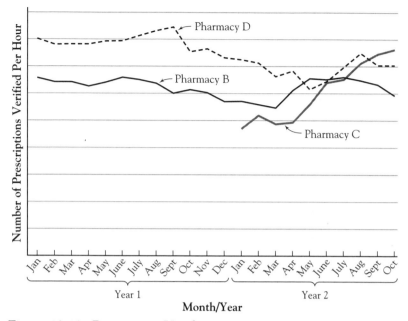

**Figure 10.10. Prescription Verification Rates**

**Table 10.14.  Project Benefits**

|  | Unit/Value | Value |
|---|---|---|
| Materials Printing (cost avoidance) |  |  |
| Training manuals for various classes | 3,538 employees trained (costs include paper and binders) | $6,559 |
| Work instructions/memos published via RxSource | 3,671,548 pages ($0.08/page) | $293,784 |
| Twelve-Month Performance Improvement |  |  |
| Employee Estimate (3.00%) | 1,012 employees trained in RxSource |  |
|  | $61,547 avg/yr (salary + benefits) | $1,868,567 |
| **Total** |  | **$2,168,850** |

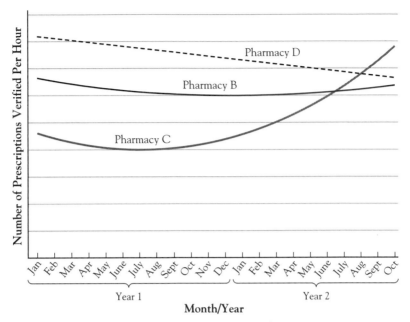

**Figure 10.11. Prescription Verification Trend Line**

page includes the cost of paper, equipment, and clerical time that would have been used to generate the documents.

### Return on Investment Calculation

The Return on Investment (ROI) for this study was calculated using the following formula:

$$ROI = \frac{\text{Net Program Benefits}}{\text{Program Costs}} \times 100$$

Based on the determined costs of $167,291 and benefits of $2,168,850 reported in the previous section, ROI is calculated as follows:

$$ROI = \frac{\$2,168,850 - \$167,291}{\$167,291} = 11.96 \times 100 = 1196\,\%$$

These results were achieved through several data decisions throughout the report:

- Calculations included major costs. These consisted of employee salaries and benefit costs for the time associated with design, implementation, and training of RxSource.

- Employee estimates of performance improvement were reduced by 35 percent to account for self-reported bias (based on research conducted by KnowledgeAdvisors, a leading learning measurement company). Furthermore, performance improvement was only calculated for those employees who were trained as of October 31 in year 1. Their responses were not extrapolated to the full number of employees using RxSource one year later. As such, it is conceivable that the total monetary value of productivity gains could exceed that calculated.

- Though RxSource was designed to eliminate the need to print memos and work instructions, document count totals were reduced by 25 percent. Potential print reduction numbers were lowered to allow that some printing still occurred. A 25 percent reduction in the calculations equates to more than 1.2 million pages (more than $97,000) of additional print elimination that was not included in the benefit calculations.

Given these results, the ROI for the RxSource project was at least 1,196 percent. Some accounting philosophies suggest that performance improvements not be included in ROI calculations because they do not always translate directly to cost savings or revenue increases on financial balance sheets. When the contribution of performance improvement is omitted, the ROI calculation still returns a significantly positive ROI as follows:

$$ROI = \frac{\$300{,}343 - \$167{,}291}{\$167{,}291} = 0.795 \times 100 = 79.5\%$$

## Intangible Results

In addition to the tangible monetary benefits that were achieved, we were able to determine some intangible benefits to the implementation of RxSource. Even though these are benefits that were not converted to monetary values, they nonetheless provide intrinsic value to the company and business units that use RxSource. Each benefit is discussed briefly in the following paragraphs.

**Identification of process variations**—One of the most important intangible results of the RxSource project was the identification of variances in processes across the seven mail-order facilities. Part of the implementation of this tool necessitated the documentation and collection of department and site business processes, work instructions, and standard operations procedures (SOP). Upon review of the documents by the content development team, significant variances were discovered across the seven facilities. This awareness led to the greater urgency for standardization and prompted the restructuring and refinement of the SOP Steering Committee.

**Process standardization**—The identification of process variances across the seven facilities highlighted the need for process analysis and cross-site coordination. As a result, coordination among departments, both internally and across the various facilities, was required to identify or modify business processes. This resulted in increased communication interdepartmentally and increased communication across the seven mail order facilities, both of which should lead to improved efficiency in reaching and maintaining process standardization.

**Risk reduction associated with outdated documents**—With the ability to store and display the most recently updated documents, the use of RxSource by employees avoids the referencing of outdated materials. Manager and employees alike can feel confident they are referencing the most current and accurate information available.

**Training portability**—RxSource has also become a critical training resource for Operations trainers. Since this system is accessible via a link within the intranet, trainers can present work instructions and training documents on shorter notice (duplication or printing of materials is no longer required for every class) and in a variety of locations or training environments. Additionally, trainees can access the same documentation via RxSource any time after the conclusion of training.

**Document portability**—As noted previously, Caremark operates seven mail service pharmacies dispersed across the nation. Having electronic documents available on RxSource has enabled access and visibility to process documentation across sites. As such, management teams are more able to distribute work across multiple locations when needed. Within moments, employees can log in to RxSource and access any document from any site with confidence that they are viewing the most current and accurate information available.

The intangible results and benefits discussed above have provided significant value to the users of RxSource. These benefits have also been observed by other mail order departments outside the original project scope who have also wanted to implement RxSource for their areas. Additionally, areas outside the mail order facilities have also wanted to take advantage of the tool to use as an efficient document repository and a training tool.

## Discussion

This study has examined the activities, costs, and impacts of creating and implementing RxSource in mail order pharmacies at Caremark. The study was designed to assess the value of RxSource from several perspectives. First, surveys were designed to provide insight to employee information search practices. Questions were also designed into the survey methodology to inquire of employees and their managers about perceived productivity improvements. Second, business data was collected in an attempt to determine whether overall metrics of productivity and quality were affected. Last, analysis of document printing activity was conducted to determine financial benefits resulting from online availability of documentation.

Overall, the benefits reported and the ROI calculated for the RxSource implementation were positive. A twelve-month ROI of 1,196 percent was calculated for the project after considering all costs and benefits associated with the project.

Much was learned during this study about the ROI process in general and about conducting ROI studies at Caremark specifically. The remainder of this section attempts to provide additional discussion of the challenges inherent in conducting this study as well as the lessons the authors have learned.

## Barriers

Throughout the study, several barriers were encountered that had to be overcome or adapted. These corrections to the data collection and analysis plans affected the continuity of the study and may limit some of the results. Each of the primary barriers is discussed here.

**Survey sample demographics**—The group of employees who completed the pre-RxSource user survey was not the same group that completed the follow-up survey. The comparison of before and after RxSource survey information was not direct. This was most apparent in two areas. One, pharmacy locations were represented by different response rates within both the pre- and post-surveys (see Table 10.3). Two, there was a significant difference in completion rates for each of the survey groups. For example, the Pre-RxSource user survey had a far higher response rate than the follow-up survey (see Table 10.15).

**Trend lines**—The data collected to identify a change in productivity was inconclusive. The analysis of prescription entry and verification rates collected prior to RxSource show a fair amount of month-to-month variance. The analysis of these same rates after RxSource implementation showed no discernable difference, mostly due to the same variance. The same was true of the quality measures. The data collected to illustrate a change in prescription entry and verification error rates collected prior to and after implementation showed no trend. Therefore, it was not possible to measure an improvement or decline in productivity or quality. As a second method of determining improvement, user post-implementation surveys contained questions asking employees to estimate the percentage of any productivity improvement following the implementation of RxSource. Using principles of isolation and error adjustment, employee estimates indicated that there was a 3 percent productivity improvement for those surveyed.

**Time tracking**—Collecting the time spent by those employees who worked on the implementation of RxSource presented a challenge. All of the employees assigned to the project were asked to log their time spent on RxSource. There was not, however,

**Table 10.15.   Survey Response Rates**

| Survey | |
|---|---|
| Pre-RxSource User Survey | 41% |
| RxSource Follow-Up Survey | 18% |
| RxSource Leader Survey | 15% |

an accepted practice or culture of doing so; neither was there an automated or easy way to track time. Unfortunately, by the end of the project, none of the employees provided the ROI team with a full-time record during the project. As an alternative, estimates of their time were used in converting data to monetary values.

**Business process changes**—The rollout of RxSource took place in phases throughout the mail order pharmacies. Because the rollout was staggered across several months, there was time available for other factors to influence the same variables of productivity and quality we were trying to measure. Additionally, several key business processes were changing or being adapted to the newly available RxSource. A significant number of documents was being loaded on a regular basis. With so much disruption in the system, there was some concern about the accuracy of the information. Many employees felt the information in RxSource, while easier to find, was out-of-date, incorrect, or conflicting. The state of constant fluctuation for a couple of months also made for longer search times and decreased some trust in the tool.

## Lessons Learned and Recommendations

Each of the barriers encountered provided valuable learning opportunities. These barriers, along with other experiences along the way, have contributed to the following lessons learned:

**Population samples**—In planning for this study, a desired sample size was calculated. The intent was to gain enough responses to be representative of the larger population that would be affected by RxSource without incurring the cost of surveying everyone. This decision, however, did not account for differences within the population. A single sample size goal is worthwhile when a population is homogeneous. At the time this study was conducted, Pharmacy Operations was operating on two primary prescription processing platforms with two residual corporate cultures in the associated sites. Additionally, some sites had different practices related to work instruction availability. A better approach would have been to determine desired sample sizes for each subgroup (in this case pharmacy location), rather than an aggregate response rate.

The importance of truly representative samples was reinforced when comparing the respondent demographics between the pre- and post-implementation surveys. There were significant differences between the two samples, primarily in the distribution of the respondents' pharmacy location. One solution would have been to ensure representative samples in each site as described above. If that is not possible, it becomes more important to at least survey the exact same group both times to ensure the validity of the comparison between the two surveys.

**Response rates**—Two primary lessons were learned regarding response rates. First, in our production-focused environment it is critical to have executive sponsorship to ensure participation of site leadership and those who control employee time. While there was strong sponsorship for the RxSource project as a whole, the authors neglected to secure continued sponsorship specifically for the survey and measurement phases of this study. As such, the response rates were wholly dependent on individual managers to allow time for the surveys. Without visible sponsorship, ROI studies like this one are subject to voluntary participation by company leaders and their teams. Secondly, those conducting ROI studies should more closely monitor response rates to ensure proper sample size is collected. The authors of this study learned that it is possible to more actively monitor and react to response rates while surveys are being collected, rather than waiting until all responses are submitted. Had we monitored those rates more closely, we could have increased survey requests to some sites in an attempt to balance overall response.

**Measurement**—Two measurements, or rather the ability to achieve desired measurement, greatly complicated this study. The simpler of the two is basic measurement of time and labor used in a project. Without a competent resource to track hours spent working in a project, it becomes difficult to calculate associated labor cost. Future ROI studies should tackle this issue early to ensure that time can be more accurately recorded and tracked, thus eliminating the need to rely on estimates.

This study also attempted to measure changes in two key business indicators: productivity and quality. As reported earlier, the authors were not able to identify trends either before or after the implementation of RxSource. While much of this was due to the nature of the data being analyzed, a few changes would have greatly helped:

- Understand the data available before conducting the study. While we had a general knowledge of the quality and productivity data we would be collecting, we had not worked with it to the degree we had to in the study. A more thorough understanding of the data, related reports, and of existing nuances before we initiated the study would have led us to choose alternative measurement approaches within our data collection and analysis plans.

- Know when to use trend analysis. Trend line analysis is useful only when extraneous changes are at a minimum during the measurement period. During the months leading up to our study, numerous business changes were occurring, including the merger of two companies and the implementation of a significant pharmacy application upgrade. These recent changes and the employees' continual adaptation to them prevented the determination of useful data trends for productivity and quality.

- Have redundancy built into data collections plans. While this study may have been jeopardized by

inconclusive trend line analyses, it was enhanced by
the inclusion of employee estimates of performance
improvement in the user surveys. The inclusion of
those questions and the eventual need for them reaf-
firms in our mind that you should always have a
"Plan B."

## Conclusion

RxSource has provided a number of benefits to Caremark Pharmacy Operations. As discussed previously, it has enabled easy
company-wide online access to business documentation, prompted
a culture of standardization, and opened a dialog about business
processes and practices, as well as departmental interdependencies.
It has reduced costs of printing documentation and reduced risk
of employees referencing outdated materials. Based on employee
estimates, it has also contributed to increases in employee productivity. These benefits, both measurable and intangible, contribute
to the overall value of RxSource. ROI calculations indicate that
the measurable benefits alone exceed the cost of designing and
implementing the system.

The RxSource tool will continue to be of growing value. The
first year following implementation has seen many changes as
departments and employees have grown accustomed to RxSource.
These changes have resulted in numerous changes within RxSource
content and some unexpected difficulty in finding information as
it has been revised. However, even during those times of added
difficulty, this study shows RxSource has still provided value. As
legacy systems are integrated and business processes are further
standardized, RxSource will become even easier to use. Employees will become more proficient at locating needed documents,
possibly resulting in even more improvements to productivity and
quality.

## Questions for Discussion

1. The authors adjusted the final ROI percentage from 1,196 percent to 79.5 percent in order to take the most conservative approach and to appease any skeptics who might not agree with including estimated performance improvement in the calculation. Do you agree with this approach? How do you think estimates of performance improvements would be viewed in your work environment?

2. The duration of this study posed challenges to measuring and isolating the effects of the new RxSource system. How would you change the evaluation methodology or approach described in this chapter to account for other unrelated variables that may have influenced business metrics?

3. In what ways could additional sponsor involvement have helped this project? Identify three to five ways to ensure adequate sponsorship for ROI projects in your workplace.

4. Identify methods that could have been used to increase survey response rates among employee groups.

5. Are there other costs that could have been included in this study but were not?

6. Some elements of the study deviated from the initial Data Collection Plan. Discuss the importance of strictly following study plans versus adapting to unforeseen circumstances.

## About the Authors

**Nathan Faylor** is a learning and performance manager at CVS Caremark. His team delivers training to Caremark Pharmacy Services employees in locations across the United States. He has more than ten years of experience in the training and development field in various industries, including healthcare, high-technology manufacturing, and retail sales. His emphasis has been in the areas of training administration, technical training, measurement, and evaluation. Faylor earned an M.A. degree in communication studies from Texas State University-San Marcos. He can be contacted at CVS Caremark, 6950 Alamo Downs Parkway, San Antonio, TX 78238; email: nrfaylor@sbcglobal.net.

**Isabelle Maisse** is an SAP Business Systems Advisor for CVS Caremark, providing services to internal clients regarding installation of new functionalities and upgrades to existing functionalities. She has had experience in a variety of departments working for an Internet company and has worked in both the clinical and training departments for CVS Caremark. She graduated with her doctor of pharmacy degree from the University of Texas at Austin and can be contacted at CVS Caremark, 2105 Eagle Parkway, Fort Worth, Texas 76177; email: isabelle_maisse@yahoo.com.

**Kristen Neal** is a pharmacist with the mail services division of CVS Caremark. She currently works in the Corporate Quality department, monitoring and evaluating phone calls for accuracy of clinical information. Her focus is identifying process improvement opportunities to enhance participant satisfaction. She has previously served as a supervisor in the Clinical Care department and a senior training analyst. Kristen earned a B.S. degree in pharmacy from The University of Texas at Austin. She can be contacted at CVS Caremark, 7034 Alamo Downs Parkway, San Antonio, TX 78238.

# 11

# Forecasting ROI in a Performance Improvement Training Program

## A Healthcare Organization

Bonnie L. Carpenter

## Abstract

The Performance Improvement Department at The Hospital District (THD) was charged with evaluating the existing performance improvement program and its effectiveness addressing performance as it relates to processes, services, and patient safety. The challenge for the district program director for performance improvement was identifying learning needs for the large healthcare organization and meeting the needs of the employees at all levels. The other challenge was to develop a training program understandable to all employees and to meet the organization's objective, to be a "Most Efficient Organization" while maintaining compliance with regulatory agencies requirements. The evaluation strategy utilizes the Phillips ROI Methodology to calculate the return on investment for the training program.

---

Note: This case was prepared to serve as a basis for discussion rather than an illustration of either effective or ineffective administrative and management practices. Names, dates, places, and data may have been disguised at the request of the author or organization.

## Background

Effectively identifying quality issues is crucial to assure safe patient care in healthcare organizations. Through the years, regulatory agencies that accredit and license hospitals have become more stringent in their evaluations of hospitals. Therefore, it has become crucial for healthcare organizations to proactively identify potential patient safety issues, conduct an analysis of the issues identified, develop and implement action plans to address the issues, educate the staff affected by the new processes being implemented, and evaluate those processes to assure compliance is maintained and resources utilized effectively.

The Hospital District (THD), a community owned healthcare organization in the State of Texas, consists of three hospitals, twelve healthcare centers, a dental center, eight school-based clinics and four mobile units. It employs more than six thousand employees and works closely with two medical schools to deliver care to the county's residents, including the indigent and homeless. To meet the needs of the organization and decrease the amount of time and human resources necessary to improve processes associated with safe patient care, the Performance Improvement Department at THD was charged with evaluating the existing performance improvement program and its effectiveness in addressing performance as it relates to processes, services, and patient safety.

Facilitation for the District Performance Improvement Committee and the Quality Review Council falls within the scope of the district program director for performance improvement. The Quality Review Council reviews all departmental performance improvement initiatives and the District Performance Improvement Committee reviews district-wide initiatives, such as patient safety issues. Contacts include senior management, directors, managers, and staff, including but not limited to nurses, physicians, security, environmental services, etc.

The mission of the organization is to "improve our community's health by delivering high-quality health care to county residents and by training the next generation of health professionals" (Carpenter, 2006). The Hospital District's strategic plan is to achieve "most efficient organization" (MEO) status. Expanding its primary focus to not only include quality care but achieve positive financial outcomes by incorporating "return on investment" processes with PDCA (plan, do, check, and act), the organization will be able to effectively and efficiently monitor new interventions.

## Learning Needs

The existing Performance Improvement (PI) Program was evaluated over a two-year period utilizing surveys, observation, and monitoring the PI initiatives reports submitted by employees. From the evaluations, a needs assessment (Exhibit 11.1) was compiled identifying the staff's deficits regarding PDCA Methodology.

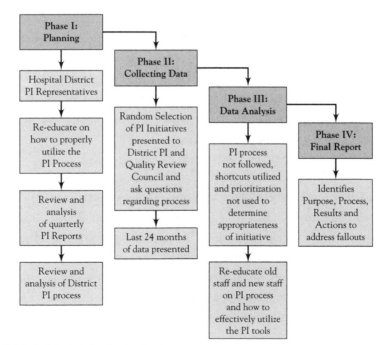

**Exhibit 11.1. Needs Analysis**

The deficits included but were not limited to the following identified results: the staff's lack of understanding and utilization of the PDCA Methodology, the ability to prioritize identified problems, and the staff's ability to proactively identify performance issues related to patient safety. In addition to developing an in-depth training program on PDCA, the district program director for performance improvement incorporated Six Sigma's requirement for completing a cause analysis on all proposed PI initiatives to assure the root of the problem would be identified and addressed. To determine the feasibility of the PI initiative, a "return on investment" module was added to the training program. The training program consists of three modules. Module 11–1 includes PDCA Methodology, definitions, objectives, and goals associated with the strategic plan for the organization. Module 11–2 offers participants the opportunity to have hands-on experience with developing a flow chart, cause-and-effect diagram, filling out the appropriate forms for reporting their initiatives, and access to the forms via their computers. Module 11–3 includes instructions on how to utilize the ROI Methodology. This enables the staff, including department directors and administrators, to evaluate the interventions deployed effectiveness. Design and implementation of appropriate instructions on how to utilize the PDCA Methodology and tools will benefit the staff, the organization as a whole, and the community the organization serves.

### Stakeholders

Partnering with stakeholders is an ongoing process that establishes rapport, credibility, and trust (Combs & Falletta, 2000). Stakeholders are those directly or indirectly affected by the change intervention. Stakeholders can include customers, suppliers, distributors, employees, and government regulators (Swanson & Holton, 2001). The primary stakeholders identified for the PDCA Methodology educational program includes, but is not limited to: Quality Management Services, Clinical Case Management, nursing departments, the executive team, and the Board of Managers.

The stakeholders identified, as well as approval and support from The Hospital District's Executive Team, Board of Managers, and department directors, are essential to the success and implementation of the educational program proposed.

The role and responsibility of THD Executive Team and the Board of Managers (BOM) is to provide support, monitor outcomes, and recognize the healthcare personnel for their actions in implementing the revised process. Exhibit 11.2 describes the stakeholders' informational needs, expectations, and priorities.

| Stakeholders | Information Needs | Expectations | Priorities |
|---|---|---|---|
| Board of Managers | • Emphasize importance of improving the performance improvement (PI) process to include detailed cause analysis and return on investment<br>• How the revised PI process impacts the district and the effects it has on providing quality healthcare to the community | • Monitors status of PI and patient safety initiatives in order to set priorities and assess the effectiveness of the intervention.<br>• Designates funds to accomplish goals | • The interventions provide positive results to accomplish quality of care efficiently and effectively creating a "most efficient organization" |
| **Stakeholders** | **Information Needs** | **Expectations** | **Priorities** |
| The Hospital District Executive Team | • Emphasize importance of improving the performance improvement (PI) process to include detailed cause analysis and return on investment<br>• How the revised PI process impacts the district and the effects it has on providing quality healthcare to the community | • Monitors status of PI and patient safety initiatives in order to set priorities and assess the effectiveness of the interventions.<br>• Designate funds to accomplish goals. | • The interventions provide positive results to accomplish quality of care efficiently and effectively creating a "most efficient organization" |
| **Stakeholders** | **Information Needs** | **Expectations** | **Priorities** |
| Quality Management Services (QMS) and Performance Improvement Departments | • Provide information on findings and educate QMS staff on revised process<br>• Develop and communicate revised PI process and timeline for implementing new process district-wide<br>• Encourage full participation in program | • Assist staff in filling appropriate utilization of revised PI process<br>• Systematically coordinate training programs to meet the needs of the staff<br>• Be available to assist staff at all times<br>• Maintain communication between staff to assure all questions about the process are addressed in a timely manner | • Schedule regular follow-up visits to troubleshoot, coach and congratulate staff on new performance successes<br>• Communicate any new initiatives or PI goals to staff<br>• Remain available to assist staff answer questions or assist with difficult issues.<br>• Report any issues to the appropriate committee |

**Exhibit 11.2. Stakeholders' Informational Needs, Expectations, and Priorities**

| Stakeholders | Information Needs | Expectations | Priorities |
|---|---|---|---|
| Other Stakeholders (Nursing, Physicians, Pharmacist, Laboratory Tech, Security, Business Office Staff) | • Participate actively in the revised performance improvement initiative <br> • Participate in selecting spokesperson to report initiative at monthly performance improvement meeting <br> • Identify the champions for the process in order to address the revised process effectively | • Participate in the educational sessions describing the new process <br> • Have a positive attitude toward the new changes within the PI process <br> • Ask questions <br> • Support co-worker <br> • Encourage all co-workers to actively participate <br> • Verbalize negative and positive experiences <br> • Communicate with each other | • Implement action plans related to the revised PI process <br> • Remain positive <br> • Work together as a team with all staff members <br> • Participate in evaluating progress <br> • Continue to report initiative results with THD through performance improvement committees |
| Stakeholders | Information Needs | Expectations | Priorities |
| Patients | • Provide feedback from the patient satisfaction surveys related to quality and safety of care | • Health care professionals will listen and communicate process improvement issues related to quality and safety of care issues | • Health care professionals will listen and communicate process improvement issues related to quality and safety of care issues |

**Exhibit 11.2. (Continued)**

## Evaluation Methodology

This ROI case study involves the evaluation of the existing performance improvement process and the revised performance improvement training program that evolved from a two-year evaluation, a needs analysis identifying weaknesses, and the potential impact on the organization's bottom line. The evaluation strategy used the Phillips ROI Methodology to calculate the return on investment (Phillips, 2003). The objective of the study was to determine the potential effectiveness of the Performance Improvement Training Program (The What, When, and How) and identify potential outcomes associated with the utilization of the program.

### Evaluation Objectives

The training program was designed after a needs analysis identified gaps in THD's performance improvement methodology, PDCA. The gaps identified by the needs assessment were confirmed by recent outcomes addressed by regulatory accreditation agencies. The stakeholders confirmed that addressing the outcomes and implementing a proactive intervention program would assist the organization in meeting compliance standards related to the regulatory accreditation agencies.

*Level 1 Objectives: Reaction and Satisfaction*

Level 1 objectives and planned actions measure participants' reaction to the program and outlines specific plans for implementation of the program as shown in Exhibit 11.3. The objectives for Level 1 (Reaction and Satisfaction) are critical in describing the immediate and long-term satisfaction of the program. Level 1 objectives include:

*Level 2 Objectives: Learning*

Level 2 (Learning) objectives measure the skills, knowledge, or attitude changes by communicating expected outcomes from instruction and describe the competent performance of the participants. The learning objectives include the participants' awareness or familiarity with terms, concepts, and processes; participants' knowledge or general understanding of concepts and processes; and participants' ability to demonstrate the knowledge and skills acquired. The Level 2 objective is "at the end of the program the participants will be able to implement the PDCA steps necessary to establish appropriate indicators and how to fill out the appropriate forms." During Part II of the program four out of five, or 80 percent, of the participants' will be able to demonstrate to the facilitator the following applications:

- The steps to the PDCA process

- Identify the appropriate graphs and learn how to use an Excel spreadsheet to create graphs

- Fill out the appropriate reporting forms for PI initiatives

**TITLE OF COURSE: Performance Improvement (The What, When & How)**

DATE:

FACILITATOR: Bonnie Carpenter

In order to continuously improve the quality of the in-services provided, please take a few minutes to evaluate the in-service course you attended today.

Please rate the in-service course using the following scale:

1 = Strongly Disagree   2 = Disagree   3 = Neutral   4 = Agree   5 = Strongly Agree

Please check a box for each item and print your comments clearly in the space provided below.

| CONTENT | 1 | 2 | 3 | 4 | 5 |
|---|---|---|---|---|---|
| The content increased my knowledge of the topic. | | | | | |
| The content was consistent with the objectives. | | | | | |
| The content was relevant to my job. | | | | | |
| The content was easily understood. | | | | | |
| The content will be useful in my job. | | | | | |
| **SETTING** | | | | | |
| The room was conducive to learning. | | | | | |
| The learning environment stimulated idea exchange. | | | | | |
| Facility was appropriate for the activity. | | | | | |

266

## INSTRUCTIONAL METHOD

| | | | | |
|---|---|---|---|---|
| The instructional material was well organized. | | | | |
| The instruction methods illustrated the concepts well. | | | | |
| The instructing strategies were appropriate for the activity. | | | | |
| My overall rating for the course is . . . . | | | | |

## PRESENTER EFFECTIVENESS

| | | | | |
|---|---|---|---|---|
| The presentation was clear and to the point. | | | | |
| The presenter demonstrated mastery of the topic. | | | | |
| The method(s) used to present the material held my attention. | | | | |
| The presenter was responsive to participant concerns. | | | | |
| My overall rating for the presenter . . . . | | | | |

COMMENTS/SUGGESTIONS

| | | | | |
|---|---|---|---|---|
| | | | | |
| | | | | |
| | | | | |

Thank you for your cooperation!

**Exhibit 11.3. Evaluation Form**

267

*Level 3 Objectives: Application and Implementation*

Level 3 (Application and Implementation) objectives describe the expected outcomes participants should demonstrate from the program (Phillips & Phillips, 2005). The Level 3 objectives for the PI program were, "Participants will apply the PDCA process effectively," four out of five, or 80 percent, of the participants will complete the prerequisite paperwork when initiating PI initiatives, continued monitoring of paperwork, presentation of paperwork, and effectively present their PI initiatives to the appropriate committee for review. The district program director for performance improvement will monitor the participants' presentations and paperwork to determine if there were barriers or enablers to the program by evaluating the information presented to be reported to the appropriate committee (Quality Review Council or District PI).

*Level 4: Business Impact*

The best impact measures contain measures linked to skills and knowledge presented in the program. Level 4 (Business Impact) objectives provide the basis for measuring the consequences of applying the skills and knowledge learned and places emphasis on achieving bottom-line results (Phillips & Phillips, 2005). There are four types of impact objectives involving hard data which include: output focused, quality focused, cost focused, and time focused. Soft data measures include: customer service focused, work climate focused, and work habits focused. The objectives for Level 4 included, but were not limited to: improve productivity/operational efficiency, improve communication between hospital departments involved in the PI process, and sustained compliance related to performance improvement initiatives. The measures for Level 4 included increase productivity/operations by increasing efficiency related to PI initiatives as indicated by the PI initiative satisfaction survey presented to participants six months after implementation of the training program. Other measures to be monitored are employee satisfaction, improved communication between departments, and sustained outcomes for a period of twelve months, as indicated from quarterly and annual reports.

*Level 5 Objectives: ROI*

Level 5 (ROI) objectives focus on the comparison of monetary values as it relates to the cost of the training program. The objective for this program was to improve and sustain performance initiatives by 40 percent, the minimum acceptable percentage of the ROI. This value was determined by the sponsor of the program. In doing so, it was anticipated that improved productivity and employee and patient satisfaction (depending on PI initiative) would occur. Exhibit 11.4 formats the above objectives in table form for easier review.

## Evaluation Results

The needs analysis developed after the two years of evaluating the existing program demonstrated the staff's lack of understanding with the existing process.

### Isolating the Effects of Performance Improvement Training

The question to ask to identify the method for isolating the effects of performance improvement training is: "How much of the improvement was caused by training?"

The methods used for isolating the effects of performance improvement training within The Hospital District would be two-fold: participants' estimate of training impact and the presenter's estimation of training impact. Due to the size and intensity of the educational training program for Performance Improvement, the facilitator used the questionnaire approach to isolate the effects. The impact questions were based on the recommended questions detailed in Table 11.1.

Evaluation Purpose: Monitor PI training program

Program: Performance Improvement (The What, When, and How) Training Program Responsibility: Bonnie L. Carpenter

Date: January 23, 2007

| Level | Broad Program Objective(s) | Measures | Data Collection Method/Instruments | Data Sources | Timing | Responsibilities |
|---|---|---|---|---|---|---|
| 1 | REACTION/SATISFACTION *Measure employees' reaction to and satisfaction with performance improvement (the what, when, and how) training program<br><br>*Participants will perceive program content relevant to identified PI initiatives<br><br>*Participants will be able to develop and submit relevant action plans for identified PI initiatives | *Four out of five or 80 percent of participants view the knowledge and skills as relevant to developing and implementing their PI initiatives and can immediately apply the knowledge and skills to existing and future PI initiatives as indicated by rating this measure on a Likert scale | *Feedback questionnaire (hard copy) immediately after presentation<br><br>*Annual mandatory evaluation of the PI Process with online evaluation questionnaire | *Employees | *At end of program presentation | *Director, Performance Improvement |
| 2 | LEARNING *Employees understand PDCA methodology<br><br>*Participants will be able to implement the PDCA steps necessary to establish appropriate indicators<br><br>*Participants will be able to fill out the appropriate forms | *During Part II of the program four out of five or 80 percent of the participants will be able to demonstrate to the facilitator the following applications:<br>*The steps to the PDCA process<br>*Identify the appropriate graphs and how to use an Excel spreadsheet to create graphs<br>*Fill out the appropriate reporting forms for PI initiatives<br>*Score on the post-test, at least 80 percent | *True/false test (hardcopy) immediately after<br>*Hands-on practicum | *Employees | *At end of program presentation | *Director, Performance Improvement *All District Employees |

| | | | | | | |
|---|---|---|---|---|---|---|
| 3 | APPLICATION/ IMPLEMENTATION **Effective and consistent implementation of the PDCA process** *Measure employees PI initiatives for frequency and relevancy as related to the PDCA methodology *Identify barriers or enablers in applying learned skills and knowledge | *Four out of five or 80 percent of the participants will complete the prerequisite paperwork when initiating PI initiatives, continued monitoring paperwork, presentation paperwork, and effectively present their PI initiatives to the appropriate committee for review *Monitor PI initiative paperwork for enablers to the process | *Monthly monitoring and review of PI initiative reports *Annual mandatory evaluation of the PI process | *Employees *Director, Performance Improvement | *Continuous monitoring of PI initiatives through the appropriate PI committee * Annual mandatory evaluation of the PI Process | *All District Employees |
| 4 | BUSINESS IMPACT **Reduce unsuccessful implementation and sustainability of PI initiatives by 40 percent during the first year.** *Improve productivity/operational efficiency *Improved communication between departments *Improve employee and customer satisfaction | *Monitor PI initiatives for compliance and sustainability *Monitor employee and customer satisfaction | *Submission and review of PI initiatives to the appropriate PI committee *Employee satisfaction survey *Customer satisfaction survey *Annual mandatory evaluation of the PI process | *Monthly PI summary reports *Board of managers annual PI report | *Analyze monthly PI initiatives presentations *Annual overall analysis of the PI initiative results | *Director, Performance Improvement |
| 5 | ROI **Target ROI: 40 percent** | Baseline Data: Evaluation of Performance Improvement Process—a two-year study determining the staff unable to effectively utilize PDCA methodology followed by a needs assessment. | | | | |
| | | Comments: Intangible Outcomes: *Employee and customer satisfaction, decreased employee stress, communication and teamwork | | | | |

## Exhibit 11.4. Data Collection Plan

Copyright © 2007 ROI Institute, Inc.

**Table 11.1.    Participants' Impact Questions**

1.   How have you and your job changed as a result of attending this program (skills and knowledge application)?

2.   What impact do these changes bring to your work or work unit?

3.   How is this impact measured (specific measure)?

4.   How much did this measure change after you participated in the program (monthly, weekly, or daily amount)?

5.   What is the unit value of the measure?

6.   What is the basis for this unit value? Please indicate the assumptions made and the specific calculations you performed to arrive at the value.

7.   What is the annual value of this change or improvement in the work unit (for the first year)?

8.   Recognizing that many other factors influence output results in addition to training, please identify the other factors that could have contributed to this performance.

9.   What percent of this improvement can be attributed directly to the application of skills and knowledge gained in the program? (0 to 100 percent)

10.  What confidence do you have in the above estimate and data expressed as a percent? (0% = no confidence; 100% = certainty)

11.  What other individuals or groups could estimate this percentage or determine the amount?

*Source:* Adapted from Phillips, J.J. (2003). *Return on Investment in Training and Performance Improvement Program* (2nd ed.). Woburn, MA: Butterworth-Heinemann.


Illustrations of the impact process were held at the end of the training program to assist the participants in completing the questionnaire. The district program director for performance improvement was also available to assist the participants, if needed. The district program director for performance improvement, who presented the program, estimated the training impact by monitoring the results of PI initiatives for accuracy and outcome sustainability. The questions answered by the PI evaluator are described in

**Table 11.2.    Supervisor/Program Presenter's Impact Questions**

| | |
|---|---|
| 1. | In addition to training, what other factors could have contributed to this success? |
| 2. | What percent of the improvement in performance measures of the participant resulted from the training program? (0 to 100 percent) |
| 3. | What is the basis for this estimate? |
| 4. | What is your confidence in this estimate, expressed as a percentage? (0% = no confidence; 100% = complete confidence) |
| 5. | What other individuals or groups would know about this improvement and could estimate this percentage? |

*Source:* Adapted from Phillips, J.J. (2003). *Return on Investment in Training and Performance Improvement Program* (2nd ed.). Woburn, MA: Butterworth-Heinemann.

Table 11.2. Utilizing the above two sources allowed THD to experiment with the different techniques and build confidence with one or both in calculating the impact for training. However, it must be remembered that the final figure(s) is only an estimate of the impact given the constraints, conditions, and resources available.

**Benefits and Cost Calculation**

Patient safety issues are a major concern for healthcare organizations. One way to assure quality care is to identify areas with less-than-quality processes. It is the responsibility of each hospital department within The Hospital District to identify at least one process to address in the attempt to provide quality care. These processes are either identified by the staff or by regulatory agencies, for example, the monitoring of intake and output for congestive heart failure, dialysis, or post-surgery patients. Once the fallout is identified, the staff develops corrective action plans, implements the new or revised intervention, monitors the success of the intervention, and evaluates the outcomes. The problem identified during the needs assessment was that the staff was unfamiliar with the District's methodology (PDCA) for addressing these issues effectively. Many of the departments had been working on PI initiatives for up to five years without sustaining positive outcomes. The standard rule of thumb is that all PI initiatives should be able to sustain compliance of at least 90 percent (JCAHO Benchmark) for a twelve-month period. Not being able to sustain compliance or fix the problem is stressful for the staff, as well as being a safety issue for patients. This causes staff and patients to become dissatisfied with the organization. The other issue associated with poor quality in healthcare is the lack of teamwork, because each pavilion and department does not realize that in healthcare no department is an island to itself. With that in mind, the other major issue within THD is communication. The action plan (Table 11.3) identifies all of the above issues as intangible benefits associated with the implementation of the PI training program. The staff was able to effectively utilize PDCA in order to save time from unnecessary rework, therefore decreasing stress levels. Patient and employee satisfaction will increase because the patients will receive the quality of care expected, and the employees will be satisfied with their accomplishments. The overall improvement will come from staff being able to communicate effectively with each other to solve problems and become team players in the organization's goal to become a "Most Efficient Organization."

The action plan also describes the objectives, evaluation period, estimate for improvement measure, current performance standard, targeted performance standard, action items completed and to be completed, and an analysis of the project with estimated projections for success. The comments section of the plan describes projected estimates for the program. After July 31, 2007, when the program has been given to an anticipated two hundred employees, a post-evaluation was administered asking the staff for their estimations of the program. The program will be re-evaluated based on this post-evaluation.

To calculate the benefits and cost, a cost estimate worksheet was developed (Exhibit 11.5). Table 11.4 summarizes the cost associated with the PI training program. The total cost of the program was used to calculate the Return on Investment (ROI) and the Benefit/Cost Ratio (BCR).

Before the BCR or the ROI could be calculated, the business impact data needed to be converted to a monetary value (Table 11.5). The estimate utilized in Table 11.5 relates to the first two hundred employees who were educated on the PDCA process. To calculate the annual benefit expected with training two hundred employees, we multiplied the number of days/year (260 days) by 200 employees for a total of 52,000 days. Then we multiplied 52,000 days by how much the measure is estimated to change for the evaluation period (40 percent), which equals 20,800. Then, we multiplied the 20,800 by the average salary cost of $35, which equals $728,000.00 per year. To calculate the adjusted value for use in identifying the BCR and ROI, we multiplied the estimated confidence rate (85 percent) by the estimated percent of change (60 percent) caused by the program, for a total of 51 percent. We multiplied $728,000.00 by 51 percent, for an adjusted value of $371,280.00.

The next step in the process was to calculate the BCR and the ROI, as illustrated in Table 11.6.

According to the calculation above, for every dollar spent on the PI training program, an estimated $10 in benefits were returned for the two hundred employees initially trained. The ROI value estimate illustrates a return of 880 percent over the estimated 40 percent ROI objective. Exhibit 11.6 summarizes the above calculations following the impact chain, or six levels of data, identified in the collection plan.

### Intangible Measures

Intangible measures are the benefits or detriments directly linked to the training program. The intangible measures identified by The Hospital District directly related to the training program and were

# Table 11.3. ROI–Action Plan: Performance Improvement Program

**Name:** The Hospital District **Department Manager/Director Signature:** Bonnie Carpenter

**Follow-Up Date:** Ongoing

**Objective:** Improve and Sustain PI initiative outcomes related process improvement

**Evaluation Period:** Quarterly    **Improvement Measure:** 40 percent of all new PI initiative submitted after 7/31/2007 will have sustained outcomes for a nine-to-twelve-month period

**Current Performance:** Unsustained, with an average of between 50 and 75 percent

**Target Performance:** 90 percent or better

| Action Items | Analysis |
|---|---|
| 1. Identified need for education on PDCA process    8/29/2006 | A. What is the unit of measure? |
| 2. Performed GAP Analysis on existing process    9/15/2006 | JCAHO Compliance Standard of 90 percent, except that National Patient Safety Goals |
| 3. Documented findings and presented information to leadership team with recommendations    12/8/2006 | Compliance is 100 percent |
| 4. Developed educational program for implementing revised PDCA Process    12/30/2006 | B. What is the value (cost) of unit? $35.00 |
|  | C. How did you arrive at this value? Average wages for participants |
| 5. Met with leaders to discuss new program and plans for rollout 1/12/2007 | D. How much did the measure change during the evaluation period? 40 percent or better (Forecast) |
| 6. In-serviced Quality Management Staff (inpatient and out-patient) in order to assist as resources in each of the pavilions | E. What percent of this change was actually caused by this program? Estimate a conservative 60 percent |

F. What level of confidence do you place on the above information? (100% = Certainty and 0% = No confidence)

85 percent

and Community Health Centers   1/30/2007

7. Set up appointments to in-service various departments within the organization until all key personnel are in-serviced on new process   2/1/2007–7/31/2007

8. Post in-service evaluations after each program Ongoing

9. Evaluate new PI initiatives for compliance with new process Ongoing

10. Present PI Program two times a year beginning 2008

**Intangible Benefits:** Communication, teamwork, decreased employee stress, employee satisfaction and patient satisfaction

**Comments:** the above analysis E is an estimate for the program. Hopefully, we will see more than a 40 percent return and the percentage of improvement with the process will exceed the estimated 60 percent.

*Source:* Adapted from Phillips, J., & Phillips, P. (2005). Using action plans to measure ROI. *Performance Improvement, 42*(1), 22–21.

| Evaluation Level for the PI Program | Methods/Process | Program Costs | Realized Benefits |
|---|---|---|---|
| Level 1—Reaction/ Satisfaction | Fully loaded costs for PI Program Trainer, PI Evaluator, and Stakeholders<br><br>Costs determined in training program, reaction questionnaire development, salaries, benefits, and travel | Total Costs equates to $3,420 | Intangible—Employee satisfaction with PI training program<br><br>Tangible—Not measurable according to test for converting intangibles to monetary values |
| Level 2—Learning | Fully loaded costs for PI Program Trainer, PI Evaluator, and Stakeholders<br><br>Costs include trainer and participants' salary/benefits | Total Costs: $28,120 | Intangible—Improved knowledge of PI Process (PDCA) and organizational commitment<br><br>Tangible—Not measurable according to test for converting intangibles to monetary values |
| Level 3—Application/ Implementation | Fully loaded costs for PI Program Trainer, PI Evaluator, and Stakeholders<br><br>Costs for 2.5 hours × 10 sessions plus materials including evaluations, salaries/benefits for trainer and participants | Total Costs: $29,670 | Intangible—Varies depending on type of PI initiatives being undertaken<br><br>Tangibles—Varies depending on type of PI initiatives being undertaken |
| Level 4—Business Impact (Forecasted) | Fully loaded costs for PI Program Trainer, PI Evaluator, and Stakeholders<br><br>Adjusted value technique for two hundred employees equates to time savings related to decreased rework of PI initiatives | Total Cost equals Analysis Costs Development Costs<br><br>Operations/Maintenance Cost and Evaluation Costs: $8,582.<br><br>Total Program Cost: $36,107<br><br>Total Benefit in Cost Savings: $371,000 | Intangible—Patient and employee satisfaction, teamwork, decreased employee stress, better communication between the three hospitals and the healthcare center<br><br>Tangible—Savings realized from time savings related to decrease rework of PI initiatives |
| Level 5—Return on Investment (ROI) (Forecasted) | Benefits to Cost Ratio (BCR)<br><br><br><br><br><br>Basic ROI Formula | BCR equals $371,280 divided by $36,107 equals 10.3:1 ratio.<br><br><br><br>ROI equals $371,280 minus $36,107 divided by $36,107 equates to 9.2 times 100 at 920 percent | Intangible—Patient and employee satisfaction, teamwork, decreased employee stress, better communication between the three hospitals and the healthcare center<br><br>Tangible—For every dollar invested, a return of $10.30 is realized at a ROI percentage of 180 percent. |

**Exhibit 11.5. Cost and Benefit Analysis**

**Table 11.4.  Program Cost Summary: Performance Improvement (The What, When, and How) Program**

| Item | | Cost ($) |
|---|---|---|
| 1. | Needs Assessment (1 × $ 50 × 38% × 48 hours) | $912 |
| 2. | Program Development Costs (Prorated for ten sessions) (1 × $50 × 38% × 100 hours) | $1,900 |
| 3. | Printing and Reproduction Costs | $400 |
| 4. | Facilitation and Coordination Costs | $475 |
| 5. | Delivery Costs (200 × $35 × 38% × 2.5 hrs Prorated for 10 sessions) | $26,600 |
| 6. | Program Materials and Supplies (Prorated for ten sessions) | $400 |
| 7. | Travel Cost | $50 |
| 8. | Operations/Maintenance Costs | $3,800 |
| 9. | Post-Training Evaluation | $1,570 |
| **Total** | | **$36,107.00** |

not converted to monetary values. These included better communication, teamwork, employee satisfaction, decreased employee stress levels, patient safety, and patient satisfaction. The latter, patient satisfaction, even though not converted to monetary values for this

**Table 11.5.  Business Impact Data: Performance Improvement Program**

| Department/ Healthcare Center Employees | Improvement ($ Values) | Measure | Contribution Estimate from Staff | Confidence Estimate | Adjusted $ Value |
|---|---|---|---|---|---|
| **200 Employees** | $728,000 | JCAHO Compliance Standard of 90% or better | 60% | 85% | (51%) $371,280 |
| **Total** | | | | $371,280 | |

**Table 11.6.   Analyze Outcome of ROI: Performance Improvement Program**

The benefit-cost ratio (BCR) and ROI are as follows:

$$BCR = \frac{\text{Program Benefits}}{\text{Program Costs}}$$

$$= \frac{\$371,280.00}{\$36,107.00}$$

$$= 10.3$$

$$ROI(\%) = \frac{\text{Program Benefits minus Program Costs (Net Program Benefits)}}{\text{Program Costs}} \times 100$$

$$= \frac{\$371,280.00 - \$36,107.00}{\$36,107.00}$$

$$= \frac{\$335,173.00}{\$36,107.00}$$

$$= 9.2 \times 100 = 920\%$$

study, will have an impact on reimbursement from the Centers for Medicare and Medicaid Services (CMS), beginning in June 2007.

Communication between the different entities within THD was a major problem. Implementing the Performance Improvement program helped open the communication channels and break down existing silos. The premise behind this is that all individuals will be required to utilize the same process to identify, develop, implement, and evaluate effective interventions throughout the organization. To eliminate duplication or different processes being used for the same situation, the staff was encouraged to communicate with their co-partners in the other facilities and worked together to disseminate the processes throughout the organization.

After the training, the employees were able to see results from their initiatives if they used the PDCA Methodology as it was laid out, step-by-step, and without shortcuts. By seeing the results or identifying unknown fallouts at the beginning of the process, the employees have greater satisfaction and see positive results from their interventions. This alleviates or decreases stress levels because their interventions are relevant to the new process or the revised process. Also, the staff is able to move to other projects/initiatives instead of being stalled and continuously reporting negative results.

Improved patient satisfaction was realized due to the processes related to patient care, such as more timely access to care and decreasing turnaround times for receiving radiology/laboratory results. For example, at this time patients needing CAT scans are waiting up to six months for routine testing. After the training, the staff should be able to effectively identify where the bottlenecks are and work as a team to implement the appropriate interventions. Not only will this make patients and their families happy, but the ordering physicians' satisfaction with the organization will improve also.

There are a number of intangible measures that can be identified within THD because for some it is not the monetary gains, but the respect and self-assurance one gains from implementing interventions with positive results.

## Anticipated Barriers and Enablers

There are many challenges to face when working for any organization and more so when working for an organization like The Hospital District. Through brainstorming, all potential barriers and enablers are identified and listed.

*Barriers*

- Communication

- Not having key individuals in on the planning sessions until after the fact

- Inadequate planning

*Enablers*

---

- Effective communication of projects/goals to all parties involved in the process/procedure at the beginning of the project

- Key individuals involved in the project from the beginning to ensure total support for project

- Identify the pros and cons associated with the project at the beginning so appropriate actions/interventions can be developed to ensure the project will be beneficial to THD

| Need for Communication | Targeted Audience | Communication Document | Distribution Method |
|---|---|---|---|
| Gain support for the project and its objectives | Senior Leadership Board of Managers | Executive Summary | Quarterly Reports |
| To reinforce the process | District PI Committee Quality Review Council Department Directors Managers/Staff | PowerPoint Presentations One-page summary | Quarterly Reports Monthly Staff Meetings |
| To prepare participants for the program | Staff and New Hires | PowerPoint Presentation | Monthly General Orientation for New Hires Monthly Staff Meetings |
| Enhance results throughout the project and the quality of future feedback | Department Directors Managers/Staff | Post Information on PI Intranet Site Organization's Newsletter | Monthly Recognition of Departments and Staff Meeting/Exceeding Compliance Standard Monthly Staff Meetings |
| To show the complete results of the training program | Future Leaders (New or Promoted) | PowerPoint Presentation One-page summary | Quarterly Leadership Orientation Monthly Staff Meetings |
| To explain techniques used to measure results | District PI Committee Quality Review Council Department Directors Managers/Staff | PowerPoint Presentations One-page summary | Ongoing Monthly Staff Meetings |
| To stimulate desire in participants to be involved in the program | Staff and New Hires Future Leaders (New or Promoted) | PowerPoint Presentations One-page summary | Ongoing Monthly Staff Meetings |
| To market future projects | Senior Leadership Department Directors Managers | Executive Summary | Ongoing |

**Exhibit 11.6. THD Plan for Communicating Evaluation Results**

## Communication Strategy

Communication is a major issue at The Hospital District. Therefore, it was essential to maintain continuous communication with all entities within the organization and at all levels. Due to the different levels and diversity of THD, communication to each of the target audience groups identified (Exhibit 11.6) needed to meet their specific needs in order for them to offer suggestions or recommendations so adjustments to the program can be made.

The skills required for communicating results effectively are as important as the skills required to obtain results. There are specific principles to address if communication is to be successful and meet the needs of the organization. Those principles include:

1. Communication must be timely.

2. Communication should be targeted to specific audiences.

3. Media should be carefully selected.

4. Communication should be unbiased and modest.

5. Communication must be consistent.

6. Testimonies are more effective coming from individuals the audience respects.

7. The audience's opinion of the PI staff and function will influence the communication strategy.

With that said, critical elements exist to assist individuals with the development of the communication plan: planning the communication, selecting the proper audience for communication, developing the information, and communicating the results. Exhibit 11.6 shows the communications plan.

Exhibit 11.7 is the timeline for the Performance Improvement Program. At each level of the development stage, communication to key stakeholders was done to inform them of the progress.

| Tasks | Responsible Persons | Aug 06 | Sept 06 | Oct 06 | Nov 06 | Dec 06 | Jan 07 | Feb 07 | Mar 07 | Apr 07 | May 07 | Jun 07 | Jul 07 |
|---|---|---|---|---|---|---|---|---|---|---|---|---|---|
| Identify Need | Administration Board of Managers | X 8/29 | | | | | | | | | | | |
| Evaluate Existing PDCA Process | Director Performance Improvement | | X 9/15 | | | | | | | | | | |
| Initiate Comparison Research for Six Sigma amd PDCA Collect Data/Information | Director Performance Improvement | | X 9/15 → | | | 12/1 | | | | | | | |
| Document Research Findings | Director Performance Improvement | | | | | X 12/8 | | | | | | | |
| Present Findings to Leadership Team with Recommendations | Director Performance Improvement | | | | | X 12/14 | | | | | | | |
| Develop Educational Program for Implementing Revised Process | Director Performance Improvement | | | | | X 12/30 | | | | | | | |
| Meet with Learning and Resource Center to Schedule Education Sessions for Organization | Director Performance Improvement | | | | | | X 1/12 | | | | | | |
| In-Service Leaders and Quality Management Staff on New Process | Director Performance Improvement | | | | | | X 1/30 | | | | | | |
| Roll Out Educational Program to Organization | Director Performance Improvement / Quality Management Staff | | | | | | | X 2/15 → | 4/13 | | | | |
| Utilization of Revised PI Process | THD Staff | | | | | | | | | | X 4/16 | Ongoing | |
| Continued Education and Follow-Up and Evaluation of Revised Process and Re-Educate If Necessary | Director Performance Improvement / Quality Management Staff | | | | | | | | | | X 4/16 | Ongoing | |
| Report Evaluation of Revised Process to Leadership | Director Performance Improvement | | | | | | | | | | | | 7/31 |

**Exhibit 11.7. Gantt Chart for the Performance Improvement Program**

As the program is implemented, continuous evaluation of the results from the program is communicated to the targeted audiences.

## Lessons Learned

Due to the large number of potential participants within THD, it was decided to use the number of employees designated to do PI initiatives (two hundred). The calculations are based on the annual cost associated with the two hundred participants using the average hourly wage. Table 11.5 demonstrates the calculations of the adjusted values associated with the confidence level multiplied by the estimates of the experts. Table 11.6 completes the estimation ROI, demonstrating a positive impact of implementing the training program as well as the potential BCR (benefit/cost ratio).

The next step will be to communicate the ROI forecast to the stakeholders and reiterate that, if two hundred employees use the training program to address patient safety and quality of care issues by the step-by-step method illustrated, the outcomes of their performance improvement initiatives will decrease stress from PI interventions that fail and also increase employee satisfaction. Patients will receive quality care, increasing patient satisfaction. The organization as a whole will benefit by meeting regulatory requirements necessary to maintain its license to provide healthcare to the community it serves. Meeting the Center for Medicare and Medicaid Services' patient satisfaction requirements will financially improve the bottom line, as well as being a "Most Efficient Organization" where the community wants to come for its healthcare services.

Therefore, it is the recommendation that the Performance Improvement (The What, When, and How) Training Program be rolled out to the other six thousand plus employees to increase and promote effective communication and teamwork and improve bottom-line outcomes.

## Questions for Discussion

1. Did the needs assessment address all of the components of the ROI impact study?

2. Is this story credible? Explain.

3. Should the forecast be made on time savings alone? Explain.

4. Do you feel the conclusion and recommendations addressed the validity of the study?

5. Were the baseline participants (two hundred) enough to forecast the impact of such a large organization? Why or why not?

6. How could the impact study be conducted differently to demonstrate positive outcomes for the organization's leaders?

## Resources

Carpenter, B. (2006). PDCA: Back to basics. An HPI project presented in partial fulfillment for ED 851: Principles of Instructional Design. Unpublished.

Combs, W., & Falletta, S. (2000). *The targeted evaluation process.* Alexandria, VA: American Society for Training and Development.

Phillips, J. (2003). *Return on investment in training and performance improvement programs* (2nd ed.). Burlington, MA: Butterworth-Heinemann.

Phillips, J., & Phillips, P. (2003). Using action plans to measure ROI. *Performance Improvement, 42*(1), 22–21. Retrieved October 1, 2005, from XanEdu course pack ED 7652.

Phillips, P., & Phillips, J. (2005). *Return on (ROI) investment: Basics.* Alexandria, VA: American Society for Training & Development.

Swanson, R., & Holton, E., III (2001). *Foundation of human resource development.* San Francisco, CA. Berrett-Koehler.

## About the Author

**Bonnie L. Carpenter**, RN, MSHS, CMAC, is the director for performance improvement for a large community-owned healthcare system in Texas. She has more than twenty-five years of experience in healthcare as a nurse, quality improvement specialist, case management director, and a paralegal, with specialties in medical litigation and corporate law. As with many nurses, quality and safe patient care are her ultimate goals. To accomplish her goals, she realized that there had to be a balance between human performance improvement and quality performance improvement. She can be reached at bonnie_carpenter@hchd.tmc.edu.

# 12

# Measuring ROI in Negotiations Skills Training

## A Mortgage Company

Kendall Kerekes, Kelly Coumbe, John Ruggiero, and
Sanam Razzaghi

## Abstract

This study presents a detailed evaluation of a negotiated skills program for mortgage associates. The evaluation approval is comprehensive with much data on all types of data categories: reaction, learning, application, impact, ROI, and intangibles. Although there is much success, there are many lessons learned.

## Background

The Home Retention Group (HRG) partnered with the Organizational Development Department to provide all HRG associates with negotiations skills training. After the training program was designed, the director of organizational development partnered with the Training Evaluation & Assessment Team (TEA) in response to a request from the stakeholders to determine the effectiveness of this program.

Note: This case was prepared to serve as a basis for discussion rather than an illustration of either effective or ineffective administrative and management practices. Names, dates, places, and data may have been disguised at the request of the author or organization.

After a series of meetings, it was identified that, if the training program was successful, the business would be positively impacted in the following ways:

- Increase in the number of deals activated

- Increase in the number of deals completed

- Increase in the offer amount for short sales

- Increase in the percentage of delinquency paid up-front

With the desired impact identified, TEA designed a measurement strategy that resulted in the following process:

- End-of-Course Evaluations—How did they react to it?

- Pre-Test—How much did the associates know before they started the training?

- Post-Test—How much did the associates know after they completed the training?

- Supervisory Observations—How much of the knowledge/skills that were learned in training are being used on the job?

- Follow-Up Assessment—Perception of how much of the training was useful and the business impact.

### Course Objectives

After the study had been designed, it was necessary to identify the objectives of the course to ensure they were quantifiable. The objectives of the negotiations course are:

- Negotiate as a business-friendly problem solver
- Use active listening skills during the negotiation process
- Apply the strategies for achieving a win-win negotiation
- Identify your personal style as it relates to negotiating situations
- Apply the strengths of four styles to negotiate in situations that are different from your natural preference
- Identify how to use and counter various negotiation tactics
- Adjust to situations when different tactics are applied
- Identify various voice tones and respond effectively

**Participant Selection**

The subject-matter experts (SMEs) for the study were then identified by the organizational development group based on the additional depth of job knowledge required for the skills assessment development task.

The SMEs were asked to select the associates for the study (August Negotiations Training Session) based on job position and level of experience. Associates from three different positions were receiving the training. Position was important because the training could potentially impact each position in a different way, and experience was equally important since the amount of time they had spent negotiating with customers could be related to how they performed on the pre-post skills assessment test and supervisor skill observation.

A control group was then selected by matching each associate who had attended the training with an associate who had not, based on level of experience and position title. The pairs had a similar amount of experience and the same position title (see Table 12.1 below).

**Table 12.1.  Level of Experience**

| Trained. Attended Training in August | | | Not Trained. Control Group | | |
|---|---|---|---|---|---|
| Name | Position | Years of Exp | Name | Position | Years of Exp |
| HRG | 1 | 4.5 months | HRG | 1 | 6 months |
| HRG | 3 | 6 years | HRG | 3 | 5.5 years |

This selection process ensured that TEA would not be able to attribute performance differences on the assessment or observations to only the training. The differences could be due to differing levels of negotiations knowledge/skills.

However, after the pre-post assessments were completed and the supervisor observations were more than 50 percent done, TEA discovered that the majority of the HRG 1s and 3s selected for the control group had actually attended the July pilot session. As a result, a new control group of non-trained associates was selected for the post-test comparison, and for the supervisory observations, those associates who had attended the training in July were removed from the overall study.

## Evaluation Tool Design

Upon completion of the measurement strategy design, SME selection, participant selection, and control group identification, the designing of the evaluation tools began. This information is covered in the following pages and is broken out by level of evaluation:

- *Level 1:*  Were they satisfied with the program?

- *Level 2:*  How much information was learned during the training?

- *Level 3:* How much of the information did they use when they returned to work?

- *Level 4:* What was the business impact as a result of applying the skills/knowledge learned in training?

- *ROI:* Was there a positive return on investment?

# Level 1: Were They Satisfied with the Program?

### Evaluation Design

The standard course evaluations were used and contained the following categories:

- *Instructor.* How was the instructor's performance during the class?

- *Courseware.* Was the content organized well and the activities helpful in the learning process?

- *Environment.* Was the environment conducive to learning?

- *Learning Effectiveness.* Did the associates feel that they learned new information?

- *Job Impact.* Was the information applicable to their jobs?

- *Business Results.* Did the associates feel that their performance improved as a result of the class?

- *ROI.* Did the course meet the associates' expectations and would they refer their colleagues to it?

### Data Collection

The associates completed an evaluation at the end of each class; the scores for the Negotiations Training (Module 1–4) are listed in Table 12.2.

**Table 12.2.    Reaction to HRG Negotiations (N = 19)**

| Content Area | Rating |
| --- | --- |
| Instructor | 6.89 |
| Courseware | 6.83 |
| Learning Effectiveness | 6.85 |
| Job Impact | 6.95 |
| Business Results | 6.58 |
| Return on Investment | 6.84 |
| Overall Rating | 6.85 |

(Strongly Agree = 7; Strongly Disagree = 1)

### Results and Analysis

Based on the information in the table, the associates were satisfied with the course. The "Job Impact," "Instructor," and "Return on Investment" categories received high ratings at 6.95, 6.89, and 6.84, respectively. No scores dropped below a 5.0, which indicates there were no areas that needed immediate attention.

## Level 2: How Much Information Was Learned During the Training?

### Skill Assessment (Pre-Post Test) Design

An SME identified the key areas of the training that were crucial for the associates to know by the time training was complete. Based on this information, TEA collaborated with the SMEs from Organizational Development and the business units to begin to develop the scenarios and answer options. The assessment was designed to move the culture "forward"; therefore, it was in a format similar to the GRE or SAT, that is, some answers were more right than others. The answers that were in alignment with the current culture were weighted as "somewhat correct," and the answers that were in alignment with the future direction of the culture were weighted as "100 percent correct."

## Data Collection

*Phase I:* The associates who attended the August training completed the online skills assessment at the beginning of Module 1 and took the same assessment two days after the program had ended.

*Phase II:* The remaining associates (everyone except for the trained group aforementioned) also completed the online skills assessment at the same time as the trained group.

Table 12.3 shows the results.

## Results/Analysis

The trained group had a positive increase in scores from the pre-assessment to the post-assessment; however, this increase was not statistically significant. From a practical significance perspective, the difference only demonstrates that, on average, the associates received one more answer right on the post-assessment. This does not demonstrate that a significant amount of learning occurred during the class. (See Table 12.4.)

When comparing the post-assessment scores of the trained versus the non-trained group, on average the HRG 1s and 3s who attended the training scored higher than those who did

**Table 12.3.  Knowledge Before vs. After Training—Trained Group**

|         | Pre-Test | Post-Test | Chg Score | Sig. Diff |
|---------|----------|-----------|-----------|-----------|
| HRG 1   | 69%      | 75%       | 6%        | No        |
| HRG 2   | 72%      | 83%       | 11%       | No        |
| HRG 3   | 77%      | 85%       | 8%        | No        |

**Table 12.4.  Knowledge Comparison After Training (Trained vs. Not Trained)**

| Position | Trained | Not Trained | Chg Score | Sig. Diff |
|----------|---------|-------------|-----------|-----------|
| HRG 1    | 75%     | 71%         | −4%       | no        |
| HRG 2    | 83%     | 83%         | 0%        | no        |
| HRG 3    | 85%     | 79%         | −6%       | no        |

not. However, again, this difference was neither statistically nor practically significant, as it amounted to the trained associates answering one more question correctly. In addition, the average score of the HRG 2s was exactly the same between the trained and the non-trained group.

**Note:** The results from Tables 12.3 and 12.4 demonstrate that, although the associates enjoyed the training, there was not a significant amount of information learned.

As shown in Table 12.5, there is a positive trend of scores increasing as the position title increases. Some of the low scores can be attributable to associates choosing the "somewhat correct" answer, showing that there is still room for improvement in associates being aware of the new techniques that should be used in business transactions.

**Table 12.5.   Overall Differences Between Positions**

| Position | Post-Test |
|---|---|
| HRG 1 | 73% |
| HRG 2 | 78% |
| HRG 3 | 79% |
| Supervisors | 81% |

## Level 3: How Much of the Information Did They Use When They Returned to Work?

### Evaluation Design

An SME identified the key skill areas of the training (nineteen in total) that were crucial for the associates to apply when they returned to their jobs. Based on this information, the TEA developed two assessment tools.

First, a one-page observation checklist was designed so the supervisors could assess how frequently, per call, the associates performed each of the skills learned at the Negotiations Training Program. The scale ranged from "Never" to "Always" and had an option of "No Opportunity" so the associate did not receive a lower score if he/she had no opportunity to demonstrate that skill.

Second, a follow-up questionnaire was developed to gather how much negotiations training the associates felt they were able to apply to their daily calls. This assessment asked associates questions that ranged from "How many of the training objectives were met?" to "How much change occurred in your negotiations skills as a result of the training?" It also requested information regarding the components within the working environment that helped them apply the skills, what prevented this from happening, and how quickly they could apply the information they learned.

Finally, to ensure the performance of each associate was observed consistently, TEA held a series of inter-rater reliability trainings with the HRG supervisors participating in the study. This training was designed to accomplish two things: (1) the supervisors needed to better understand the human error that is involved in observing the performance of associates (rating someone higher because he/she does things the way you do, rating someone lower because you compare him/her to the last person you observed, etc.), and (2) it was important for the supervisors to agree on the level of performance they felt meets, exceeds, and falls below expectations. After these two goals were accomplished, the supervisors would understand how to objectively assess an associate and how to do so in a manner that was in alignment with the overall vision of the HRG Department.

## Data Collection

To determine if the negotiation skills learned in class were utilized when the associates returned to the phones, the HRG supervisors were asked to listen to one phone (of both the trained and non-trained associates), every week for six weeks. Originally, it was assumed that all associates were on a dialer, which would allow the supervisor to request a call that had taken place so he/she could listen to the recording at any time. However, many of the associates were not on a dialer, which resulted in supervisors being "on the associate's line" until he/she took a live call that supervisors could review. In addition, the supervisors could not review their own associates, to avoid any potential bias. This too presented a problem as the supervisors in one location were scheduled to review associates in the other location and vice versa, but because the calls could not be "requested," the matching had to be altered so that Location 1 supervisors could observe Location 1 associates and Location 2 supervisors could review Location 2 associates.

Furthermore, so the associate could receive coaching feedback regarding his/her performance on each call, the reviewing supervisor provided the direct supervisor with the feedback from each call. This was done so the associate would receive coaching from his/her direct supervisor, which was felt by the group to be the most appropriate solution.

To ensure the data was collected from each participant, TEA went to both locations to administer them in person. This ensured that all questions asked in the questionnaire could be clarified immediately and that all assessments were returned.

**Results/Analysis**

The supervisors used the following scale to assess the observations:

- Always = 5
- Usually = 4
- About $\frac{1}{2}$ = 3
- Seldom = 2
- Never = 1
- No Opportunity = No score

A comparative analysis is shown in Table 12.6.

When comparing the HRG 2s who attended training and those who did not, there were no significant differences. See Table 12.7 for a comparison across positions.

**Table 12.6.  HRG 2 Comparative Analysis**

|  | Trained (N = 11) | Not Trained (N = 7) | Difference | Sig Change |
|---|---|---|---|---|
| Average Call Rating | 4.54 | 4.46 | .08 | no |

**Table 12.7.  HRG Comparative Analysis Across Positions**

|  | HRG 1 | HRG 2 | HRG 3 | Sig Diff |
|---|---|---|---|---|
| Average Call Rating | 3.6 | 4.5 | 3.6 | no |

Both HRG 2 groups demonstrated the skills, on average, between usually and always; therefore the training did not provide any additional skill sets that those who hadn't received training weren't already demonstrating. The HRG 1s and 3s are demonstrating the skills, on average, between half the time and usually. There is room for improvement in these areas.

The results of the follow-up questionnaire are shown in Table 12.8. When asked to indicate the degree of success in meeting the goals of the training program:

- HRG 1s rated the degree of success slightly lower than "generally successful" (3.85).

- HRG 2s (N = 11) rated the negotiations training as slightly higher than "generally successful" (4.18) in meeting the goals.

- HRG 3s (N = 1) rated the degree of success between "limited success" and "generally successful" (3.67).

See further results in Table 12.9.

**Table 12.8.    Meeting HRG Negotiations Objectives**

Listed below are the goals of the *Negotiations Program* you completed in August. After reflecting on the program, please indicate the degree of success in meeting these goals.

| Question | HRG 1 (N = 3) | HRG 2 (N = 11) | HRG 3 (N = 1) |
|---|---|---|---|
| 1 = No Success, 2 = Very Little Success, 3 = Limited Success, 4 = Generally Successful, 5 = Completely Successful | | | |
| Negotiate as a business-friendly problem solver | 3.67 | 4.27 | 3.00 |
| Use active listening skills during the negotiation process | 4.00 | 4.45 | 4.00 |
| Apply the strategies for achieving a win-win negotiation | 3.67 | 4.27 | 3.00 |
| Identify your personal style as it relates to negotiating situations | 3.33 | 4.00 | 4.00 |
| Apply the strengths of your style to negotiate in situations that are different from your natural preferences | 4.00 | 3.91 | 3.00 |
| Identify how to use and counter various negotiation tactics | 4.33 | 4.09 | 3.00 |
| Adjust to situation when different tactics are applied | 4.00 | 4.27 | 4.00 |
| Identify various voice tones and respond effectively | 4.00 | 4.27 | 5.00 |
| Respond appropriately to both positive and negative voice dynamics | 3.67 | 4.09 | 4.00 |

**Table 12.9.  Relevance of HRG Negotiations Program**

Please rate, on a scale of 1 to 5, the relevance of each of the *negotiation program* elements to your job:

| Question | HRG 1 (N = 3) | HRG 2 (N = 11) | HRG 3 (N = 1) |
|---|---|---|---|
| 1 = No relevance, 5 = Very relevant | | | |
| Interactive Activities (Role Plays) | 4.33 | 4.36 | 3.00 |
| Training Workbook | 3.67 | 4.18 | 4.00 |
| Instructor Lecture | 4.33 | 4.64 | 4.00 |
| Take-Home Negotiation Cards | 3.33 | 2.36 | 4.00 |

The instructor lecture and interactive activities (role plays) were rated as having the most relevance to their jobs by all associates. More results are shown in Tables 12.10 through 12.17.

**Table 12.10.  Use of HRG Negotiations Tools**

| Question | HRG 1 (N = 3) | HRG 2 (N = 11) | HRG 3 (N = 1) |
|---|---|---|---|
| Have you used the Training Workbook? | 33% Yes | 36% Yes | 100% Yes |

None of the associates used the take-home negotiations cards (Table 12.11). Some associates even stated that they never received them.

**Table 12.11.  Use of HRG Negotiations Tools**

| Question | HRG 1 (N = 3) | HRG 2 (N = 11) | HRG 3 (N = 1) |
|---|---|---|---|
| Have you used the Take Home Negotiations cards? | 0% Yes | 0% Yes | 0% Yes |

### Table 12.12.    Use of HRG Negotiations Skills

Please indicate the degree to which you have positively changed the use of the following behaviors **as a result of your participation** in the *negotiations program*:

| Question | HRG 1 (N = 3) | HRG 2 (N = 11) | HRG 3 (N = 1) |
|---|---|---|---|
| 1 = No Change, 2 = Some Change, 3 = Moderate Change, 4 = Significant Change | | | |
| Developing a good rapport with the borrower in the first three minutes of the phone call | 3.00 | 2.27 | 3.00 |
| Demonstrating the ability to empathize with the borrower (put myself in his/her shoes and respond in a manner appropriate to the situation) | 3.00 | 2.55 | 2.00 |
| Appropriately matching my tone with the borrower's tone when necessary | 3.00 | 2.09 | 4.00 |
| Delivering information in a business-friendly voice when negotiating with the borrower (maintaining a professionalism in tone and language) | 2.00 | 2.00 | 4.00 |
| Demonstrating a solid awareness of how my verbal reactions affect the borrower when a comment/statement evoked a negative reaction | 3.00 | 2.55 | 3.00 |
| Understanding the assumptions and facts that I was negotiating on (clear understanding of the facts provided by borrower) | 2.33 | 2.45 | 2.00 |

**Table 12.12.**    *(continued)*

| Question | HRG 1 (N = 3) | HRG 2 (N = 11) | HRG 3 (N = 1) |
|---|---|---|---|
| Asking follow-up questions to get more information (when the borrower gave information that warranted clarification) | 2.33 | 2.18 | 2.00 |
| Summarizing what the borrower just said so there was shared understanding (recapped what was said to ensure we were on the same page) | 2.33 | 2.27 | 3.00 |
| Offering explanations and information (providing additional information about the options and explaining why those were appropriate for the situation) | 1.67 | 2.36 | 2.00 |
| Effectively staying in control of the call (or regarding control if the borrower was dictating the direction) | 2.67 | 2.09 | 2.00 |
| Recognizing the AMC policy framework when negotiating with borrowers (abiding by HRG policies/procedures) | 1.33 | 2.18 | 2.00 |
| Recognizing friendly negotiating tactics (ability to identify when a borrower was attempting to negotiate in a friendly non-confrontational way) | 2.00 | 2.27 | 1.00 |

*(continued)*

**Table 12.12.**   (*continued*)

| Question | HRG 1 (N = 3) | HRG 2 (N = 11) | HRG 3 (N = 1) |
|---|---|---|---|
| Effectively countering unfriendly tactics (able to identify when an unfriendly tactic was being used and could respond appropriately) | 2.00 | 2.55 | 4.00 |
| Utilizing concession effectively (seizing an opportunity to use them or ensuring the borrower offered something before a concession was offered) | 2.67 | 2.36 | 3.00 |
| Effectively claiming the limit (articulating to the client the conditions that cannot be negotiated; holding my ground) | 1.67 | 2.36 | 4.00 |
| Continuing the negotiation process when the borrower says "no" (demonstrating the knowledge of "What is it you don't understand about 'No' ") | 2.33 | 2.64 | 2.00 |
| Maintaining the focus on what was in the best interest of the customer instead of giving an ultimatum (negotiating "Interests" not "Positions") | 3.00 | 2.36 | 2.00 |
| Ensuring the final outcome meets the needs of both AMQ and the borrower (negotiating for a win-win outcome) | 2.67 | 2.27 | 2.00 |

*No opportunity to use was removed from the overall score

**Table 12.13.  Use of HRG Negotiations Skills**

| Question | HRG 1 (N = 3) | HRG 2 (N = 11) | HRG 3 (N = 1) |
|---|---|---|---|
| What percent of your total work time have you spent on tasks that require the knowledge/ skills presented in this training? | 57% | 58% | 60% |

**Table 12.14.  Critical Perspective to HRG Negotiations**

| Question | HRG 1 (N = 3) | HRG 2 (N = 11) | HRG 3 (N = 1) |
|---|---|---|---|
| On a scale of 0 percent (not at all) to 100 percent (extremely critical), how critical was applying the content of this training to your job success? | 52% | 72% | 40% |

When asked to indicate the degree to which they had positively changed the behaviors targeted in the training, all associates felt that they experienced between some change and a moderate change, (HRG 1 = 2.39, HRG 2 = 2.32, HRG 3 = 2.61).

The behaviors used most frequently since the training were:

- HRG 1 = Empathizing

- HRG 2 = Developing rapport

- HRG 3 = Recognizing friendly negotiating tactics

**Table 12.15.  Timing of Use of HRG Negotiations**

| Question | HRG 1 (N = 3) | HRG 2 (N = 11) | HRG 3 (N = 1) |
|---|---|---|---|
| I was able to apply the training to my job within: | 100%—The first few days | 100%—The first few days/1 week | 100%—The first few days |

Table 12.16.    Most Appropriate Job for HRG Negotiations

Question: Please indicate the HRG associate position the *negotiations program would be the most useful for*:

| | HRG 1 (N = 3) | HRG 2 (N = 11) | HRG 3 (N = 1) |
|---|---|---|---|
| HRG 1s with little/no experience in negotiations | 100% | 73% | 100% |
| HRG 1s with experience in negotiations | 67% | 73% | 100% |
| HRG 2s | 33% | 91% | 0% |
| HRG 3s | 33% | 73% | 0% |
| Supervisor/Managers | 33% | 55% | 0% |

Table 12.17.    Enablers to HRG Negotiations Use

Question: What enablers, if any, are present to help you use the skills or knowledge gained from the *negotiations program*:

| | HRG 1 (N = 3) | HRG 2 (N = 11) | HRG 3 (N = 1) |
|---|---|---|---|
| I am provided opportunities to use the skills | 100% | 73% | 0% |
| I have enough time in my work day to apply the skills | 100% | 45% | 0% |
| My work environment supports the use of these skills/behaviors | 100% | 64% | 0% |
| My supervisor helps reinforce the information I learned in negotiations training | 33% | 45% | 0% |
| My manager helps reinforce the information I learned in negotiations training | 33% | 45% | 0% |
| This material applies directly to my job situation | 33% | 73% | 0% |

Associates felt that about 60 percent of their total work time was spent on tasks requiring the skills learned in training (Table 12.13).

When asked how critical the application of these skills were to their job success on a scale of 0 percent (not at all) to 100 percent (extremely critical), the criticality was rated lower than expected (Table 12.14). For a class designed to address the fundamentals of a business, these percentages should have been higher.

All associates were able to apply the training within one week (Table 12.15). When asked what HRG associate position this training would be used for (Table 12.16):

- HRG 1s felt that it would be most useful for HRG 1s with little or no experience

- HRG 2s felt that it would be most useful for HRG 1s with experience in negotiations

- The HRG 3 stated that this training was most useful for HRG 2s

**Note:** Caution should be taken due to the fact that only one HRG 3 was included in this study.

When asked what enablers were present to help use the skills gained from training (Table 12.17):

- HRG 1s and 2s felt that they had the opportunity, the time, and a supportive environment to enable their use of the skills.

- HRG 3s felt that there were no enablers.

Barriers were also inquired about, and only one associate stated that a barrier existed. It was noted that there was not enough time to apply the skills.

## Level 4: What Was the Business Impact?

### Evaluation Design

To determine whether the training had a positive impact on the HRG business (that is, increase in number of deals activated, etc.), data had to be collected on each of these outcomes. In order to obtain the most accurate measure of this, the decision was made to gather participant estimation data. Originally, an attempt was made to collect tangible business data at the associate level; however, only the "total delinquency amount" metric was provided. In addition, the analyst who provided the data commented:

> "The associate names will not be as accurate or complete the further back the course completed because Resolve is a transactional system and we began a snapshot of the associate data only a short time ago."

Therefore, the data was not accurate, which meant it would be unclear as to the increase due to the training. Therefore, during the follow-up questionnaire session, a series of questions were asked surrounding each of the four business outcomes identified on the first page. They are listed below:

- Increase in the number of deals activated

- Increase in the number of deals completed

- Increase in the offer amount for short sales

- Increase in the percentage of the delinquency paid up-front

### Data Collection/Isolation Technique

During the follow-up questionnaire session, each associate was asked if he or she felt the knowledge/skills learned impacted any of the targeted business outcomes. If he/she felt the knowledge/skills learned had influence, the associate was asked to identify the amount ranging from "Some Influence" to "Very Significant Influence." After the amount of influence was identified, the associates were asked to provide information on the following:

- How much of an increase per month did they see before versus after the training?

- What percent of that improvement was a direct result of attending the training?

- How confident were they in their responses to the two questions above (this is to conservatively account for any lack of confidence in the estimations)?

- What is the average monetary value for each unit of that outcome?

**Note:** The isolation technique used to determine how much improvement was a result of the training is accounted for in the second and third bullets.

### Results/Analysis

Tables 12.18 through 12.20 include data on results. Most associates saw the connection of the HRG Training Program affecting this business outcome.

**Table 12.18.  Number of Deals Completed—Monetary Value Was Attributable**

|  | Total Value | Percentage of Improvement Due to the Training | Average Value Per Unit | Confidence Level in the Estimate | Adjusted Value |
|---|---|---|---|---|---|
| HRG 1 | 0 | 0% | $20,000 | 0% | $      0 |
| HRG 1 | 0 | 0% | $20,000 | 0% | $      0 |
| HRG 1 | 3 | 5% | $20,000 | 15% | $    450 |
| HRG 2 | 0 | 0% | $20,000 | 0% | $      0 |
| HRG 2 | 5 | 50% | $20,000 | 40% | $ 20,000 |
| HRG 2 | 0 | 0% | $20,000 | 95% | $      0 |

(*continued overleaf*)

**Table 12.18.** (*continued*)

|  | Total Value | Percentage of Improvement Due to the Training | Average Value Per Unit | Confidence Level in the Estimate | Adjusted Value |
|---|---|---|---|---|---|
| HRG 2 | 15 | 80% | $20,000 | 90% | $216,000* |
| HRG 2 | 0 | 0% | $20,000 | 0% | $        0 |
| HRG 2 | 10 | 50% | $20,000 | 60% | $  60,000 |
| HRG 2 | 4 | 20% | $20,000 | 90% | $  14,400 |
| HRG 2 | 8 | 15% | $20,000 | 90% | $  21,600 |
| HRG 2 | 15 | 10% | $20,000 | 70% | $  21,000 |
| HRG 2 | 0 | 0% | $20,000 | 0% | $        0 |
| HRG 2 | 0 | 20% | $20,000 | 90% | $        0 |
| HRG 3 | 0 | 10% | $20,000 | 50% | $        0 |

Total = $137,450.00

*Removed in order to keep estimate conservative (Total with = $353,450.00)

**Table 12.19.    Percentage of Delinquency Paid Up-Front—Monetary Value Was Attributable**

|  | Total Value | Percentage of Improvement Due to the Training | Average Value Per Unit | Confidence Level in the Estimate | Adjusted Value |
|---|---|---|---|---|---|
| HRG 1 | 10 | 50% | $10,000 | 75% | $37,500 |
| HRG 1 | 50 | 0% | $10,000 | 0% | $      0 |
| HRG 1 | 0 | 0% | $10,000 | 0% | $      0 |
| HRG 2 | 0 | 0% | $10,000 | 0% | $      0 |
| HRG 2 | 10 | 50% | $10,000 | 80% | $40,000 |
| HRG 2 | 0 | 0% | $10,000 | 0% | $      0 |
| HRG 2 | 10 | 75% | $10,000 | 80% | $60,000 |
| HRG 2 | 0 | 0% | $10,000 | 0% | $      0 |
| HRG 2 | 10 | 50% | $10,000 | 60% | $30,000 |
| HRG 2 | 15 | 50% | $10,000 | 90% | $67,500 |
| HRG 2 | 10 | 15% | $10,000 | 80% | $12,000 |
| HRG 2 | 0 | 0% | $10,000 | 0% | $      0 |
| HRG 2 | 0 | 0% | $10,000 | 0% | $      0 |
| HRG 2 | 0 | 0% | $10,000 | 0% | $      0 |
| HRG 3 | 0 | 0% | $10,000 | 0% | $      0 |

Total = $247,000.00

**Table 12.20.   Number of Deals Activated—No Monetary Value Was Attributable**

|  | Total Value | Percentage of Improvement Due to the Training | Average Value Per Unit | Confidence Level in the Estimate | Total |
|---|---|---|---|---|---|
| HRG 1 | 20 | 50% | X | 80% | 8.00 |
| HRG 1 | 12 | 10% | X | 20% | .24 |
| HRG 1 | 10 | 70% | X | 85% | 5.95 |
| HRG 2 | 0 | 0% | X | 0% | 0 |
| HRG 2 | 15 | 10% | X | 80% | 1.20 |
| HRG 2 | 15 | 30% | X | 90% | 4.05 |
| HRG 2 | 5 | 20% | X | 85% | .85 |
| HRG 2 | 10 | 50% | X | 60% | 3.00 |
| HRG 2 | 0 | 0% | X | 0% | 0 |
| HRG 2 | 0 | 0% | X | 0% | 0 |
| HRG 2 | 0 | 0% | X | 0% | 0 |
| HRG 2 | 10 | 50% | X | 40% | 2.00 |
| HRG 2 | 10 | 80% | X | 90% | 7.20 |
| HRG 2 | 0 | 0% | X | 0% | 0 |
| HRG 3 | 0 | 0% | X | 0% | 0 |

Total Benefit = Thirty-Three Deals

## ROI: Was There a Positive Return on Investment?

The benefit cost ratio and return on investment calculation are as follows:

BCR : Benefits/Cost

ROI : Net Program Benefits/Cost × 100

Based on the monetary benefit isolated by participants, the Negotiations Training Program resulted in a 12.15:1 BCR and an ROI of 1,114.62 percent. This suggests that for every $1 invested in the Negotiations Training Program, HRG receives $11.14 back after costs.

$$\text{BCR} = \$384,450.00/\$31,651.98 = 12.15:1$$

$$\text{ROI} = \frac{(\$384,450.00 - \$31,651.98)}{\$31,651.98} \times 100 = 1,114.62\%$$

## Intangible Benefits

*Follow-Up Questionnaire*

- Increase in customer service

- Decrease in calls escalated to a supervisor

- Increase in confidence level

### Anecdotal Information

After the supervisors completed the training and subsequent performance calibration exercises on how to consistently and objectively review the HRG associates' performance, extensive feedback was provided. Comments were made that this was the most valuable training they had ever received.

The supervisors felt that there was extreme value in integrating the supervisory observation process into the current culture to facilitate coaching conversations and focus on quality as well as production.

Finally, the observation checklist that was utilized is also being considered as a valuable tool to integrate into the performance management process with the HRG associates.

## Limitations

Throughout the ROI study, limitations were collected and subsequently documented. First, all associates did not write their names on the pre-tests; therefore, a manual matching process was used so change scores from before the training versus after the training so the results could be assessed. Second, the control group that was identified by the SMEs was unknowingly comprised of associates who had already attended the training; therefore, part of the control group had to be removed from the study. As a result, this alleviated our ability to compare the HRG 1s and 3s in the supervisor observation section, which would have been valuable data. Third, many of the scenarios and answer options provided by the SMEs were not correct. The HRG group was going through a large culture change and the items provided to the evaluation group were not in alignment with the new culture. Therefore, a series of items were removed from the August and September overall scores so accurate scores could be communicated to the executive sponsor. And, per the request of the executive team, the questions were rewritten so accurate tests could be administered to the October and November sessions. The ability to compare August/September to October/November scores was removed; however, the executive team was able to gauge whether some of the associates truly understood the culture changes that had been implemented.

In addition to those already discussed, the following limitations were also experienced. First, the Supervisor Observation Checklist was designed on the assumption that "new" negotiating techniques would be taught to each level of associates. However, after receiving qualitative information from the participants, the curriculum did not differ depending on experience. All associates (Levels 1 through 3) received the same information. Second, the SMEs' design of "how" the supervisors could observe each associate's performance was not applicable to all supervisors. After the observation process started, it was discovered that only some associates' conversations with customers were recorded. Therefore, some supervisors could not request a copy of the recorded call and actually had to wait on the line until the associate took a live call. Finally, Hurricane Katrina occurred in the middle of the study, which delayed the supervisor observation process and provided complications sufficient enough for some supervisors to not complete the observation process at all.

## Lessons Learned

In light of the myriad of limitations that were encountered, there were many valuable lessons learned. First, always ensure the subject-matter experts chosen for you to collaborate with are agreed on by **both** the client requesting the training and the department delivering the training. This will allow for accurate information to be conveyed and ensure everyone is in agreement on the information that is presented.

Second, ensure you either have timelines to review tests and observation strategies long enough or a back-up reviewer in case an executive does not have time for the final review. This will ensure that the project moves along at the pace necessary to gather data.

Third, if the key executive stakeholder has made a specific request for a data collection methodology, ensure the final draft is reviewed and approved **prior** to implementation. This will ensure your level of confidence that you are meeting all expectations.

Fourth, ensure you have planned the study in full detail prior to project kick-off. Gather all impact data (to ensure it is obtainable), account for culture, technology, and resources allocation for all methodologies, and ensure you are impacting the environment as little as possible with your study. You want to be relatively invisible if possible.

Fifth, make sure all t's are crossed and i's are dotted. Do not "assume" that your business partners or SMEs think the way you do. Ensure you have provided detailed instructions for all steps and be physically present as often as possible to account for any confounding variables or challenging situations that may affect your study.

Sixth, when collecting participant estimation data at the end of the study, do these sessions with as few people as possible. One or two people should be the maximum if you have very complex outcome variables and entry-level associates. If you have associates who hold positions with more responsibility, three to five associates is recommended.

Finally, if you are holding calibration sessions so all performance observers are assessing "successful performance" the same way, ensure you allow enough time so everyone agrees. Approximately three sessions prior to observations beginning (approximately two hours apiece) is recommended, and refresher calibration calls were also requested by the supervisors who went through this exercise.

## Communication Strategy

The results of the data were communicated within two weeks after it was collected. This information was discussed with the trainer, the organizational development director, as well as the HRG executives to ensure adequate progress was being made and any quick changes could be acted upon to maximize impact. In addition, the final ROI study was presented to the executive vice president of special services, his executive team, and the team of associates that we partnered with from the Organizational Development Department. Results were shared and a debriefing session on aspects to continue moving forward with and opportunities for enhancement was held.

### Questions for Discussion

1. What steps should be taken if the training program has already started, but the objectives to what the training program is intended to accomplish have not been identified yet?

2. When choosing the subject-matter experts, how do you assess whether you have the correct people or not?

3. What other methodologies could have been used to measure the amount of knowledge the HRG associates had obtained?

4. How can you ensure your Level 3 plan will impact production the least while gathering the most accurate data?

5. What type of preparation should you do when you are communicating a positive ROI, but the "problem" that has been identified would be better solved with a technology solution versus a training solution?

6. How frequently should the data be communicated to the stakeholders and the training department you are working with?

7. What type of confidentiality should you consider prior to beginning an ROI study? Who should be considered, and how do you set these expectations up-front?

8. How do you manage the expectations of the client before you begin an ROI study? And is this even important?

## About the Authors

For the past seven years, **Kendall Kerekes** has had the privilege of developing tools and strategies to develop and assess human capital development, surveys/assessments, selection and retention strategies, leadership development programs, succession planning methodologies, and training evaluation programs, which include implementing the Phillips ROI Methodology for both public and private sectors. In addition, Kendall has led a high performing evaluation team of I/O psychology practitioners who specialized in evaluating the impact of talent development programs for corporate shared services, home loan origination and processing, loan servicing and executive management. This team was responsible for a cost savings of over $5 million due to the series of impact studies that were completed and acted upon.

Kendall is currently employed with Indymac Bank as the First Vice President of HR for the Client Consumer Direct groups (Sales, Servicing, and Banks), overseeing the strategic design and development of the Recruiting, Training, Compensation and Employee Relations Departments. Kendall graduated with a B.A. in Psychology from Westmont College and an M.S. in Industrial/Organizational Psychology from CSU San Bernardino. Kendall can be contacted at 1 Banting Rd, Irvine, CA, 92618; e-mail: Kendall.Kerekes@imb.com

**Kelly Coumbe** has been involved in company-wide selection, retention, training, promotion, and Six Sigma business initiatives for more than five years in both the public and private sectors. She helped build an internal training evaluation department with Kendall Kerekes, including process and tool design, implementation of the Phillips ROI Methodology, and helped the company achieve large savings based on the data analyses conducted.

Previously, she acted as the project manager for implementing a nation-wide selection system and a job specification tool for effective hiring of top tier managers for a Fortune 500 company. Recently, she redesigned a retail loan process from the initial sale through funding, designing automated risk mitigation software, and led Six Sigma Green Belt training in the financial services industry. Currently, she serves in a Black Belt role for a Fortune Global 50 company, where she is designing and improving business processes and helping with the overall implementation of Six Sigma across the company.

Ms. Coumbe graduated with a B.A. in psychology from Minnesota State University and an M.S. in industrial/organizational psychology from California State University, San Bernardino. She can be contacted at ING, 200 N. Sepulveda Boulevard, El Segundo, CA, 90245; email: coumbek@ingadvisors.com or kelly-lynncoumbe@hotmail.com

**John Ruggiero** attended Rutgers College with a double major in psychology (B.S.) and journalism (B.A.). During college, he worked as a counselor for adults with pervasive mental illnesses and children in a behavioral modification program. After graduation from college, John pursued a master's degree in social-organizational psychology from Columbia University, where he completed internships that provided practical experience in large organizations. After completing his master's degree, John has worked in large organizations in the realm of organizational development and performance management. He is currently a program manager in Learning Analytics at Southern California Edison.

**Sanam Razzaghi** pursued a graduate degree from Columbia University, where she obtained her master's degree in social-organizational psychology. While in graduate school, she completed internships with large corporations that provided her with practical experience in organizational development. Ms. Razzaghi has since worked for large corporations in various areas of organizational effectiveness, such as training evaluation and change management. She currently works for Watson Wyatt Worldwide as a consultant. Prior to graduate school, Ms. Razzaghi obtained a bachelor's degree in psychology from McGill University in Montreal, where she completed her thesis, "Social Roles and the Perceptions of Others in a Work Environment."

# 13

# Measuring ROI in Manage by Fact (MBF) Training
## An Automotive Wheels Manufacturing Company

Alaster Nyaude

## Abstract

Quality Wheels International (QWI) wanted all two hundred employees, including first- and second-level managers, to attend the Manage by Fact (MBF) training. A Level 4 evaluation of the MBF impact was conducted based on one group of ten participants who completed the training. To isolate the effects of the training, participants' estimates, supervisor estimate, and finance department estimates were used. A fully loaded cost of the program was computed at $187,600. An ROI of 332 percent and a BCR of 4.3:1 were determined.

## Background

Quality Wheels International produces automobile wheels for a number of customers in North America, South America, Asia, Africa, and Europe. The strategic vision for the organization is to become the best and leading automotive supplier. The thrust of the company is to work toward creating greater value in the

Note: This case was prepared to serve as a basis for discussion rather than an illustration of either effective or ineffective administrative and management practices.

eyes of its constituents by achieving the following strategies: (1) growth by satisfying customers—QWI believes that its customers require systemic customer service in which the company employs an integrated business approach that includes maximizing continuous improvement, quality, technology, innovation, and safety performance throughout the company and cross-functional groups are used to ensure business excellence across all company divisions; (2) growth by producing less costly products and by implementing and continuing to research new ways to minimize operational expenses; and (3) growth by investing in intellectual human capital as a competitive strength and to ensure perpetual growth for QWI. The company is a learning organization that continues to promote and foster a winning team of trained, talented employees at all levels. QWI's philosophical culture is that of continuous improvement, open communication, organizational learning, close interaction, and employee responsibility.

## Business Problem

QWI has been experiencing some problems of high external and internal product rejects due to quality issues of non-conformance, late deliveries, high inventory stocks (work in progress), and low sales volume at one of its plants in Georgia.

## Gap and Needs Assessment

The performance improvement practitioner and the client agreed to conduct a gap and needs assessment of the organization before recommending solutions. The goal of the gap analysis was to find the difference between what should be and what was. In Table 13.1, the expected performance column shows what the level of performance should be. The current performance column represents what it actually is. The gap column is the difference.

**Table 13.1. Gap Analysis**

| Process or Activity | Expected Performance (A) | Current Performance (B) | Performance Gap (A minus B) | Effect of Gap on Organization |
|---|---|---|---|---|
| Scrap rate is too high | 5% scrap | 29% scrap | −24% | The company might end up shutting down operations or transferring business to another country. |
| External and internal rejects (customer complaints) | 0 complaints per month | 8 complaints per month | less than 8 | The chances of losing business are so high. The company needs to reverse this trend and focus more on quality and on customer satisfaction. |
| Cost associated with scrap | US$150 000 per month is considered acceptable | $1.2 million per month | −$1,050 000 | The cost is too high and unsustainable. |
| Supply spending | 10 percent of the operational expense costs | 35 percent of operational expense costs | −25 percent an unfavorable position | Unsustainable business position. The company needs to reduce costs to survive. |
| Delivery time | 95 percent on time | 65 percent | 30 percent is required to improve on-time delivery | The company may lose customers to competitors. |

The worksheet was adapted from Gupta (1999, p. 145).

319

## Intervention Selection

A business analysis of the gap and needs assessment revealed that the business problems were due to lack of problem-solving techniques and teamwork training. A training solution/intervention was proposed to bridge and inspire employees and management to greater performance. A Manage by Fact (MBF) training program was therefore designed and developed. The purpose of the course is to introduce participants to principles of business excellence and to teach participants how to work in teams and solve business problems through a step-by-step problem-solving process. Topics included safety, employee contribution, economic value adding, employee code of conduct, business ethics, and institutionalization of the principles of business excellence that include problem-solving tools such as run chart, check sheet, Pareto, fishbone, five whys, problem simulation, role plays, negotiation, and mediation activities.

## Objectives of the MBF Training

At the end of the eight-hour training, the participants will:

- Be equipped with the skills to apply principles of business excellence to their jobs within a day of receiving training and improve standard production per hour by at least 25 percent.

- Be able to add value to business performance by employing tools to improve quality and ensure customer satisfaction, as measured by a reduction in the number of internal product rejects (complaints) to zero or one per week within one week of receiving training.

- Be able to implement the MBF standard problem-solving methodology to improve equipment optimization and uptime by at least 20 percent within one week of receiving training.

- Be able to add value to the flow of business processes by being cost-effective and reducing supply spending by 20 percent.

## Data Collection Plan

Data collection methods included a survey questionnaire, observations, self-assessments, and interviews. Table 13.2 is a breakdown of the data collection plan.

## Training Effects Isolation Methods

The issue of isolating the effects of training should come into play when there are different owners of the processes influencing business results. The question that remains will be to answer how much improvement training alone can exert on performance.

While several techniques are available to isolate the impact of training, QWI chose to use participants' estimates, supervisors/management estimates, and expert estimates. These identified techniques were chosen based on: (1) feasibility to implement and manage, (2) accuracy provided by the technique when compared to the accuracy needed, (3) credibility of the technique with the target audience, and (4) for being simple and inexpensive to manage.

## Plan for Calculating Benefits and Costs for the MBF ROI Impact Study

*Measures Taken to Ensure Data Credibility*

A communication plan entails that every milestone of the project be communicated clearly to all stakeholders. The metrics in use are the standard business day-to-day metrics that are credible to all stakeholders. These are sales volume, number of external and internal rejects, work in progress, on-time delivery, scrap, supply spending, and percent of in-house chips melt. Primary business data comes from daily, weekly, and monthly recorded performance reports. Data in Table 13.3 was pulled from Business Objects, software that stores data as measured by the standard accounting and

**Table 13.2. Data Collection**

| Level | Broad Program Objective(s) | Measures | Data Collection Method/Instruments | Data Sources | Timing | Responsibilities |
|---|---|---|---|---|---|---|
| 1 | **Reaction/Satisfaction.** Participants to rate the program as relevant, important, and deployable to their jobs | 4 out of 5 on a 5-point Likert rating scale | Survey questionnaire designed on the Likert scale of 1 to 5 | Employees, supervisors, trainers | One day after training | Operational excellence manager and facilitator |
| 2 | **Learning.** Participants to demonstrate ability to transfer skills learned onto their jobs | At least 85 percent completion of Statistical Process Control (SPC) charts and calibration records | Observation, performance record, and self-assessment | Employees and supervisors, calibration charts, SPC records, and production records | Expected at end of training | Business excellence manager and facilitator |
| 3 | **Application/ Implementation.** Participants to practice and apply the acquired competencies on a routine basis | Equipment uptime expected to increase by at least 20 percent; expected training impact of at least 25 percent increase in productivity per hour; operational efficiency to be at least 85 percent; on-time deliveries/shipments with 45 percent reduction in delayed deliveries | Survey questionnaires and structured interviews, observations, and performance records | Employees, supervisors, employee subordinates, peer employees | Two weeks after receiving training | Operational excellence manager and facilitator |

| | | | | | |
|---|---|---|---|---|---|
| 4 | **Business Impact.** Participants to derive improvement initiatives in all key areas of the business: productivity, equipment uptime, internal and external rejects, sales volume, on-time delivery, and reduced work in progress | At least 30 percent increase in throughput per individual, internal, and external rejects of products to be reduced by 50 percent; zero missed deliveries; reduce work in progress by 90 percent and continue to produce and deliver on time. | Survey questionnaires | Employees, supervisors, visual system management (VMS) | Two weeks after receiving training | Operational excellence manager and facilitator |
| 5 | **ROI.** An ROI of at least 25 percent is expected | **Baseline Data:** Based on available business metrics on productivity, equipment uptime, production efficiency, sales volume, internal and external rejects, work in progress, and shipping information **Comments:** ROI will be demonstrated through monetary values attached to increase in productivity, efficiency, sales volume, reduced internal rejects, reduced external rejects, and less work in progress. The stakeholders believe in these metrics and are committed to remain enlisted in measuring ROI impact. | | | | |

*Source:* From ROI Institute (2006). *ROI Certification: Building Capability and Expertise with ROI Implementation.* Birmingham, AL: Author, p. 127.

Table 13.3.    Baseline Data Before
Training Intervention

| Performance Metric | August | September |
|---|---|---|
| External rejects | 8 | 9 |
| Internal rejects | 8 | 11 |
| Work in progress | 10 | 11 |
| Sales volume | 8 | 7 |
| On-time delivery | 65 | 60 |
| Scrap | 28.57 | 30.22 |
| Supply spending | 35 | 37 |
| In-house chips melt | 54 | 40 |
| Equipment uptime | 65 | 60 |

process metrics. On every visual management system (VMS) plant performance data is posted and displayed for communication purposes with all stakeholders, including employees. Table 13.3 and Figure 13.1 show plant performance as measured in terms of percentages prior to MBF training.

## Methods for Converting Data to Money

There are several methods for converting data to money. In QWI they have already been converted. For each measure there was a standard value, except for one measure: in-house chips mount. We use the standard value for the vendor. This makes this step easy and credible.

## Approaches for ROI Calculation

Two approaches stand out as the preferred methods to determine ROI annualized impact in terms of dollar values: benefit-cost ratio (BCR) and the basic ROI formula. BCR compares the annual economic benefits of the program to the cost of the program. ROI is the most appropriate method for evaluating training investment and is expressed as the ratio of net program benefits divided by

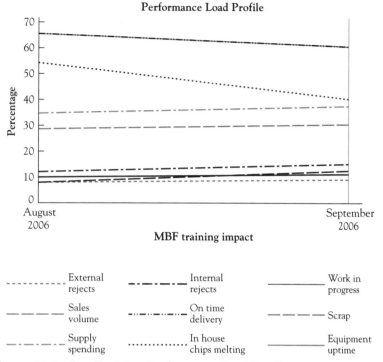

**Figure 13.1. Pre-Training Performance Load Profile**

program costs. These two ratios will be used in determining ROI on MBF training and have been communicated explicitly to all stakeholders from the beginning of the training program to enlist stakeholder support.

## Training Program ROI

MBF training was conducted on October 6, 2006, for a group of ten participants. Performance baseline data was collected between the months of August and September of 2006 and tabulated against key business measures as shown in Table 13.3. Table 13.4 and Figure 13.2 show the new graphical and trend line display of the MBF impact analysis for the months of October to November 2006. A visible improvement is noted in all key business areas: reduced number of external and internal rejects, increased sales volume,

**Table 13.4.  Performance Data Trend Analysis**

| Performance Metric | August | September | October | November |
|---|---|---|---|---|
| External Rejects | 8 | 9 | 3 | 1 |
| Internal rejects | 8 | 11 | 3 | 2 |
| Work in progress | 10 | 11 | 5 | 4 |
| Sales volume | 8 | 7 | 15 | 40 |
| On-time delivery | 65 | 60 | 81 | 90 |
| Scrap | 28.57 | 30.22 | 22.7 | 15.4 |
| Supply spending | 35 | 37 | 18 | 12.7 |
| In-house chips melt | 54 | 40 | 78 | 88 |
| Equipment uptime | 65 | 60 | 70 | 85 |

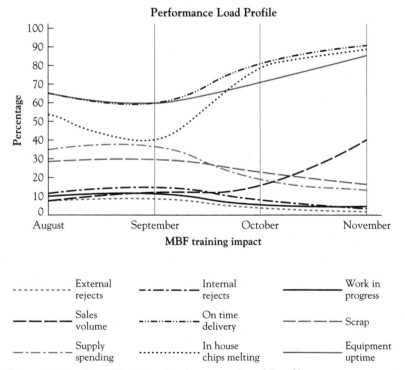

**Figure 13.2.  Post-Training Performance Load Profile**

**Table 13.5.  Business Measures and Planned Analysis**

| Data Item | Method of Isolating the Effects of Training | Method of Converting Data |
|---|---|---|
| External rejects | Quality assurance manager estimation | Standard value |
| Internal rejects | Quality assurance manager estimation | Standard value |
| Work in progress | Supervisor estimation | Standard value |
| Delivery time | Shipping manager estimate | Standard value |
| Sales volume | Plant controller estimation | Standard value |
| Supply spending | Materials manager estimation | Standard value |
| Scrap | Plant manager estimation | Standard value |
| In-house chips melt | Materials manager estimation | Vendor standard value |
| Equipment uptime | Supervisor estimation | Standard value |

reduced work in progress, reduced supply spending, increased chips melt in-house, improved equipment uptime, reduced scrap, and on-time delivery.

**Calculating ROI**

The ROI and BCR ratios have been used to calculate the MBF impact on business performance. Table 13.5 is a summary of the business measures and strategy for isolating the effects of training and converting data to monetary value. Table 13.6 shows the ROI business impact analysis and an estimation of the impact attributed to the program.

The original data sets represented the data for ten employees, and they have been extrapolated for the entire plant. Consequently, Table 13.6 shows the impact analysis for the plant assuming the

Table 13.6. ROI Business Impact Analysis (Level 4)

| Participant | Performance Measure | Annual Improvement $ | Contribution from Program % | Confidence Estimate % | Adjusted Value $ |
|---|---|---|---|---|---|
| Quality Assurance Managers | External rejects | 120,000.00 | 87.7 | 90 | 95,040.00 |
| Quality Assurance Managers | Internal rejects | 72,000.00 | 75 | 85 | 45,900.00 |
| Supervisor | Work in progress | 145,000.00 | 60 | 95 | 82,650.00 |
| Plant Controller | Sales volume (profit) | 350,000.00 | 40 | 94 | 131,600.00 |
| Shipping Manager Estimate | On-time delivery | 75,000.00 | 25 | 100 | 18,750.00 |
| Plant Manager Estimation | Scrap | 568,000.00 | 46 | 95 | 248,216.00 |
| Materials Managers Estimation | Supply spending | 75,000.00 | 64 | 85 | 40,800.00 |
| Materials Managers Estimation | In-house chips melt (money maker) | 250,000.00 | 34 | 100 | 85,000.00 |
| Supervisor Estimation | Equipment uptime | 105,000.00 | 20 | 90 | 18,900.00 |
| | | | | Total: | $766,856 |

other 190 employees have the same success as the ten in the initial pilot.

From Table 13.6, the total adjusted benefit value was $766,856.

## Program Costs Calculation

Table 13.7 shows the estimated fully loaded annual program costs associated with the development and delivery of the MBF training intervention. The program costs involved needs analysis, design, development, delivery, and ROI evaluation components. The table is a summary of the MBF program costs.

$$\text{Total Adjusted Benefit Value} = \$766,856$$

$$\text{Total Program Costs} = \$187,600$$

$$\text{BCR} = \text{Program Benefits/Program Costs} = 766,856/187,600 = 4.09:1$$

The ratio means that for every dollar invested in the MBF training program, approximately $4 in benefits were returned.

$$\text{Therefore ROI (\%)} = \text{Net Program Benefits/Program Costs} \times 100$$
$$= \$766,856 - 187,600/\$187,600 \times 100$$

$$\text{ROI\%} = 309\%$$

## Intangible Benefits

Intangible measures are defined as measures that are purposely not converted to monetary values. QWI believes in three main strategic business goals: to grow business by satisfying customers through high-quality products, to develop the best people, and to produce economically. QWI subscribes greatly improving to employee commitment, employee satisfaction, customer satisfaction, employee retention, employee tardiness, innovativeness, competencies, and teamwork. Interviews were held with supervisors and area managers

## Table 13.7.    Estimated MBF Program Costs

| Content Acquisition | Cost Estimate |
| --- | --- |
| 1. Needs assessment costs | $2,000.00 |
| 2. Subject-matter expert consultancy fee (400 hours at $60.00 per hour) | $24,000.00 |
| Total *hours* for content acquisition: 400 | |
| Total *cost* for content acquisition and needs assessments<br>   [(400 × $60.00) + $2000.00] | $26,000.00 |
| Development of standards, including scripting for eight-hour course.<br>   Assume one-hour course takes 50 hours to develop<br>   (8 × 50 × 50.00 per hour = $20,000.00). Team of five people from<br>   XX Wheels International on the project on the course design team<br>   (5 × 20,000.00) | $100,000.00 |
| Total *hours* for development of standards: 400 hours | |
| Total *cost* for development of standards: $50 per hour | $100,000.00 |
| **Per Class Cost** | |
| 1. Two hundred employees (8 hours each at $14.50 per hour) | $23,200.000 |
| 2. Management and engineering staff (8 hours each at $50 per hour) | $10,000.00 |
| 3. Instructor salary (8 hours at $50 per hour) | $400.00 |
| 4. Total per class cost | $33,600.00 |
| **Data Collection and Analysis** | |
| 1. Evaluation survey through surveymonkey.com (10 × $50) | $500.00 |
| 2. Interviews (10 hours at $45 per hour) | $450.00 |
| 3. Focus groups (10 hours at $45 per hour) | $450.00 |
| Total *hours* for data collection: 30 | |
| Total *cost* for data collection | $1,400 |
| Data Analysis Cost (2 × 10 sessions at $45 per hour) | $900.00 |
| Training room at a hotel | |
| 1. (80 hours at $200 per hour) | $16,000.00 |
| 2. Lunch and snacks ($5.00 per person × 200) | $1,000.00 |
| Total *cost* room rental, lunch and snacks | $17,000.00 |
| Reference Manuals | |
| 1. MBF Manual (200 × $20 each) | $4,000.00 |
| 3. Duplication costs | $200.00 |
| 4. Name tags, roster, overhead projector, video projector ($200 × 10) | $2,000.00 |
| 5. Packaging (200 × $5) | $1,000.00 |
| Total | $7,200.00 |
| ROI Evaluation cost | $1,500.00 |
| **Total cost of providing the MBF training to two hundred employees per year** | **$187,600.00** |

to measure the training impact on the intangible benefits. The intangible benefits were:

- Increased Commitment

- Less Employee Tardiness

- More Innovativeness

- Increased Employee Satisfaction

- Broadened Competencies

- Increased Employee Retention

- Better Teamwork

## Communicating Results

The presentation to the stakeholders should cover the impact of the MBF training intervention on business performance as measured in all five evaluation levels. A communication presentation plan described the program and explained why it was being evaluated, presented the methodology process, presented reaction, learning, application, barriers, enablers, business impact, the ROI, and the intangibles, reviewed the credibility of the data, summarized the conclusions, and presented the recommendations. Table 13.8 is a summary of the results that brought the most performance impact. The presentation plan included the results in Table 13.4.

## Conclusion

Stakeholders' support is required throughout the ROI process in order to acquire a credible and acceptable ROI and BCR values. The MBF training promises to have a greater business performance impact. The estimated ROI value of 332 percent is a good forecast of the impact the training will have on the whole plant when all two hundred employees and management have been trained.

**Table 13.8.  Communicating Results**

| Level 1: Reaction | Level 2: Learning | Level 3: Application | Level 4: Impact | Level 5: ROI | Intangible Benefits |
|---|---|---|---|---|---|
| Overall rating 4.3 out of 5 | 60 percent increase post-quality versus pre-quality evaluations | Equipment uptime went up from 65 percent to 95 percent | 30 percent increase in throughput per individual; internal and external rejects of products reduced by 50 percent; zero missed deliveries; 90 percent reduction in work in progress | 309 percent | Job satisfaction, commitment, innovativeness, employee satisfaction, employee retention, less employee tardiness, more teamwork, increased competencies |

## Questions for Discussion

1. Assess the credibility of the data in Table 13.6. What issues do you have with the data? Explain.

2. The shipping manager's reported confidence level was 100 percent. How does this affect the results of the ROI calculation? What would be the best approach to fix the problem?

3. What would be the ROI and BCR if all two hundred employees had received training in the same year, assuming similar conditions as the first group of ten employees?

4. Given the profile of the participants who provided information for use in ROI impact analysis, how would you justify the credibility of the ROI value obtained?

5. Analyze the objectives of the MBF training and compare with the ROI value obtained. Is the MBF training a value-adding program to QWI?

6. 309 percent ROI value seem to be a big figure of investment return. How would you justify the credibility of this figure to senior QWI executives?

## About the Author

**Alaster Nyaude** is a doctoral student at Capella University specializing in training and performance improvement and is expected to graduate in February 2008. Mr. Nyaude has more than ten years of training and organization development experience with a passion for performance improvement, coaching, and building human capacity. He has a diversified managerial background after having worked in Sweden, The Netherlands, Africa, and the United States. He is a respected manager, with expertise and experience in presentations, curriculum design, and training and development. He received his master's degree in organizational development from Brenau University of Gainesville, Georgia, and a B.S. in computer information systems from Emmanuel College of Franklin Springs, Georgia. He is also a telecommunications engineer with specialty in microwave radio communications. He can be reached at nyaudea@bellsouth.net.

# 14

# Measuring ROI in an Employee Retraining Program
## A Global Copper Mining and Manufacturing Company

Christian Faune Hormazabal,
Marcelo Mardones Coronado,
Jaime Rosas Saraniti, and
Rodrigo Lara Fernández

## Abstract

Organizational needs change over time, and personnel should be willing to address those changes. Codelco, the biggest copper producer organization in the world, implemented a conversion program to move some personnel from one mining activity to another. A full ROI evaluation was conducted.

## Background

Chile is a long and thin country, located in South America. About fifteen million people live there, either in the Pacific Coast, in the central valleys, or near the Andes Mountains. Argentina, Peru, and Bolivia are neighboring countries. This country is recognized world-wide because of its products. Everyone has heard about the wood, the seafood, and the Chilean wine. However, its main product is copper.

Note: This case was prepared to serve as a basis for discussion rather than an illustration of either effective or ineffective administrative and management practices.

Codelco is a public sector copper extractor and processor company that works mostly in the central and north side of the country. It has become as one of Chile's, and the world's, most important companies, reaching huge production levels. In fact, Codelco is a fundamental part of the Chilean economy.

## Program Context: North Expansion of South Mine (NESM)

One of the mines from which the copper is extracted, which belongs to North Codelco, was in a growth process to maintain production levels. This is not just a mining expansion, but they also have to create a new plant, a mineral treatment plant. This plant will process all the minerals extracted from the new portion of the mine called South Mine.

This growth generated a great need for trained personnel because there was more new work. Because of that, the operation area temporarily increased from 170 to 330 people to cover the operational needs of South Mine and the new plant.

The recruitment process was achieved using surplus personnel from other areas of Codelco, so it was necessary to convert them from their original functions to the new ones. Table 14.1 shows the conversion needed.

The training plan was based in the competency requirements of the mining operator team. The same scheme was conducted to work either in the mine or the plant. It must be highlighted that from this format, a training plan was made for the first individual development plans from the North Codelco division.

The program was separated into two stages:

1. *Theoretical Stage* In which the people would acquire new knowledge and abilities to accomplish the mining team operation and general operator functions.

2. *Practical Stage* In which the people developed the abilities at work, that is, running the equipment in normal condition of production on a one-by-one lesson basis.

**Table 14.1.  Conversion Needed**

| Action | Number of People |
|---|---|
| Converting Refinery Operators to General Mine Operator | 12 |
| Converting Refinery Operators to Mining Equipment Operator | 29 |
| Refreshing Multifunctional Operator Competences from the Digger and Transport Area | 38 |
| Certification on Operators' Competences | 81 |
| Refreshing South Mine Operator Competences | 170 |

## The Evaluated Program

### Original Personnel from South Mine

The ROI Methodology was applied to the operators of the mining equipment of South Mine. They are competent workers who were retrained throughout a seventy-six-hour program, fifty-two for the theoretical stage and twenty-four for the practical stage.

Theoretical training included:

- South Mine management induction

- South Mine operational security

- Operational procedures of mining equipment

- Symptom analysis and failing detection

- Emergency local brigade

Practical training included:

- Operational procedures

- Operational security in the mine

- Equipment test

The evaluation program was focused on performance of one kind of personnel: the extraction truck operator (CAEX, in Spanish) from South Mine, mainly for experimental reasons.

In this group it was possible to compare the operators' performance before and after the program was conducted, because they were operating under the same conditions and equivalent technologies. There was objective information to set up the performance difference between the trained people and those who were not trained. The performance indicators will show that kind of information.

In this case, an ex-post evaluation of training activities was conducted, that is, the evaluation began after the training activities were finished.

## Evaluation Plan

### Objectives and Levels of Evaluation

The main objective of the activity consisted of knowing the productivity difference (transported tons, traveled distance average, and effective use of available hours) in the Extraction Truck Operation (CAEX) of Caterpillar 789 and Dresser 685 trucks in South Mine (SM) and the North Expansion of South Mine (NESM), after the training program was conducted.

The NESM project was evaluated due to its strategic relevance within the corporation and because of the high training inversion that was involved. Early, the goal was to measure the five ROI levels, however, Level 1 data (reaction surveys) did not exist so the first level was not analyzed.

Level 2 was measured trough theoretical tests and showed the new knowledge the participants acquired. Application tests were used to measure Level 3, which let us know how much of that knowledge was transferred to the real work scenario.

Measuring Level 4 was no problem. There were a lot of data and all kinds of precedents in the information systems that South Mine consistently uses. Dispatch and Power View are examples of that kind of online system. Historic and individual information were relevant, too.

Therefore, for this evaluation, the evaluation planning was conducted in the same way as a typical program, but it was conducted after the training program was completed. Table 14.2 shows the evaluation plan, and Table 14.3 describes the ROI analysis plan.

### Data Collection

Data collection was made just as defined in the data collection plan. Nevertheless, as this was an ex-post evaluation, there were some problems regarding the difficulty of finding the data.

For Level 1, the evaluation team found that the information was non-existent, due to the fact that no Level 1 evaluation was conducted at the time of the program.

For Level 2, learning was measured through knowledge-based tests applied by the instructors at the end of each course. The scale used was a standard 1 to 7 scale (7 = excellent, 6 = very good, 5 = good, 4 = sufficient, 3 = insufficient, 2 = poor, 1 = very bad). A score of 4 was considered enough for approving. Final average was 6.82, as shown in Figure 14.1.

Level 3 data was recollected through a series of methods that measured the application of daily basis work practices structured in pre-operational, operational, and post-operational aspects of mining equipment.

- *Practical Test:* Two-hour process in which the operator shows how qualified he is in the operation of a certain mining machine. The result (approved or rejected)

**Table 14.2. Data Collection Plan**

Program: South Mine North Expansion Project Responsible: GMS/GOP/GDP

| Level | Objectives | Indicators | Data Collection Method | Source of Data | Time | Responsible |
|---|---|---|---|---|---|---|
| 2 | Technical knowledge evaluation: Operational security; symptom analysis and failing detection; emergency local brigade; operational procedures | 1 to 7 scale with 60 percent of exigency | Knowledge based tests | Participants | At the end of each theoretical activity | Facilitator |
| 3 | Use the new theoretical knowledge in the operation | Percentage defined by each area, depending on the relevance of the item | Practical test/Checklist/ Certification | Instructor | At the end of each practical activity | Facilitator |
| 4 | Increase performance indicators due to the training process | Dispatch and power view indicators in process that follows the same work conditions either in 2003 and 2004 with and without training | Indicators overview | Operators/ Dispatch/GOP (Operator Management System) | June-July | GOP/Impact Evaluator |
| 5 | R.O.I. >10 percent | The ROI value will be determined by the economical benefit due to the change on the indicators | | | | |

**Table 14.3. ROI Analysis Plan**

Program: South Mine North Expansion Project Responsible: GMS/GOP/GDP

| Data Items (Usually Level 4) | Method to Isolate the Effects of the Program | Method to Convert Data to Monetary Value | Costs | Intangible Benefits | Communication Destinies to the Final Report |
|---|---|---|---|---|---|
| Tons; Distance (in kilometres); CAEX effective hours | Control Group | Operational Earnings/Savings and Use of Internal Standards Values | Hours of administration and coordination/Participant costs/Materials/Translates and hosting/Facilitator fees/Equipment and installations/Evaluation and ROI case elaboration | Better climate/Stability/New communication network/Satisfaction | Participants/Client areas/Development area teams/Development corporative management |

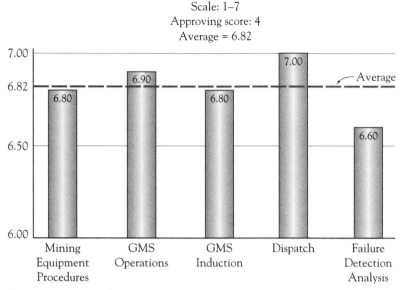

**Figure 14.1. Level 2: Learning**

defines whether he is qualified to work in the NESM project.

- *Checklist:* Instrument that measures certain abilities for operating mining machines.

- *Certification:* Work site process that certifies whether a worker has certain core competences.

Figure 14.2 shows that all the participants approved the Level 3 evaluation with a 90 percent average. The practical test is 30 percent and the checklist is the 70 percent of the final score.

Level 4 data was collected together with the GOP unit. They had all the information required for the proper analysis in their database systems: dispatch systems, power view, and costs, among others. This allowed exact information of individual performance on a daily basis. Specifically, the data collection was a 2003, 2004,

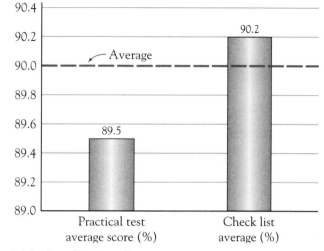

**Figure 14.2. Level 3: Results**

and beginning of 2005 analysis between the program participants and workers who did not attend the program. Both groups worked under similar conditions and operation standards. The 2003 data was used to define the similarities between the groups. The evaluation was made comparing metrics of both groups (transported tons, traveled distance average, and effective use of available hours). January 2004 to February 2005 data was analyzed to compare the differences in both groups.

The key indicator was defined as "performance," and it includes all three metrics:

$$\text{Performance} = \frac{\text{Transported Tons} \times \text{Traveled Average Distance}}{\text{Effective Time}}$$

An improvement on this indicator shows a greater efficiency on the use of the resources. The analysis was made following three types of criteria.

- Type of truck: CAT 789/Dresser 685.

- Extraction sector: North Expansion of South Mine (NESM)/South Mine (SM)

- Trained/not trained operators

## Data Analysis

### Isolating the Effects of the Program

As mentioned before, control groups were used as an isolation method. The experimental group had fifty-five operators who attended the program; those results were compared to the control group, twenty-two operators who did not attend the program and worked under similar conditions and operation standards.

The results of the CAT 789 trucks are shown in Figure 14.3.

Table 14.4 shows a similar performance during 2003. In 2004 the situation changes, as trained operators begin to have a better performance than untrained operators.

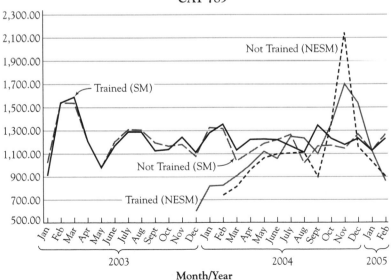

Figure 14.3. CAT 789 Results

**Table 14.4.  2004–2005 CAT 789 Average**

|  |  | NESM | | SM | |
|---|---|---|---|---|---|
|  |  | Trained | Not Trained | Trained | Not Trained |
| CAT 789 | 2004–2005 Average | 1.085,97 | 1.047,96 | 1.200,51 | 1.163,45 |
|  | Trained/not trained difference | 38,01 | | 37,07 | |

**Table 14.5.  Level 4 Results**

|  | NESM | SM |
|---|---|---|
| **CAT 789** | 38,01 | 37,07 |
| **Dresser 685** | 58,61 | 45,65 |

The Dresser 685 trucks also showed positive results, although they were not as good as the CAT 789. In summary, final Level 4 results are shown in Table 14.5.

**Converting to Monetary Values**

This was a very difficult process due to the complexity of the metric. Success was achieved by working as a team with the expert areas.

1. First, the performance metric was developed so a ton/effective hour indicator could be calculated.

$$\text{Performance} = \frac{\text{Transported Tons} \times \text{Traveled Average Distance}}{\text{Effective Time}}$$

is equivalent to

$$\frac{\text{Transported Tons}}{\text{Effective Time}} = \frac{\text{Performance}}{\text{Traveled Average Distance}}$$

2. The Traveled Average Distances had the figures shown in Table 14.6.

Table 14.6.    Traveled Average Distances

|  | NESM | SM |
|---|---|---|
| Average Distance | 2,01 | 2,65 |

Table 14.7.    Transported Tons/Effective Time Metric Results

|  | CAT 789 |  | DRESSER 685 |  |
|---|---|---|---|---|
|  | NESM | SM | NESM | SM |
| Performance | 38,01 | 37,01 | 58,61 | 35,14 |
| Average Distance | 2,01 | 2,65 | 2,01 | 2,65 |
| Tons/effective time | 19,0 | 14 | 29,2 | 17 |

3. Next, the results in Table 14.7 were calculated for the Transported Tons/Effective Time metric.

4. The following step is to calculate the tons that are related to the performance improvement. In order to do this we have to multiply transported tons/effective time times the difference between effective times of operators with and without training in both North Expansion of South Mine and South Mine. The average times are shown In Table 14.8.

5. Next it has to be defined how much mineral and how much gravel were in the tons. According to production registers, in South Mine 20 percent was mineral and 80 percent gravel. In North Expansion of South Mine, 100 percent was gravel, as shown in Table 14.9.

6. Finally, a monetary value was calculated. To do this, in order to be conservative, only the benefits from the gravel tons was considered, as shown in Table 14.10.

**Table 14.8.  Tons Related to Performance**

|            | NESM | | | SM | | |
|------------|------------------|---------------------|------------|------------------|---------------------|------------|
|            | With Training | Without Training | Difference | With Training | Without Training | Difference |
| **CAT 789** | 2.822,28 | 882,99 | **1.939,29** | 17.346,21 | 10.248,96 | **7.097,96** |
| **Dresser 685** | 20.435,37 | 5.446,43 | **14.998,94** | 608,18 | 258,14 | **350,04** |

|          | CAT 789 | | DRESSER 685 | |
|----------|-----------------|----------------|-----------------|----------------|
|          | NESM | SM | NESM | SM |
|          | $19 \times 1.939,29$ | $14 \times 7.097,96$ | $29,2 \times 14.998,92$ | $17 \times 350,04$ |
| **Tons** | **36.753** | **99.441** | **437.978** | **6.041** |

**Table 14.9.  Mineral Tons vs. Gravel Tons**

|              | CAT 789 | | DRESSER 685 | |
|--------------|----------|----------|----------|----------|
|              | NESM | SM | NESM | SM |
| **Mineral Tons** | | 19.888 | | 1.208 |
| **Gravel Tons** | 36.753 | 79.553 | 437.978 | 4.833 |

**Table 14.10.  Benefits from Gravel Tons**

|                       | CAT 789 | | DRESSER 685 | |
|-----------------------|----------|----------|----------|----------|
|                       | NESM | SM | NESM | SM |
| **Gravel Benefit (US$)** | 47.172 | 111.507 | 562.143 | 6.774 |
| **Total Benefit (US$)** | **727.596** | | | |

## Costs of the Program

The costs of the program (shown in Table 14.11) were defined using a matrix that has all the project variables, stages, and costs. The main items were:

- Needs assessment, consulting, and evaluating costs.

- Design and development costs

Table 14.11.  Program Costs

| | | |
|---|---|---|
| Needs Assessment | | 11.386 |
| Salary | 9.756 | |
| Consultants | 1.630 | |
| Design and Development | | 8.033 |
| Salary | 8.033 | |
| Delivery | | 306.937 |
| Salary | 81.127 | |
| Coordination | 44.097 | |
| Logistics | 31.808 | |
| Consultants | 149.905 | |
| Evaluation | | 11.995 |
| Salary | 10.683 | |
| Travel and Lodging | 1.312 | |
| TOTAL US$ | | 338.351 |

- Delivery: participants' time, consulting, logistics, coordination, etc.

- Evaluation: evaluators, travel, meals, lodging, etc.

*ROI Calculation*

$$BCR = \frac{727.596}{338.351} = 2.15 : 1$$

$$ROI = \frac{727.596 - 338.352}{338.351 \times 100} = 115\%$$

These results show a well-planned program, and it is a scientific demonstration that activities regarding the project were extremely successful. Some intangible benefits, including stability, a new communication network, and satisfaction were achieved as well.

## Lessons Learned

There were some difficulties, such as the lack of Level 1 data, that should be considered in future programs. The information obtained from this level can be extremely important, such as the data regarding future application.

Instruments for all levels should be developed to have valid data and make assumptions based on historic values.

An ex-post-evaluation has a lot of difficulties, such as the lack of data and the impossibility to follow a data analysis plan. It is convenient to use the ROI Methodology from the very beginning, especially when a needs assessment process is conducted. This is a good way to have reliable data.

With the development of this process, the importance of this methodology is clear. The ROI process should be fully integrated to other human resources processes, such as career development, competences, training, and improvement.

### Questions for Discussion

1. What do you think were the advantages of dividing the study into two stages (theoretical and practical)?

2. Is Level 1 data necessary? What could have been done to ensure that more Level 1 data were collected?

3. Is this study credible? Explain.

4. Do you have enough data to understand the ROI analysis? Explain.

### About the Authors

**Christian Faune Hormazabal** is a psychologist and leads North Codelco's People Development area. He specializes in learning, development, and performance management.

**Marcelo Mardones Coronado** has a degree in engineering and worked in Codelco's Human Resources area. Currently, he works as a SAP consultant.

**Rodrigo Lara Fernández** has bachelor's degrees in both psychology and business administration and a master's degree in human resources. He has had fourteen years of experience in training and development. Rodrigo began his career in a bank and has worked as a consultant for the last twelve years with MAS Consultores (www.masconsultores.cl), a Chilean company in which he is a partner. MAS Consultores has branches in Chile, Peru, and Venezuela. Through his company, he has had the chance to work not only in Chile, but also in Europe, the USA, and several South American countries. With Jack Phillips, he created Instituto ROI Chile (www.institutoroi.com), a company to deliver ROI Methodology workshops and consultancy in Latin America, and has built the first ROI Network in South America. He has also been a college professor for many years and has participated in various investigation projects. He holds the ROI Methodology Certification and he currently is ROI Institute's Regional Director for Latin America (www.roiinstitute.net). He is a member of ASTD, where he also has participated as an advisor for the Evaluation and ROI Network and as an evaluator for the ASTD awards.

**Jaime Rosas Saraniti**, psychologist and MBA, is certified in ROI Methodology and works as a senior HR consultant with MAS Consultores specializing in needs assessments, team building, and ROI. He is project director for Instituto ROI.

# Index

# About the Editors

**Patricia Pulliam Phillips, Ph.D.,** is president of ROI Institute, Inc., the leading source of ROI competency building, implementation support, networking, and research. She is also chair and CEO of The Chelsea Group, Inc., an international consulting organization supporting organizations and their efforts to build accountability into their training, human resources, and performance improvement programs with a primary focus on building accountability in public sector organizations. She helps organizations implement the ROI Methodology domestically and abroad.

After a thirteen-year career in the electrical utility industry, Phillips has embraced the ROI Methodology since 1997 by committing herself to ongoing research and practice. Phillips has implemented ROI in private sector and public sector organizations, conducting ROI impact studies on programs such as leadership development, sales, new-hire orientation, human performance improvement, K-12 educator development, educators' National Board Certification mentoring, and faculty fellowship. Phillips is currently expanding her interest in public sector and nonprofit accountability through application of the ROI Methodology in community- and faith-based initiatives, including Citizen Corps, AmeriCorps, and the Compassion Capital Fund.

Phillips helps others build capacity in the ROI Methodology through the ROI certification process, as a facilitator for ASTD's

ROI and Measuring and Evaluating Learning Workshops, and as adjunct professor for graduate-level evaluation courses. She speaks on the topic of ROI at conferences worldwide.

Phillips's academic accomplishments include a Ph.D. in international development and a master's degree in public and private management. She is certified in ROI evaluation and has earned the designation of Certified Performance Technologist. She has authored a number of publications on the subject of accountability and ROI, including her most recent books: *The Value of Learning* (Pfeiffer, 2007); *Show Me the Money: How to Determine ROI in People, Projects, and Programs* (Berrett-Koehler, 2007); *Return on Investment Basics* (ASTD, 2005); *Proving the Value of HR: How and Why to Measure ROI* (SHRM, 2005); and *Make Evaluation Work* (ASTD, 2004). Phillips can be reached at patti@roiinstitute.net.

**Jack J. Phillips, Ph.D.**, a world-renowned expert on accountability, measurement, and evaluation, provides consulting services for Fortune 500 companies and major global organizations. The author or editor of more than fifty books, Phillips conducts workshops and makes conference presentations throughout the world.

His expertise in measurement and evaluation is based on more than twenty-seven years of corporate experience in the aerospace, textile, metals, construction materials, and banking industries. He has served as training and development manager at two Fortune 500 firms, as senior human resource officer at two firms, as president of a regional bank, and as management professor at a major state university.

This background led Phillips to develop the ROI Methodology, a revolutionary process that provides bottom-line figures and accountability for all types of learning, performance improvement, human resource, technology, and public policy programs. Phillips regularly consults with clients in manufacturing, service, and government organizations in forty-four countries in North and South America, Europe, Africa, Australia, and Asia.

Books most recently authored by Phillips include *The Value of Learning* (Pfeiffer, 2007); *Show Me the Money: How to Determine ROI in People, Projects, and Programs* (Berrett-Koehler, 2007); *Proving the Value of Meetings & Events: How and Why to Measure ROI* (ROI Institute, MPI, 2007); *Building a Successful Consulting Practice* (McGraw-Hill, 2006); *Investing in Your Company's Human Capital: Strategies to Avoid Spending Too Much or Too Little* (AMACOM, 2005); *Proving the Value of HR: How and Why to Measure ROI* (SHRM, 2005); *The Leadership Scorecard* (Elsevier Butterworth-Heinemann, 2004); *Managing Employee Retention* (Elsevier Butterworth-Heinemann, 2003); *Return on Investment in Training and Performance Improvement Programs* (2nd ed.) (Elsevier Butterworth-Heinemann, 2003); *The Project Management Scorecard* (Elsevier Butterworth-Heinemann, 2002); and *How to Measure Training Results* (McGraw-Hill, 2002). Phillips served as series editor for ASTD's *In Action* casebook series, an ambitious publishing project featuring thirty titles. He currently serves as series editor for Elsevier Butterworth-Heinemann's *Improving Human Performance* series, and for Pfeiffer's new series on Measurement and Evaluation.

Phillips has received several awards for his books and work. The Society for Human Resource Management presented him an award for one of his books and honored a Phillips ROI study with its highest award for creativity. The American Society for Training and Development gave him its highest award, Distinguished Contribution to Workplace Learning and Development, based on his work with ROI. *Meeting News* has twice named him one of the twenty-five most influential people in the meetings and events industry, based on his work on ROI for the industry. Phillips has undergraduate degrees in electrical engineering, physics, and mathematics; a master's degree in decision sciences from Georgia State University; and a Ph.D. in human resource management from the University of Alabama. He has served on the boards of several private businesses and several nonprofits and associations, including the American Society for Training and Development. He is chairman of ROI Institute, Inc., and can be reached at (205) 678–8101, or by e-mail at jack@roiinstitute.net.

# Pfeiffer Publications Guide

This guide is designed to familiarize you with the various types of Pfeiffer publications. The formats section describes the various types of products that we publish; the methodologies section describes the many different ways that content might be provided within a product. We also provide a list of the topic areas in which we publish.

## FORMATS

In addition to its extensive book-publishing program, Pfeiffer offers content in an array of formats, from fieldbooks for the practitioner to complete, ready-to-use training packages that support group learning.

**FIELDBOOK** Designed to provide information and guidance to practitioners in the midst of action. Most fieldbooks are companions to another, sometimes earlier, work, from which its ideas are derived; the fieldbook makes practical what was theoretical in the original text. Fieldbooks can certainly be read from cover to cover. More likely, though, you'll find yourself bouncing around following a particular theme, or dipping in as the mood, and the situation, dictate.

**HANDBOOK** A contributed volume of work on a single topic, comprising an eclectic mix of ideas, case studies, and best practices sourced by practitioners and experts in the field.

An editor or team of editors usually is appointed to seek out contributors and to evaluate content for relevance to the topic. Think of a handbook not as a ready-to-eat meal, but as a cookbook of ingredients that enables you to create the most fitting experience for the occasion.

**RESOURCE** Materials designed to support group learning. They come in many forms: a complete, ready-to-use exercise (such as a game); a comprehensive resource on one topic (such as conflict management) containing a variety of methods and approaches; or a collection of like-minded activities (such as icebreakers) on multiple subjects and situations.

**TRAINING PACKAGE** An entire, ready-to-use learning program that focuses on a particular topic or skill. All packages comprise a guide for the facilitator/trainer and a workbook for the participants. Some packages are supported with additional media—such as video—or learning aids, instruments, or other devices to help participants understand concepts or practice and develop skills.

- *Facilitator/trainer's guide* Contains an introduction to the program, advice on how to organize and facilitate the learning event, and step-by-step instructor notes. The guide also contains copies of presentation materials—handouts, presentations, and overhead designs, for example—used in the program.

- *Participant's workbook* Contains exercises and reading materials that support the learning goal and serves as a valuable reference and support guide for participants in the weeks and months that follow the learning event. Typically, each participant will require his or her own workbook.

**ELECTRONIC** CD-ROMs and web-based products transform static Pfeiffer content into dynamic, interactive experiences. Designed to take advantage of the searchability, automation, and ease-of-use that technology provides, our e-products bring convenience and immediate accessibility to your workspace.

# METHODOLOGIES

**CASE STUDY** A presentation, in narrative form, of an actual event that has occurred inside an organization. Case studies are not prescriptive, nor are they used to prove a point; they are designed to develop critical analysis and decision-making skills. A case study has a specific time frame, specifies a sequence of events, is narrative in structure, and contains a plot structure—an issue (what should be/have been done?). Use case studies when the goal is to enable participants to apply previously learned theories to the circumstances in the case, decide what is pertinent, identify the real issues, decide what should have been done, and develop a plan of action.

**ENERGIZER** A short activity that develops readiness for the next session or learning event. Energizers are most commonly used after a break or lunch to stimulate or refocus the group. Many involve some form of physical activity, so they are a useful way to counter post-lunch lethargy. Other uses include transitioning from one topic to another, where "mental" distancing is important.

**EXPERIENTIAL LEARNING ACTIVITY (ELA)** A facilitator-led intervention that moves participants through the learning cycle from experience to application (also known as a Structured Experience). ELAs are carefully thought-out designs in which there is a definite learning purpose and intended outcome. Each step—everything that participants do during the activity—facilitates the accomplishment of the stated goal. Each ELA includes complete instructions for facilitating the intervention and a clear statement of goals, suggested group size and timing, materials required, an explanation of the process, and, where appropriate, possible variations to the activity. (For more detail on Experiential Learning Activities, see the Introduction to the *Reference Guide to Handbooks and Annuals*, 1999 edition, Pfeiffer, San Francisco.)

**GAME** A group activity that has the purpose of fostering team spirit and togetherness in addition to the achievement of a pre-stated goal. Usually contrived—undertaking a desert expedition, for example—this type of learning method offers an engaging means for participants to demonstrate and practice business and interpersonal skills. Games are effective for team building and personal development mainly because the goal is subordinate to the process—the means through which participants reach decisions, collaborate, communicate, and generate trust and understanding. Games often engage teams in "friendly" competition.

**ICEBREAKER** A (usually) short activity designed to help participants overcome initial anxiety in a training session and/or to acquaint the participants with one another. An icebreaker can be a fun activity or can be tied to specific topics or training goals. While a useful tool in itself, the icebreaker comes into its own in situations where tension or resistance exists within a group.

**INSTRUMENT** A device used to assess, appraise, evaluate, describe, classify, and summarize various aspects of human behavior. The term used to describe an instrument depends primarily on its format and purpose. These terms include survey, questionnaire, inventory, diagnostic, survey, and poll. Some uses of instruments include providing instrumental feedback to group members, studying here-and-now processes or functioning within a group, manipulating group composition, and evaluating outcomes of training and other interventions.

Instruments are popular in the training and HR field because, in general, more growth can occur if an individual is provided with a method for focusing specifically on his or her own behavior. Instruments also are used to obtain information that will serve as a basis for change and to assist in workforce planning efforts.

Paper-and-pencil tests still dominate the instrument landscape with a typical package comprising a facilitator's guide, which offers advice on administering the instrument and interpreting the collected data, and an initial set of instruments. Additional instruments are available separately. Pfeiffer, though, is investing heavily in e-instruments. Electronic instrumentation provides effortless distribution and, for larger groups particularly, offers advantages over paper-and-pencil tests in the time it takes to analyze data and provide feedback.

**LECTURETTE** A short talk that provides an explanation of a principle, model, or process that is pertinent to the participants' current learning needs. A lecturette is intended to establish a common language bond between the trainer and the participants by providing a mutual frame of reference. Use a lecturette as an introduction to a group activity or event, as an interjection during an event, or as a handout.

**MODEL** A graphic depiction of a system or process and the relationship among its elements. Models provide a frame of reference and something more tangible, and more easily remembered, than a verbal explanation. They also give participants something to "go on," enabling them to track their own progress as they experience the dynamics, processes, and relationships being depicted in the model.

**ROLE PLAY** A technique in which people assume a role in a situation/scenario: a customer service rep in an angry-customer exchange, for example. The way in which the role is approached is then discussed and feedback is offered. The role play is often repeated using a different approach and/or incorporating changes made based on feedback received. In other words, role playing is a spontaneous interaction involving realistic behavior under artificial (and safe) conditions.

**SIMULATION** A methodology for understanding the interrelationships among components of a system or process. Simulations differ from games in that they test or use a model that depicts or mirrors some aspect of reality in form, if not necessarily in content. Learning occurs by studying the effects of change on one or more factors of the model. Simulations are commonly used to test hypotheses about what happens in a system—often referred to as "what if?" analysis—or to examine best-case/worst-case scenarios.

**THEORY** A presentation of an idea from a conjectural perspective. Theories are useful because they encourage us to examine behavior and phenomena through a different lens.

## TOPICS

The twin goals of providing effective and practical solutions for workforce training and organization development and meeting the educational needs of training and human resource professionals shape Pfeiffer's publishing program. Core topics include the following:

Leadership & Management

Communication & Presentation

Coaching & Mentoring

Training & Development

E-Learning

Teams & Collaboration

OD & Strategic Planning

Human Resources

Consulting

# What will you find on pfeiffer.com?

- The best in workplace performance solutions for training and HR professionals

- Downloadable training tools, exercises, and content

- Web-exclusive offers

- Training tips, articles, and news

- Seamless on-line ordering

- Author guidelines, information on becoming a Pfeiffer Affiliate, and much more

Discover more at www.pfeiffer.com

# Special Offer from ROI Institute

Send for your own ROI Process Model, an indispensable tool for implementing and presenting ROI in your organization. ROI Institute is offering an exclusive gift to readers of the *ROI in Action Casebook*. This 11-inch by 25-inch multicolor foldout shows the ROI Methodology flow model and the key issues surrounding the implementation of the ROI Methodology. This easy-to-understand overview of the ROI Methodology has proven invaluable to countless professionals when implementing the ROI Methodology. Please return this page or e-mail your information to the address below to receive your free foldout (a $6 value). Please check your area(s) of interest in ROI.

Please send me the ROI Process Model described in the book. I am interested in learning more about the following ROI materials and services:

☐ Workshops and briefing on ROI

☐ Books and support materials on ROI

☐ Certification in the ROI Methodology

☐ ROI software

☐ ROI consulting services

☐ ROI Network information

☐ ROI benchmarking

☐ ROI research

Name:

Title:

Organization:

Address:

Phone:

E-Mail Address:

## *Functional Area of Interest*

☐ General Human Resources/Human Capital

☐ General Learning and Development/Performance Improvement

☐ Technical/Training/ Government Relations

☐ Talent Management

☐ Sales/Marketing Training

☐ Technology/IT Systems Training

☐ Diversity

☐ Quality/Six Sigma Training

☐ Consulting/OD

☐ Change Management/ Research and Development/ Innovations

☐ Compensation

☐ Recruiting and Selection

☐ Wellness/Fitness

☐ Leadership Development

☐ Compliance/Ethics

## Organizational Level

☐ executive          ☐ student

☐ management         ☐ evaluator

☐ consultant         ☐ researcher

☐ specialist

Return this form or contact
   ROI Institute
   P.O. Box 380637
   Birmingham, AL 35238–0637
   www.roiinstitute.net
Or e-mail information to info@roiinstitute.net
Please allow four to six weeks for delivery.